T0354340

Hey, God!
What went wrong and when are You going to fix it?

Samuel Heath

iUniverse, Inc.
New York   Bloomington

iUniverse books may be ordered through booksellers or by contacting:

iUniverse
1663 Liberty Drive
Bloomington, IN 47403
www.iuniverse.com
1-800-Authors (1-800-288-4677)

Because of the dynamic nature of the Internet, any Web addresses or links contained in this book may have changed since publication and may no longer be valid. The views expressed in this work are solely those of the author and do not necessarily reflect the views of the publisher, and the publisher hereby disclaims any responsibility for them.

ISBN: 978-1-4401-4521-6 (sc)
ISBN: 978-1-4401-4522-3 (ebook)

Printed in the United States of America

iUniverse rev. date: 05/18/2009

Table of Contents

Chapter one

Welcome to "HEY GOD! What went wrong and when are You going to fix it?" You surely know the title of this book is not intended to convey the idea it is all up to God to fix that which is our responsibility. But to sincerely ask, "Hey, God! What went wrong and when are you going to fix it?" is a perfectly legitimate question; and one that often crosses most of our minds.

I'm Sam Heath, the author of this book and I hope you will benefit from it. I want to thank you for the opportunity to bring this subject to your attention; a subject that I guarantee will cause you to reflect on some of your beliefs in a new and positive way.

The book is very controversial because it exposes some of the hard-held tenets of religion as the superstitions that they are, superstitions that have caused immeasurable suffering in the world, things like the inquisition and the crusades, the burning of men, women and children called heretics and witches at the stake.

Because of twisted and distorted religious views of God and the Bible, some of the greatest crimes against humanity have been committed in the name of God and Jesus Christ. Everyone knows there is something horribly wrong with this. But no one has come up with a solution of the problem. People are still killing others in the name of God throughout the world today.

I will suggest several things that might, if considered, be approaches to understanding of this subject of the nature of God and his dealings with humanity. And if I am right in some of these things, we may yet be able to deal with the problem of so much suffering in the name of religion.

Not belonging to the camp of "You just have to accept it on blind faith (actually blind prejudice, but it makes such people feel spiritually superior and therefore adds pride to their sins)", I struggle with the questions just like those Psalmists of old. And these questions will never

have answers unless they are searched out diligently! But because I am a humorist in the vein of Sam Clemens, Will Rogers and Walt Kelly, the reader is cautioned in advance. The reader is further cautioned by the following example from an ex-friend of mine of many years; Gary North. His comments will give you an idea of what you have to look forward to in this book:

"After reading your book I will only say this...you are so far into flagrant heresy that it is highly unlikely that you are saved...you are in the position of a self-excommunicated man...that you are on the road to hell. I would not waste even this much time on you except for my personal debt to you for having presented the gospel to me. That would be the great irony: the man who led me to Christ roasts in the lake of fire forever...you are a perpetually lawless man whose wives treated you just as you have treated the Church... be not surprised at your present lonely condition. It will get worse. Much, much worse. In hell, it will be forever... here is my counsel...recant publicly and send out a newsletter telling your readers that you have done so."

The above was in response to a book I wrote some time ago where I raised some questions that prompted my old friend's dire warning. Among several other things, I suggested that God has admitted, according to the Bible, making errors! This present book goes beyond even those things that caused Gary's concern for my soul. I can only imagine what he, and many others, might say in response to the questions I raise in this volume.

Gary could be right. It may well be that having written some of these things my soul is destined to be stir-fried in the infernal regions. Not unlike poor old Rushdie of Satanic Verses infamy will this book result in some Baptist or Four Square Ayatollah putting out a contract on me? Or, at the very least, can I expect to get horsewhipped like that poor fellow in Elmer Gantry? Time will tell. Of one thing I am certain; if I am right in some of the suggestions I make I'll most certainly have the Devil's attention! To aggravate the matter of my self-excommunication even further, I have expanded considerably in this book on the early views that earned Gary's dire warning of my soul's peril.

I believe there is a Devil. But there is much to the fellow's comment that if he didn't exist, we would have to invent him anyway; and if so what a marvelous position he has held since his invention. When all else fails, we can blame it on the Devil. That is, when we're not blaming it on God.

Another old acquaintance adds his advice to Gary's:

"You raise a number of issues in your material ... The Church has languished at times under leaders whose theology was more historically systematic than Biblical ... (But) The questions you raise serve as very dangerous doctrines!" John MacArthur, a contemporary of the author at Biola/Talbot and pastor of Grace Community Church in Sun Valley and founder of The Master's College.

But some have profited by the book. For example this comment by a friend: "You have my eternal gratitude for relieving me from the tyranny of religion." D.R.

You, the reader, will judge whether this book is a service to humankind and honors God or if it consigns me to the outer reaches. But there is something dreadfully wrong about our world, the constant turmoil and warfare, so many suffering because of the greed and avarice of those that abuse their power and authority. And this something seems no closer of a solution by Gary or any others in the churches than it ever was.

I used to have a very comfortable, orthodox Christian view of things. I ministered in pulpits and even started three Christian schools after years of working in the public schools. As long as I did not admit of those reasonable, legitimate but very unsettling questions of the faith like what happens to babies when they die and why so many parts of the Bible are virtually impossible to reconcile with facts and realities, I could go along to get along with the brethren.

But once I admitted these legitimate questions do exist and theologians have not answered them, that the churches themselves are filled with ignorance and superstitions, I opened the floodgates of questioning my smug, comfortable orthodoxy. All hell broke loose! as per my friend Gary and others. I had to resign myself to being a leper to the churches and the people I loved. A very lonely position that no one would choose, it is a compulsion.

I no longer consider myself a religious man. But I know the myths and fables of past civilizations have much to offer by way of understanding. The various scriptures of ancient peoples, particularly the Old and New Testaments, with which so many are familiar, are of special interest. For this reason, I treat of them in some detail in the following pages.

The difficulty of addressing the problems raised by the study of ancient writings like the Bible is the result of the lack of common cause and cooperation of those that think of themselves as enlightened. And especially those that think of themselves as Christians.

As to what went wrong and when is God going to fix it, I think God needs our help. A very heretical idea at best. But when it comes to the paradox of good and evil, the responsibility has to lie somewhere. Good Jews and Christians immediately point to Sin. But who, and what, made it possible for Sin and evil in the world? This is not as simple a question as most good synagogue and church people have been led to believe.

In the Talmud, Rabbi Simelai makes an interesting point when he calls attention to Jewish thinking in regard to the interpretation of the Law; Moses, he says, lists 613 commandments, Isaiah reduces them to 6 (Isaiah 33:25,26), Micah reduces them to 3 (Micah 6:8) and, finally, Habakkuk to one: The righteous shall live by his faith (Habakkuk 2:4).

It would seem that Rabbi Simelai and Christian theology are in agreement at this point. However, the fighting that surrounds a definition of this faith continues unabated.

A large part of the debate and conflict centers on issues like the teleological and eschatological interpretation of Scripture. But the resulting cosmologies should not make any soteriological demands on believers, as, I fear, is coming more and more into vogue and creating widening schisms.

This book is an attempt to examine what constitutes real understanding of God, if such is possible, and what saving faith consists of. What part is the responsibility of God and what part is that of the people who claim to worship him in working together in understanding and cooperation to fix this mess the world is in?

At a time when books about Spiritism, angels and demons, experiences of all kinds are selling as never before, I think it good to take heed to Isaiah 8:19-20: When men tell you to consult mediums and spiritists, who whisper and mutter, should not a people inquire of their God? Why consult the dead on behalf of the living? To the law and to the testimony! If they do not speak according to this word, they have no light of dawn.

I wish every proponent of the Glossalallia, especially, would take heed to the wisdom of Isaiah. You can trace this gibberish, mutterings, far back in time before the prophet. Long the stock in trade of conjurors, seers and idol-worshiping priests of every description, such angelic language has an ancient and ignoble history.

Where it is not used to simply call attention to the practitioner as an exercise of the fleshly ego, it is simply a continuation of a religious fraud of past centuries or outright hysteria. And such people are going to condemn Joe Smith and his golden tablets and peepstone?

The New International Version of the Bible, one I use and quote often, perpetuates this heretical fraud by using the word tongues instead of languages in the NT. Why? Because of fear of alienating the fastest growing segment of Bible purchasers, the charismatics. Pure intellectual fraud and dishonest, prostituted scholarship for the sake of a buck!

It is generally agreed that a properly defined problem is half of its solution. The continuing, and growing, problems of the human race are obviously the result of a failure to cooperate in arriving at solutions. This lack of cooperation comes from a distrust and lack of agreement among the peoples of the world, a failure to define a common and saving faith, if you will.

Religion, by whatever definition and however practiced, is a commonality of all people, even those pre-Homo sapiens (pre-Adamic to the religious) hominids. But it seems that most religions do not hold up very well to honest and sensible examination, much of Christianity included. Personally, I would like to credit God with more common sense than the churches seem to.

For example, while I fully expect to meet my loved ones already gone on before me, I also expect heaven to include trout streams, forests with birds and animals and oceans with pounding surf to delight us with the continuing magic of such things. Being free to express my own opinion, heaven without the best of creation would be a cheat.

And heaven must have the laughter and wonder of children. What could possibly substitute for this? And Jesus did say: For of such is the Kingdom of Heaven! I hope he was right.

There are many questions the Bible does not answer. Haven't you
ever wondered, for example, what Eve told Adam at the time of The
Fall? She must have said something because God condemns Adam for
listening to his wife!

In the following chapters, we are going to plunge into some
common sense questions that the churches refuse to acknowledge. You
may well not agree with some of the suggestions I make but I guarantee
they will stir your thought processes.

For example the Genesis creation: Let us make man in our image,
after our likeness. The US is Elohim, a plural noun. Just who is the US?
It cannot, according to the rules of good scholarship and the Hebrew,
be the so-called pluralis majestatis.

Why is it that translator's, Hebrew and Christian, do not correctly
use Yahweh (or Yahvah) thy Elohim as it actually occurs in the Ten
Commandments?

A difficult problem of reconciling the origins of the human race
with the Bible increasingly demands the attention of Christians as well
as those of other religions. There are certain facts of science that will
not go away with fanciful interpretations or wishful thinking.

Were Adam and Eve vegetarians? The Genesis narrative would lead
to this conclusion. After the flood, God gives Noah express permission
to eat meat, thus implying it was not acceptable previously.

But Abel brought animal sacrifice to God while Cain brought the
produce of the soil. What led one son to be a tiller of the soil and the
other to raise sheep? And why raise flocks if you are not supposed to eat
meat? Cain's offering was rejected and Abel's was accepted. What, then,
was the real difference between the two? There is a great deal more to
this than Bible commentators have discovered.

A rather unique idea is that of viewing the Bible as a Romance,
keeping in mind that the course of true love never runs smoothly. I
contend that God is motivated by love and the Bible manifests his need
and his search to love and be loved, for true worship as defined by this
love.

Where did Cain, in fact, get his wife? Since God is so obviously
opposed to incest, it isn't likely she could have been a sister.

Who are these sons of God as opposed to the daughters of men
in Genesis 6:1,2 the commingling of the two resulting in the race of

Nephilim and causing God's great anger and the Flood? What went wrong that enabled the race of the evil Cainites to overcome the godly Sethites?

Discounting the probable apocryphal origin of the story, why was astrology so important to the ancients like those magi who appeared at the birth of Christ and even some of the church fathers? Who were those post-Neolithic hominids that buried their dead with ceremony long before Adam is supposed to have come on the scene?

Did God give Satan the power to create? Were dinosaurs and a proto-race of creatures like man a part of Satan's creative efforts that turned out so badly God (more probably Mr. and Mrs. God) had to destroy them and create man in his (their?) image? Did this result in Satan's great hatred of mankind and motivate him in getting Adam and Eve to fail?

Jesus says God is a Spirit. The Apostle John says no one has seen God at any time. But didn't Adam and Eve see God?

God appears to Abraham on his way to check out things in Sodom and Gomorrah. Who did Abraham see?

How is it that the Bible declares Moses and Elijah saw God; that God spoke to them face-to-face?

It is a weariness to encounter so much ignorance concerning the Bible.

When I was a very young man, I had the privilege of the intimate friendship of one of the greatest scholars of the Bible of modern times, Charles Lee Feinberg, Ph.D., Th.D.

Dr. Feinberg, a converted Jew, was the Dean of Talbot Theological Seminary at the time we met. For whatever reason, he took me under his wing and one of my most prized possessions is an autographed, Pilot Edition of the New American Standard Bible for which he was the head translator.

A master of Semitic languages, his major area of study at Johns Hopkins University, Uncle Charles, as he asked me to refer to him, gave me much needed and expert guidance in my own scholarly study of the Bible for which I will always be grateful.

As a Christian (at the time), I firmly believed in the historicity of the resurrection. In regard to the Bible, I had always maintained that no one has any right to consider themselves truly educated who has not read the one book that has had a greater impact on civilization than that of any ever written, the Bible. And I still believe this.

In the course of my own study, I amassed a personal library of some 5,000 volumes of the finest, most scholarly works about the Bible, its history, the geography, languages, and mores of the peoples of Bible times. From earliest childhood I was raised in a church environment and taught the lessons of Scripture. The study of this book has been, virtually, a lifetime habit.

Because of our extraordinary relationship, Uncle Charles advised me to get a university education from non-religious schools. Which I did. As a result, I was thrust into an academic environment that saved me from many of the myths and superstitions that hold sway in religious institutions, something that Uncle Charles recognized would eventually be my undoing as a scholar in my own right.

Early on, I realized there was something fundamentally wrong with a gospel that could not discriminate between an Albert Schweitzer and a David Livingston. What kind of a gospel would allow Livingston into heaven and consign Schweitzer to hell? Both men lived sacrificially for others.

Yet to watch the average minister struggle with such a question is a study in human behavior as they attempt to contrive an answer that is inevitably a conflict with the very doctrine of soteriology they espouse.

No one has a higher regard for the Bible as literature than I. But my regard for the book does not blind me to scholarly, textual criticism.

One of the marvels of the Bible is that it is so free of many of the myths and superstitions that held sway during the historical period covered. One could say it is a virtual miracle that stories such as that of the fabulous Phoenix are not contained in the book (this is not to say that it is free of fabulous stories like the sun standing still for Joshua. It is not).

But the book is in some ways a credible history of the times covered by it. Yet, to say that it is without error flies in the face of irrefutable, scholarly evidence to the contrary.

Orthodox Jews and fundamentalists claim the book to be without error in the original autographs. But none such exist. The best manuscript evidence at our disposal shows corruption's of the texts in several places, even some, what I call, holy tampering of the texts by both Jewish and Christian copyists and translators. Some people make the ignorant statement that the Bible is without contradictions. I will cite only two of many examples I could give:

In the 27th chapter of Matthew, Judas goes to the chief priests, throws the betrayal money into the temple and goes out and hangs himself. They pick up the money and buy the potter's field to bury strangers.

But the story as given in the first chapter of the Acts of the Apostles is that Judas, personally, used the money for a real estate investment!

In the 2nd chapter of Exodus, Moses flees Egypt in fear of his life. But in the 11th chapter of Hebrews, Moses is portrayed as not fearing the wrath of Pharaoh!

In both of these examples, the contradictions are evident. Yet the twisted and distorted attempts by otherwise honest commentators and preachers have been a history of obfuscatory language and reasoning that flies in the face of honest scholarship.

Such attempts to reconcile the irreconcilable have brought rightful suspicion of ministers and Bible commentators. If they cannot be honest in regards to textual criticism, where else might they be practicing such intellectual dishonesty?

My years dedicated to work in the churches, among the books of the great Bible scholastics, led eventually to an honest appraisal of much dishonesty and, even, the hypocrisy of much so-called orthodoxy.

And in my studies I have found the attraction for the New Age Movement. Whether a stream (or ocean) of consciousness, the stream of nature, such things may have a basis in fact and often prove preferable in many cases to the mysticism and hypocrisies of organized religions that try to dismiss legitimate questions in the name of God.

The greatest of the heresies of which I am accused of the brethren, the thing that brought a breach between me and those orthodox brethren with whom I used to have sweet fellowship, was my finally accepting the fact that in the Bible God has admitted to making errors.

Granted these errors were made in love, they remain. The most obvious was God admitting he was sorry he made man and determined to destroy him from the face of the earth. But God risked it all again, in love, on Noah. The Bible is filled with such errors of love as God sought for men to do his will; men like David and Solomon who failed of his expectations for them.

I have made many errors of love. They are those of loving and trusting only to have that love and trust betrayed. Yet neither God nor I have given up loving and trusting again and again.

If God is love, and I believe he is, love always takes such a risk. An error? If so, it is a risk all those that follow the teaching of Jesus take in practicing the real Gospel, that of loving others. The blind orthodoxy of religious men led to the Dark Ages and some of the cruelest treatment of human beings imaginable, all in the name of God and Jesus Christ.

Christianity was to be distinguished by love as opposed to the false religions of the world. Tragically, the churches took a wrong turn and are noted for the confusion and chaos of today.

In examining the history of religion, especially Hebrew and Christian, I believe I have discovered some of these wrong turns. Not in the sense of an Ah, ha! The plot here begins its gelatinous coagulation but in the sense of someone who has gone window shopping for fun and found themselves in a funeral home, admiring the latest models of caskets in the display room.

In the words of an old friend, J. Vernon McGee: These Christians may love God but they sure seem to hate each other! And once the reader gets into the following chapters and finds out how misleading, even dishonest, religious history and theology, Jewish and Christian has been, I believe there will be justifiable anger.

At a time when the charismatic antics of pulpit, TV and radio so-called evangelists are making every attempt to make God look foolish, when men seem to think God places a premium on ignorance, the world has a right to look askance at the churches.

The very superstitions and charlatanism perpetrated by these scoundrels would, you would think, cause reasonable human beings with an I.Q. anywhere between trusting used car and real estate salesmen and the ability to tie their own shoelaces to come up with a: These stories are as phony and self-serving as a politician's smile!

But we know differently, since so many still give their money to these holy thieves and liars. Unhappily, the opinion of these divinely anointed mullahs of the folks who support their so-called ministries as ignorant sheep to be shorn is sadly born out by the continued ministries of frauds like Jimmy Swaggart and Tammy Faye!

And what of the scholarly holy liars who perpetuate the myths and superstitions of the churches, schools and universities? An accounting of these people is long past due! Tragically, this condition will persist until Christians are willing to question their own blind orthodoxies and honestly seek answers to the legitimate questions we all have a right to ask of God.

Anyone who has read the Psalms knows these men were not afraid to confront God on the issues of the pain, suffering and injustices of the world. Where did the churches take a wrong turn in attempting to make God something he is not? God is not perfect by the definition of men; he is perfect by his own. And he is a lot more human, for lack of a better word, according to the Bible, than the churches give him credit.

Omniscience, Omnipotence and Omnipresence are religious inventions of men; they are not characteristics God claims for himself. Until those who profess to speak in the name of God begin to be honest, I have small hope things will change for the better in the churches.

If the churches are to lead as agents of change for the better, they are going to have to get their act together and agree on courses of action rather than practice theological juggling acts.

One example of real action would be to see the churches agree on a Constitutional Amendment against the perversion of child molestation. If the majority of Christians agree this is a bad thing, what better institution than the Church to take the leadership in this area?

Self-flagellation, terror and apocalyptic sermons have never accomplished anything of substantive change for the better. On the contrary, they have proven delusional and destructive. How about some leadership for positive action from pulpits for the sake of our posterity?

But, unhappily, that would require the churches giving up their cherished tax-exempt status, refusing to face the truth of the fact: They who feed at Caesar's table are Caesar's dogs!

There is no doubt in my mind that many will join Gary in their warning that I will be consigned to the outer reaches and the eternal flames by some of the things I cover in this book.

I can only take a small degree of comfort that these things will arouse the indiscriminate ire of all, evolutionists, and religious persons of all persuasions as well as a sub-species of which too many lawyers, politicians and all those that abuse their authority comprise a large majority.

The greatest impetus for this book came from my obligation to my children and others that responded to an essay I published under the title: THE AMERICAN POET. The response was so overwhelmingly favorable for such a book as this that I could not, in good conscience, fail to follow through. You will find that original and seminal essay at the end of this book.

But there is another reason for this book. In sharing some of these ideas with others, they have expressed great appreciation at being freed from the contradictions, even superstitious fears of their own blind orthodoxy.

And there is something else, a *something* that has plagued humankind. As we look at the stars in the canopy of heaven, who has not thought: What a beautiful world it can be! If only it weren't for some of the people in it! Could such things as the stars, of creation, of life be the result of chance, of some ethereal cosmic force without intelligence?

But who will ever be able to present a sensible answer to the paradox of good and evil in the midst of any kind of divine plan, of a loving sentience as the primal cause of truth and beauty? How to make sense of the power of love being unable to gain the ascendancy over evil? Why does the evil always seem to prevail? There are inexplicable things, anomalies for which science has no answer. But answers must come if there is to be any hope for the human race.

Will they come by way of men and women taking the initiative of opening the door to new, philosophical thought? Or will they come by the advances of science? Or will they come by some amalgamating of the two? And who will be willing to pay the price of such a thing?

The images of war, the carnage of the battlefield, the mangled, bloody bodies of so many men, women and children. And to what purpose? In view of such senseless slaughter, who has not wanted to shake his fist in the face of God himself?

Where is truth to be found in ideological hatred, whether religious or political? Must the seeking for truth always result in the carnage of a battlefield strewn with broken and maimed, bloody bodies? Why must truth and justice be bought with bomb, cannon and rifle, sword and bayonet?

And does an honest search for truth and justice always require the sacrifice of those innocent that don't even know why they are being maimed and killed? Must some bloodthirsty deity representing itself as truth demand continual human sacrifice to appease its hatred and anger toward humanity and the human failure to meet divine expectations? Insanity!

Bloody religion! Bloody humankind!

Jesus used great plainness of speech and the common people heard him gladly. I have attempted to do the same. For this reason, HEY, GOD! is not intended to be a textbook. The subjects treated can be researched at length in scholarly tomes. But you will be forewarned, by reading the following chapters, not to blindly trust the conclusions of many of these scholars.

Chapter two

Gods Funny Bone: People!

It was in a discussion with some friends that my mind turned, once more, to the lack of God's sense of humor. When Sam Clemens said: He was as happy as if he had just gotten out of church! he expressed the sentiment of many folks. Although the more spiritual among us would never admit it.

I recall being raised not to hit girls. Now we boys enjoyed hitting. We were always hitting one another. Somehow it seemed imminently unfair that girls weren't allowed to indulge in this popular pastime.

We boys could wrestle and hit, rolling in the dust and dirt, bleed on each other and, in general, just have a good time. Girls? No way! Unfair.

Yet, it may be just as well that girls aren't raised hitting and wrestling like boys. Girls really are different in some respects and there just seems to be something about them that makes them look better in dresses having tea parties rather than cussing, spitting and hitting.

And boys might smell like an open graveyard or have eaten something too-long-dead but girls are supposed to smell nice at all times.

Girls should never aspire to be preachers. I have to agree with Spurgeon who, when asked about this said: "I once saw a dog that had been trained to walk upright on its hind legs. I didn't wonder that the dog did it badly; the wonder was that it did it at all?"

My real point is that if such damage to society is done in the name of religion, why should girls want to be a party to such a thing? I can more readily understand women wanting to join the army or air force where they can legitimately shoot at men, but, ladies, take my advice and stay out of the pulpits. They are no place for a decent woman with any self-respect.

14

Sam had a way with words. Few people know of his talents as Theologian and Political Philosopher. Who but Sam could sum up Congress as succinctly as calling Judas Iscariot a premature congressman?

In respect to championing the virtue and purity of fair maidenhood, it was Sam who said he was against giving women the franchise because it would reduce them to the level of men and Negroes. How far-sighted his assessment of the situation.

I believe Sam recognized the ploy of spineless men at the time whose solitary goal in supporting this was to be able to make women equally guilty for the mess in government and further the cause of numberless husbands who, like old Adam, could take the resulting chaos like men and blame it on their wives.

So if the reader should misconstrue Sam's and my words concerning the franchise in the hands of women by trying to make us say: "We should never have given them the vote!" please keep our pure and selfless motives in mind.

And as a champion of the Gospel, who but Sam could sum up the role of the churches in America with such a straightforward assessment as his observation: "He was as happy as if he had just gotten out of church!"

I recall Sam making a point concerning an Episcopal minister, a Reverend Sabine, who refused the offices of the church in properly burying a play actor, one George Holland. The good reverend did not hold with the corrupting influence of the stage and theater.

Sam's reaction to this was somewhat volatile concerning the good priest of the church describing this noble man of the cloth as a "... crawling, slimy, sanctimonious, self-righteous reptile."

Sam is one of my favorite theologians (along with Will Rogers and Walt Kelly). He faced the hypocrisy of the churches of his time with rare wit and humor, using the realities of life to confront the hypocrites. What a field day he would be having with today's TV evangelists!

I love women. I love writing about them and the relationships between men and women.

About four years ago I wrote an essay entitled: "Fathers and Daughters." This was the foundation for a book: "Birds With Broken Wings."

This led to an examination of the historical problem of the relationship between men and women, one that led Sam Clemens to call men and women natural born enemies.

Being unwilling to accept Sam's dismal assessment of the situation, largely because of what I learned as a man from my beautiful daughters, I began to write of what I call The Missing Half of Humankind: Women!

As an academic, I have been immersed in the studies of philosophy and theology. It finally penetrated my thick skull that women were conspicuous by their absence from such philosophies, philosophies that have determined the course of history and nations.

The specifics of such attention by me as a man has led to the greatest challenge of my life, an attempt to find a solution to the historical problem of relationships, to discover the reasons that the philosophies of men have determinedly excluded women throughout the history of humankind.

That this is an enormously complex problem is proved by the thousands of books and innumerable talk shows directed at the problem. It is my considered opinion that it is treated far too simplistically.

One example. I asked a beautiful woman friend of mine to ask an organization of 150 women to whom she had access to ask them this question:

Since the number one complaint of women concerning men is that men don't listen to them, what, exactly, is it that women are trying to say that legitimizes their complaint?

My friend was astounded at the resulting confusion and lack of being able to formalize and articulate an answer to this question.

The historical basis of Solomon's jaundiced statement: "A virtuous woman who can find, for her price is far above rubies" cannot be denied and even Mr. Kierkegaard's comments on the subject have factual relevance to the problem as well. There is a pronounced lack on the part of both men and women to be honest and candid concerning the nature of either. It is, as I say repeatedly, a problem of immense complexity and proportion. The solution to the problem of a lack of romance in a relationship, for example, is most often thought to be: "Get someone else!"

Women have far fewer options than men. They know this and

retaliate the best they can. And, historically, they have always lost the war. Understandable resentment is the norm.

The obvious answer would be virtuous men and women, men and women whose characters were ruled by the principles of love rather than lust and selfishness. But it takes an entire society to move together in cooperation of the emphasis on the supreme importance and sanctity of family to bring such a thing to pass.

I'm asked if I know of any successful marriages. Yes. But very few. For example the longevity of a marriage is not necessarily the criteria. It is most certainly one of the criteria but a couple may celebrate a fiftieth wedding anniversary and not really care much about each other.

Such a successful relationship must have a basis of mutual love and esteem. On this basis, I know of very few successful marriages.

Since love is an art, since it demands the self discipline of learning any art in order to do it well, it fails when we lack artists. And a large part of such failure is the loss of romance.

The great majority of married men and women quickly lose the romance of the relationship. There are a host of factors involved which contribute to such a loss.

Most lose those things which first attracted them to each other. That is the result of not practicing the art of love. And it takes both to make it work.

This loss breeds resentment. The resentment grows worse with the growing realization in many cases that the thrill of romance is no longer possible. And this frequently happens. And the resentment frequently results in growing hostility and outright warfare.

But when real romance is missing, when only books supply a vicarious substitute to enliven that missing dimension in a relationship if only in imagination, you have a problem of huge proportions in a society.

In attempting an understanding of the problem, it has to be accepted that the real equality of the sexes is in the compatibility of differences which should result in mutual love and esteem. But this is seldom the actual case between men and women.

The Apostle Paul makes the point succinctly in the New Testament (I Corinthians 11:11) that a man and a woman are co-dependent, that while the woman was created for the man both were created with the capacity to become One on the basis of that mutual love and esteem and that compatibility of differences.

The too often despotic and tyrannical rule of men over women is inexcusable. But as a point of understanding, women should consider the fact that men face a very difficult role as providers and protectors. It is a hard, often cruel world out there.

In facing the difficulties of making it in this world men have, historically, as the stronger, more aggressive sex to contend with other men and the forces of nature in order to provide and protect. That this results in a distinctive character trait of hardness on the part of men is necessary, reasonable and normal.

I have to confess to that hardness which is a part of me as a man. While I would like to devote my life to writing of the softer and gentler things of the relationships between men and women, of love and romance, that part of me as a man which contends against evil and the dangers of the world must be operative as well.

Here is a point where the compatibility of differences should come into play. While women should represent the softer and gentler elements of humanity distinctive to them, men must be accepted by them for the strength of provider and protector, the necessary harder element.

The utility of steel is based on the alloying of materials which results in a metal which is useful for many purposes. Iron, by itself, is very limited; it is hard, brittle and breaks easily. But with the addition of other things like tungsten, the resulting product, steel, has many diverse uses.

The alloying of the softness of the woman and the hardness of the man amalgamating is the steel of the family which can withstand much more of the difficult forces of life, is far more useful to society than either one alone.

To carry the analogy a little further, steel is made through a process of fire. The fires of life should give a relationship the necessary tempering and melding of a man and a woman in a marriage that makes the two, One.

It is in the art of steel-making to bring the diverse elements together as one. In the art of love there must be the essential elements in the two that would produce that One.

The arts of steel-making and love-making require things to be in proper balance and proportion. If there is too much of one material, if there is too much emphasis on a point of difference, the result is a useless material or a failed relationship.

No, I don't think God lacks a sense of humor. But I do believe the religious professionals have been vastly successful in making people believe the same God who gave us humor and laughter doesn't know anything about it. Strange thinking. And to what purpose?

Yet, when I asked these friends to give me an example of God's humor, they couldn't. My friends are Bible literate and good churchgoers. But aside from stories like God made the monkey and some of you folks, they were hard pressed for an answer to my question.

But they agreed that surely God must have a sense of humor, they just couldn't come up with any examples.

Some preachers have really strained to make a few Bible stories sources of humor. But let's face it folks, humor isn't the strong suit of Scripture.

Not that it is non-existent. Jesus was, according to the Pharisees, a Party Kind of Guy. I've said that since Jesus made about 120 gallons of wine for that marriage in Cana he must have intended they all have a good time of it. And considering the sourpusses who called him a glutton and drunkard, I kind of wish I had been at the party.

I've often said that if the churches could make heaven half as exciting as hell, they would be crowded. And let's face it folks, hell seems to be where all the action is as opposed to floating on clouds, plucking harps and singing your lungs out to some high and mighty tyrant that doesn't seem to understand what having fun and a good time is all about.

As Sam put it in the words of Huckleberry Finn: If his friend Tom Sawyer wasn't going to heaven, he would rather go to that other place. Huck had a pretty good grasp of the situation.

If it were God's intention to keep humor out of the Bible, one would have to say he was enormously successful. But the Bible wasn't written to be funny. On that score, anyone would have to agree.

The Bible deals with serious issues. Apparently it wasn't intended to be funny. Among other things, it relates stories of antiquity about creation, The Fall, the history of God's dealing with humanity throughout the ages, and the depravity of evil.

Well, if we don't find the humor of God in the Bible, where shall we look? And why?

First and foremost, the absence of humor on the part of God would be a deadly thing indeed. In spite of the gravity of the subject, He does stress a merry heart, Jesus did mix with people who were having fun, and I am certain that he and the Apostles did share some laughs together.

But God's humor must be found in his supreme creation: People. We may safely assume that in God's creation of humans, one of his attributes is reflected in our capacity for humor. It is a gift of God.

He undoubtedly knew we would need such a gift to deal with the somber, sober issues of life. It is that image of God, US! that proves God has a sense of humor.

I make much of this because the problems we face as human beings cannot be handled without that medicine of the soul, laughter and joy! There is also another point. The humanity of God expressed by His humor in us. I intend to exercise this gift of God in some of the following material to help the less palatable medicine go down.

I never tire of philosophical discussion and exchange of ideas concerning the nature of God, His Creation, and humanity. And I've learned a few things during my years of study of such things.

Any basic philosophy text will acquaint the reader with systems and ideologies that attempt explanations of God, nature and humanity. Plato, Aristotle, Sartre, Skinner, Lorenz, Freud, Darwin, Marx, Thoreau, Kierkegaard are common names to philosophy.

When comparing ideologies that derive from philosophies, there are things common to all. Not surprising since all philosophies are the work of men. Religious philosophies like Christianity, Islam and Judaism have evolved from the questions of men and women (though women are generally excluded from any scholarly discussion of the subject) in attempts to systematize a relationship between God and humankind.

In the religion of Christianity there is a Savior, Jesus Christ, who is supposed to have given himself as a sacrifice for sins. Christians believe he rose from the dead and will return in glory to redeem the world and make all things right.

But do systematic and dogmatic theologies explain the problems and answer the questions all rational people have? No.

I've made the point many times that the Bible does not have the answers to many legitimate questions. But it is a basic text, a Primer, and as such, the study of it helps us to pursue answers to these questions since it reflects so much of the thinking of men concerning origins and philosophies.

It should go without saying that ignorance of this book dooms one to philosophical illiteracy. No matter how many other texts you study by all the great thinkers of the world, ignorance of a book that has had such an impact on mankind is to be abysmally and inexcusably ignorant in any philosophical discussion or study.

I will also state the obvious: No one, religious or non-religious who has not read the Bible has any right to think of him or herself as an educated person.

In attempting to find the answers to so many difficult questions, a study of the Bible together with a study of those systems of philosophies derived from men like Plato and Freud is essential. It is in the exchange of ideas that the path to answers will be found, the path to realizing the potential of the human race.

No discussion of philosophy can ignore the mythologies of the human race, including those of the Bible. Much of philosophy derives from such mythologies. Understanding of these things is essential for progress in attempting solutions to the problems that plague humankind.

Theology, Philosophy and Mythology are attempts to make sense of God and human nature, of the relationship between God, people and the natural creation. I will not plow ground so thoroughly covered by others in the particular areas of mythology. My peculiar task is to confront the presumptuousness of Christian scholars, theologians, who have neglected to consider the wisdom outside their own areas of expertise; and, I will add, their areas of presumptive knowledge.

We read in Paul's epistle to the Romans that humanity suffered terribly by forsaking the true knowledge and worship of God and turning to idols and immorality. The result being the total obfuscation of the real nature of God and His relationship with mankind.

This corruption of the truth of God is summed up in Romans 1:21-25:

For although they knew God, they neither glorified him as God nor gave thanks to him, but their thinking became futile and their foolish hearts were darkened. Although they claimed to be wise, they became fools and exchanged the glory of the immortal God for images made to look like mortal man and birds and animals and reptiles. Therefore God gave them over in the sinful desires of their hearts to sexual impurity for the degrading of their bodies with one another. They exchanged the truth of God for a lie, and worshiped and served created things rather than the Creator.

As a result of forsaking the truth and real knowledge of God, mythologies, as well as the things enumerated in Romans, evolved. In general, these stories attempted to explain God and the supernatural.

Cultures began to become distinctive and their mythologies show their imprint. The Greek culture was replete with a pantheon of demigods, gods and goddesses. The Egyptians had a great inventory of such, as did the Romans.

Such stories have a basis in truth. The credit I accord them is the humanity ascribed to these deities. In spite of the corruption of the truth, there remained a common element throughout that no matter how exalted; these deities were susceptible to common, human frailties.

I do not attempt to make a god in my image. I believe God made us in His. But I do want to confront the hypocrisy of the churches in their making God inhuman; to confront them for the grievous errors and for the damage done by the churches and other religions like Judaism and Muslimism in making God inhuman.

For example, the hypocrisy of things such as the Inquisition and the Salem Witch Trials. Can anyone believe God should take the blame for such things done in his name?

It is the faulty thinking of the philosophies of men that have made the character of God appear as something he is not. And I cannot help but believe that if men had included women and children in such philosophies, a lot of the harm done by them would have been avoided. It isn't a question of equal rights, but one of equal value.

Theologians, Jewish, Christian, and Moslem have resorted to all kinds of foolish mechanisms to protect God's honor.

Reading some of this material in various commentaries one cannot help thinking: With friends like these, God doesn't need enemies!

From portrayals as an inept and superstitious fool to a bloodthirsty despot, you find it all in the philosophies of men and their "scriptures" who, most of them self-deceived, have tried to uphold the honor of God.

I think it fitting at this point to give the reader a fuller appreciation of my credentials to address this matter. And these credentials are more than academic. They come from living experiences as well. So before I go any further, I will take an excerpt from my book "The Lord and The Weedpatcher" so you will know I am writing for the benefit of people who are earnestly seeking answers to the same questions I have:

I am grateful for the fact that The Lord has a sense of humor. He has, of course, the finest sense of humor of all. In spite of the fact that He must be the best parent, thereby seeming to spoil all the fun while we are growing up, He does bear with a lot.

My grandparent's church in Little Oklahoma was a happy place. I am an Honorary Okie myself by virtue of my birth in Weedpatch and early raisin' in Southeast Bakersfield.

The little, tarpaper and dirt floor temple had an actual steeple and bell. One of life's little pleasures was ringing that bell on Sunday mornings.

Cottonwood and Padre. Dirt roads, floors and living but proud people. No one stole from friends or relatives. Tookin' wasn't stealing and considerable tookin' took place from the local rail yard and packing plant. The aroma of the plant together with the oil fields gave Bakersfield an early start on air pollution.

But, as with the outhouses, there is a perverted kind of nostalgia I associate with these fumes. Blue and Austin Hall were my closest, childhood friends. Their mother was the literal spitting image (thanks to the ubiquitous snuff and chewing tobacco) of Mammy Yokum. Being honest pagans, Blue and Austin's parents didn't often attend church but sent the kids.

The war was on and here and there you saw the small flags in the windows with blue, and, tragically, occasionally, gold stars. We children bought war stamps at school (Mt. Vernon) and turned in toys for metal drives. I helped grandad flatten tin cans for this purpose. Since nylon wasn't available, being needed for parachutes, my mother along with many young women of the time, dutifully painted stockings on her legs and my brother and I helped her peel the foil from cigarette packages and roll it in a ball for the war effort. Meat was rationed and we raised rabbits.

We saved grease and lard and listened to Gabriel Heatter and the Lone Ranger. We watched from the schoolyard as planes from Minter Field engaged in mock combat overhead. Teachers warned about finding any strange items on the school grounds as they might be explosive devices cleverly left by saboteurs. Israeli and Arabian children know this drill too well.

The war was made very real to us as children and we were thoroughly propagandized. The media from comic books to movies taught us to hate the rotten Japs and Knocksies. I can imagine how children in other countries are taught to hate us.

But we were simple folks, believing in the righteousness of our cause and our leaders, even, I'm sure, as do the simple folks in other lands now. There were few social services and we didn't think of ourselves as poor or underprivileged because there was no TV or bureaucrats coming around telling us we were poor and underprivileged.

The uniform deguere for children was bare feet and bib overhalls for summer (sans shirts) and, if you had them, shoes and overhalls for winter (with shirts). Socks and underwear were sometime things. While Bakersfield winters could be cruel, the summers were glorious. We could swim in the weir or the irrigation canals, shoot marbles, catch frogs and catfish, pick cotton (my brother and I were forbidden this noble occupation, I suspect from the exalted position my grandparents held in the community) catch lizards and other local reptiles and, in sum, enjoy being children.

Shoes, if you had them, were the first things to go in summer. And not just among the children. Most of the womenfolk went barefoot as well. The warm, alkali dust felt marvelous to our feet, particularly if you had spent the winter shod. At night, if you chanced around an electric light (they were scarce in Little Oklahoma) you could find June bugs and mammoth moths. Worlds of fun with these critters.

You shouldn't get the impression that we children were perfectly innocent of worldly things just because we lacked the preeminent teacher, TV, in that area. There were certain ones that exhibited a certain savoir-faire and knowledge of things illegitimate and carnal beyond their tender years.

Fortunately, any trouble my brother and I got into in this regard was easily attributable to wicked companions, not our own proclivity for evil. Or so our grandparents believed to our good fortune. When memory turns back to that simple church and time, the old songs of Zion (from the very popular Latter Rain Revival hymnbook) come to mind.

What memories does recalling the sylvan cacophony of mingled guitars, tambourines, triangles and piano evoke. Perhaps you too remember some of those old favorites: If I Could Hear My Mother Pray Again, God's Radio, Oh Why Tonight?, Over The Top For Jesus, You'll Wish You Were One Of Us By and By (there's a real message in that one), When I Can Read My Title Clear, 'Twas Rum That Spoiled My Boy, but we really swung into high gear on When The Roll Is Called Up Yonder and Beulah Land.

A problem of course with a dirt floor is that if a lot of people really get into the spirit, all that toe-tapping and hand slapping music can raise a good deal of dust.

But the sensitive reader might be offended by elaboration on this theme so I will relegate it to the chapter on spit-washing young faces and other less tidy subjects of dust-bowl memorabilia. In a more serious vein I will tell you of the little queer.

Now my brother and I didn't know about homosexuals when we were children. Of course, we didn't know about sex of any kind. The delicacy of the subject prevented our grandparents from ever talking about it (I suspect our mother could have given us a few hints).

But, on the whole, sex was simply a taboo of our youth. The intriguing mystery was before us in the conversation and actions of our more knowledgeable playmates, especially since several of them seemed to derive some special pleasure in playing with themselves before an audience.

It is very much to our grandparent's credit that we boys were definitely taught right from wrong, that we never used profanity and that we had a strict, moral code worthy of a conqueror knight seeking the Holy Grail (This did cause some slight adjustment as we grew older, particularly in regard to the weaker and fairer sex). Oh yes, about the little queer.

This kid definitely had bubbles in his think-tank. As Good Samaritans, our grandparents occasionally did take in some of the walking wounded of this world system. Two such were this kid and his mother.

Other than a clubfoot that required the strangest shoe we had ever seen and a right hand that went 90 degrees from the normal, the boy seemed quite average (there was also some facial disfigurement from small pox). Anyhow, they were both shouting fundies, raging warm on the need to live good Christian lives.

This kid held my brother and I spellbound on such lively topics as sodomy and descriptive anatomy. While utterly lacking any experiential frame of reference, we did not wish to appear unappreciative in the presence of such a learned and enlightened one, and one who was so obviously willing to tell anyone who would listen of his exploits into that forbidden world of It! On more than one occasion my brother and I felt we were listening to an episode of Inner Sanctum.

Such was the tender delicacy of our minds compared to this august personage. But, Ronnie (my brother, also called Dee Dee by me and Fuzz, because of his curly hair, by my grandad. Dee Dee hated that name, Fuzz) and I were well acquainted with hell-fire and damnation and did not want to intrude too far into that dark and enticing, evil world no matter how good its practitioner made it sound. Homosexuality was a term and a fact neither of us boys had ever heard of or had any knowledge.

But one night during the evening Sunday service it was Testimony Time and the saints were popping up like fleas shouting that they were glad they were saved and had the Holy Ghost! While this inspiring display of religious fervor was going on, this kid was putting his arm around me and trying to kiss me. Somehow this didn't strike me as the work of The Lord, especially as his hand was feeling my leg.

I moved away from him and suddenly he leaped up with an "I'm glad I'm saved and got the Holy Ghost and God's called me to be a preacher!" I was certainly surprised by this revelation under the circumstances but the kid sat down amid shouted Hallelujahs! Amens! and the proud, beaming look of his mother. Then he said to me: Now it's your turn, you gotta testify!

A rather peculiar thing then occurred. No one had ever asked me if I was saved; I guess my grandparents just took it for granted that no boy could be loved and preached at with such fervor as I had been and not be a sure-fire contender for salvation. Well, I thought, Whatever 'saved' means, I'm not and I sure don't have that 'Holy Ghost' that knocks old lady Walker off her hinges.

Nor was I at all sure I wanted that dreadful power pushing me all over the place making me cluck, spit and moan in strange ways. And, so, I remained nailed to my bench, refusing to be this kid's first convert to holy-rollerism (not that many of them really rolled much, but they sure twitched a lot). I knew I was a sinner but I also knew that being saved must be a different thing than what this kid was.

Later, as a teenager, a kindly, old man was to ask me directly, for the first time, if I was saved. I will never forget, since my grandad was present, saying I was just to satisfy him. I felt intense guilt for this deception. I still didn't know what Saved was then.

It wasn't that the Bible and Jesus weren't made prominent in the little church or that I lacked examples of real Christians. But the Gospel was so distorted by ignorance and, sometimes, terrible hypocrisy, that it was never really explained in its pure simplicity. It was not until I read the Bible for myself that I discovered this.

One of the greater things I found by reading the Bible for myself was that so much of what others had told me was Scriptural was nowhere contained in the book. It does seem that the world our children will inherit will be filled with ignorance. Not the ignorance of being able to use a VCR or flip hamburgers, but the hurtful ignorance of prejudice and bigotry, ignorance of science and real art and literature, ignorance of what a clear, mountain stream and a starry sky represent.

In order to give the reader a fuller appreciation of the function of our little church, Faith Tabernacle, in Dust Bowl Era Little Oklahoma, I will describe a typical service.

Call to worship was accomplished by ringing the bell Sunday

morning. This was the only sound to be heard at this time and day in our little community. No lawns so no mowers. No loud radios (and no TV's of course). No cars so no traffic. Only, in summer, the noise of flitting insects and birds and the occasional yap of some hound.

The congregation filtered in, women in flour sack dresses and straw hats, children in the conventional overhalls and, mostly, shoeless. The men tried to dress in Sunday-go-to-meeting attire of miscellaneous items, some with uncomfortable bow ties and, here and there, a white shirt might be seen. Folks tried to dress up the little girls but the boys, while clean, escaped such nonsense. We would begin with a few rousers like Come and Dine to warm up the audience. The cardboard fans donated by a mortuary in Bakersfield that grandad did business with would begin to flutter by now.

Bakersfield summers were hot and it didn't take much to work up a sweat among the faithful. Prayer requests were taken and testimonies given of what The Lord had done for (or to) various people in the neighborhood. At prayer time, The Lord's favor was implored for all our boys overseas and His righteous judgment against the enemies of Democracy. After the people had prayed (we had no Amen corner, everybody had the liberty to interject Amen and Hallelujah as the spirit moved them) it was Show time! I do not mean to interject irreverence. We all took the service seriously. But, to us children, it was definitely show time.

While we enjoyed the singing and Sunday school lessons very much, it was the grown-ups that could be counted on to gay-up the time something fierce. How we looked forward to the fun as people began to warm to grandad's preaching. My grandfather's face would contort with rage against the iniquitous Philistines and Pharisees.

His voice boomed out like thunder as his fist pounded again and again on the old, wood pulpit. His whole body lurched in cadence with the words and seemed to help hurl them out like bullets at the helpless spectators in the pews (actually the pews were ramshackle benches more or less nailed together and sitting on the dirt floor).

Old lady Walker suddenly jumped to her feet, flang her arms toward heaven, threw her head back, and with eyes closed began shouting in tongues. To my childish ears she seemed to be spouting a kind of sound like our make-believe Indian talk. O lalla lalla keba o notchaway,

O lalla lalla keba o notchaway she repeated over and over, her voice growing softer until she was finally slain by the spirit and slipped to the ground.

Another old saint, Mrs. Hall, taking her cue, jumped to her feet and took off on Helagumba, hellagumba, hellagumba, hellagumba until this terrible force of heaven also mowed her down. I thought again for the umpteenth time that old lady Walker sure had it all over Mrs. Hall. After all, an entire sentence must be a greater accomplishment than one word.

Also, old lady Walker had a certain way of falling which left her in a more decorous position than Mrs. Hall. We children took great notice of how each dear old saint fell and writhed and twitched; not just their facility with grunts, yelling, jumping, tongue clicking and enthusiasm in general.

My grandfather would halt his thunderous barrage against all sorts of wickedness from bob-hair to hug-dancing each time the spirit moved on one of the saints. I always admired my grandfather's great sense of delicate timing. When the spirit moved he had sense enough not to interfere with such a terrifying power. No sooner had this dread force accomplished its work and felled its victim but grandad would pick up as though nothing had interrupted his discourse.

Up jumped Mrs. Young as though goosed forcefully and indiscreetly. Geeda geeda lamasabathany, geeda geeda lamasabathany, geeda geeda lamasabathany until the ambushing spirit polled her like an ox. This was one part we children really liked because Mrs. Young had the heft of a cord of wood. We often wondered how Mr. Young, who could have posed as the 90-pound weakling for Charles Atlas advertisements, controlled this pulchritudinous behemoth. And Mrs. Young had class. No twitching, groaning or moaning.

After the performance, she just lay quiet with flecks of spittle on her hairy, upper lip. At the end of the service (performance?), there was the altar call. This was the opportunity for each member of the congregation to come to the front of the church and kneel and pray. If the spirit really moved a real catharsis of sins, real and imagined, would be poured out with much crying and shouting. This was a treat for the children as we heard many things our parents would never say in front of us otherwise.

Lest the reader misunderstand, the altar call was real in many cases. People often needed the gathering together to confess and pray for one another. Many wounds were healed in this fashion and fellowship restored. On rare occasions, we would have a baptism. This was accomplished only during the summer because we had to make a day of it at the Jordan (otherwise known as the Kern River).

Real baptism must be done by completely submerging the penitent in a real river. None of that sissy bathtub or sprinkled Dandy stuff for Little Oklahoma believers. And, you wore your Sunday best, not baptismal robes. Grandad would remove his shoes and roll up his pants, but it was still Black suit, black bow tie and white shirt.

A picnic atmosphere was always a part of the ceremony and a great time would be had by all. If the congregation was not so small, I'm sure many a sinner would have gone back for seconds just for the fun of it. Fried chicken, rabbit, catfish and frog legs were plentiful. Pies and cakes. In all, with everything deep-fried, there was enough cholesterol to make a mortician smile.

We children would be occupied catching crawdads for the feast. The summer Mrs. Young was baptized was especially entertaining. She kept bobbing up like a cork and grandad had to have two of the deacons help him to get her under. At that, she proceeded to float downstream and it took half the congregation to beach her.

My grandfather always dressed the part. Black suit and black bow tie. He was a large, raw-boned man, over six foot and about 200 pounds. He had a commanding presence and a thunderous voice. He had actually played a gambler in a silent movie made locally and he and my grandmother had done a stint in a circus, he as a Barker and my grandmother as the Fat Lady.

Grandma played the piano marvelously but grandad couldn't carry a tune in a bucket. However, he loved music and, keeping time with a tambourine, his deep, loud and resonant voice overpowered us. Faith Tabernacle could always be counted on to make a truly joyous noise unto The Lord.

My grandma's piano playing and the spirited singing meant a lot to culturally starved Okies and Arkies and the success of the church. The church was truly a great social need-fulfilling thing as well as meeting the spiritual needs of the poor white trash, as they were known to the greater Bakersfield City dwellers.

While it was true that the community was dirt poor and many were on the lam and had criminal records, there was no shame attached. We were all aware of the frailty of the law in understanding some of the injustices of extremity. Many were criminals for things like stealing food or material to put a makeshift roof on a shack.

But no deputy sheriff ever intruded into Little Oklahoma in those days. My grandad was sworn in as a Special Deputy, complete with uniform, Sam Brown, a Smith and Wesson .32-20 (peculiar caliber), clamshell breakaway holster, handcuffs and a copy of the California Penal Code. He, like Judge Roy Bean, became The Law and arbiter of justice in the community. His primary function was that of liaison with the powers in Bakersfield.

But back to our church meetin'. Grandad's preaching was dynamic. The format was to have my grandmother read from The Scriptures and when she came to a spot that hit my grandad right, he would take off.

Grandad, of course, had no formal training for his calling. But, like many that heeded the call, knew The Lord would give him the message. Now my grandfather tolerated exaggerated behavior on the part of the saints and expected them to have a good time and a certain flexibility was needed amid the shouts of hallelujah and amen in order for them to enjoy their religion.

When one of the sisters would feel the moving of the spirit and jump up to speak in tongues, my grandfather would halt his thunderous barrage and wait for the fit to pass. He did not hold with most of this nonsense but had enough insight to understand the need of his constituents. When the spirit finally fled, grandad would resume his discourse as though nothing had happened.

While he looked askance at women speaking in the church (believing Paul's admonition that this was a shameful thing) he also knew that human nature and culture required outlets of expression. His own as well. I suspect he also realized that it was a lot of fun for us children. Curiously, it was always the women that spoke in tongues, never the men. Years later I would read: If the women in the church stopped speaking in tongues, the movement would soon cease to move!

But this was before the formal churches like the Roman Catholic and Anglicans got into the act and legitimatized the gibberish, even giving it a good, solid Greek name; Glossolalia. Too bad Amy Simple wasn't around to cash in on that. But, Swaggart, Baker, et al. would make up for her and then some.

My grandfather's own conversion experience needs a little elaboration. It was supposed to have occurred during a tent meeting somewhere in the South. Being a real heller as a young man, he obviously presented one of those challenges that so inspire the fervent, holy pursuit of the godly. As he told the story, he went to the meeting with some other young bloods to heckle and enjoy the show.

But one dear, old saint who recognized him decided the time was ripe for his call to repentance. So enthusiastic did she become under the influence of the spirit that she literally began to chase my grandfather around the meeting place shouting the imprecations of his lost condition and his need to call on the mercy of God for salvation. No fire-breathing dragon could have so consumed its prey as effectively.

The woman, aided by several that had joined in the chase, finally brought grandad to ground. Turning to face his tormenters, grandad said that the Spirit suddenly took hold of me and rattled me good! To the holy delight of his hounds of heaven, he cried out to God and began to speak in tongues (grandad never did this as long as I knew him. This was the only occasion of which he gave any credence to this hysteria). There was no doubt to any that such a Saul-like experience could betoken anything but a divine call to preach.

And it was thus that my grandfather was impelled on his colorful career in the Lord's army. Buying himself a Pharisee Bible (these are large Bibles, usually with thumb indexing, color plates, glossary, index, concordance, doctrinal notes, maps, short histories, biographies and pebble grained leather bindings weighing enough to tire any but the most energetic thumper and providing a not inconsiderable weapon should need arise) a Cruden's Concordance and equipping himself further with a few well-selected hell-fire and damnation verses, he, like so many others of similar background, was in the preaching business.

While my grandfather did not believe in Theology and might not even have heard the word, or use any commentaries, he had a pretty fair grasp of what was reasonable in religion and what was not and preached accordingly. A curious aberration was his refusing to take up a collection or to ever ask for money from the pulpit. His curious response when pressed on the issue was to reply: God never made a beggar out of any man or His church! What heresy! Not even a Bingo night!

Grandad had built the little church on his own lot at the corner of Cottonwood and Padre. It was built, like our house next door, of material he had scrounged from various places. The bulk of the wood was from a wrecked boxcar at the rail yard. The last couple of years we lived in Bakersfield, grandad acquired a PA system for the church.

By attaching two large speakers outside, the entire neighborhood received the benefit of hearing sin denounced in the booming thunder of grandad's preaching. I'm sure the local sinners thought the terror of the heavens had descended upon them when they were first bombarded with this wrath and vengeance unleashed upon the ungodly.

No doubt the local sink of iniquity (a combination cuttin', shootin', liquor and grocery store where you could steal Bull Durham by holding the bell with your hand as you opened the door) profited mightily. They must have as they were the only ones to complain of this counterpoint to their customer's lively language and cultural pursuits.

But my brother and I had an interregnum from this period of our religious training provided by our mother and a Polish stepfather. While staying with them back east, we were properly catechized into the Roman Catholic Church. Bit of a culture shock. We even were made to attend a year at a Catholic Military Academy, St. Joseph's in Florida.

I've always been grateful for this training in Roman Catholicism as it gave me needed insights to address the problems peculiar to this institution.

Since those early years of learning religion, I have attended some 40 different denominational churches including Lutheran, Presbyterian, Episcopalian, Baptist of all kinds, and many non-denominational community churches.

With this kind of experience in religion, together with my academic training and having served as a minister myself, I will continue with my argument that God is much more human than the churches will admit.

And I will be bringing in the subject of those mythologies where appropriate together with the superstitions that will help explain both the truths of the matter and the fallacies.

But I have to warn the reader of one thing. God did not miraculously put ancient bones and artifacts in the earth to test our faith. These things exist because of actual events, actual creatures and cultures, that preceded Homo sapiens (or, Adam and Eve if you will).

A faith that cannot stand up to the facts is not a faith that honors God.

Chapter three

There is Dumb and then there is Terminally Dumb!

It is all too true that the difference between genius and stupidity is that genius has its limits.

I could dwell on this subject at length. But I am not going to give in to that. In fact, at the end of this chapter you will find a love story. Why? Because at heart I'm a poet. And poets are the impractical people who believe love is the strongest force in the world. And, perhaps, out of the world as well. If you believe in Heaven.

In the biblical story of Abraham's argument with God over the proposed destruction of Sodom and Gomorrah, it is evident that Abraham believed God was capable of making a mistake.

Abraham is called in Scripture a Friend of God. He did not engage in arguing with God, as a friend, for any other motive than friendship. He loved God and did not want him to do anything that would impugn his character.

But Abraham evidently knew God in a different light than Hebrew and Christian scholars would have us believe.

I was in love once. Well, more than once but anyhow.... When I love someone I am prone to overlook, even not see, what others might consider imperfections in the one I love. In other words, objectivity isn't the name of the game when someone is in love.

I've known many beautiful women and fallen in love with some of them. Eventually, I had to admit they weren't perfect. A couple of them, arguably and subjectively of course, might try to say they discovered the same thing about me.

Now as a mere man, I have an ideal in my mind of the perfect woman. To begin with, she thinks I'm a perfect man. I won't bore the reader with the rest of the list (which, with the exception of a couple of constants, changes from time-to-time anyhow).

Somewhere along the line, Hebrew and Christian scholars decided God had to be perfect according to their definitions of perfection. A real burden, I'm sure, to God.

Three words finally found Orthodox legitimacy among the faithful to define God's perfection: Omniscience, Omnipotence, and Omnipresence. God was to be understood as all knowing, all-powerful and everywhere at the same time.

The problem remained, however, that these are not characteristics that God claims for himself! And it seems the Ancients, secular and religious including Abraham, didn't think about God in these terms either.

I've said many times that God is much more human than the churches give him credit. The Ancients, again including Abraham, were in agreement with this.

By Abraham's time, superstitions and mythologies were abundant. God did, according to the Bible, work through dreams and visions; several people in Scripture heard the audible voice of God, and there were miracles of God's intervention in the affairs of men.

God is said to have appeared to men like Abraham and Moses, angels were seen and the Devil was busy. All in all, an interesting time in history.

But to listen to some of these TV evangelists and their radio and pulpit counterparts tell about it, those folks hadn't seen anything! If I believed some of these religion producers of today, angels, miracles and demons are thick as fleas on a camel, popping up all over the place! After listening to some of these charlatans I'm tempted to start my own Ghostbusters!

You'll have to forgive me my lack of spirituality at this point but I confess that I have never heard the audible voice of God, an angel or the Devil. To compound the matter, I haven't seen any of them either.

Now I maybe ought to feel cheated in this matter, snubbed, in fact. In that event, I could take it personal and change deodorants or feel righteous indignation.

After all, I've never raped, murdered or pillaged (at least not yet). In short, I'm really a pretty nice guy compared to Attila the Hun, the Boston Strangler or the Marquis de Sade; in other words, the kind of guy a nice girl would take home to meet the folks.

Yet, in spite of such an illustrious pedigree, I'm ignored in terms of overt, supernatural manifestations.

I know this is my fault. Why? I'm being ignored, I'm told by any number of people who have a direct line to God (according to them), because I haven't sent any of them any money!

There are many of these gospel-peddlers that have told me, in no uncertain terms, that my lack of faith in them (evidenced by my pecuniary tight-fistedness, i.e. cheap) in not giving them money has resulted in my insulting God Himself!

And God isn't about to take such doubt of the bono fides of these people lying down! No siree! He is not about to bless someone like me with spirits popping out of the closet, from under the bed or the hood of my car on the freeway. Not that my old ticker could handle such blessings, but God's mad at me anyhow for not writing those checks.

Well, I know I've done things to get the Deity ticked off at me but I somehow don't think it's because I didn't give to Jim and Tammy or Jimmy Swaggart et al. Proving my own recalcitrant attitude to people like these, I'm more inclined to think I would incur God's displeasure if I had given them money!

But when you've got enough suckers, what does another one, more or less, count? They can struggle through with a few million a year and afford to tell people like me to take a flying leap.

Now I've met a few people who didn't seem to have a full clip. They're the kind who would play Russian roulette with an automatic. They remind me of the guy who, in despair and rage because of his marriage to a nagging shrew of a wife, couldn't take it any more and decided to end it all. As he put the gun to his head, his wife came in the room and laughing, said: You idiot, what do you think you're doing now? Go ahead and laugh, he said, you're next!

Now there is dumb, and then there is terminally dumb. Realizing this, having met a few of these folks, it shouldn't be surprising there are always going to be those who are willing to support religious charlatans of every description.

UFOs might be your thing; I don't know. I don't discount them simply because I have never shaken hands with any little green men. But I draw the line at outright fraud. And especially fraud in the name of God and Jesus.

The mental health industry is a booming one. Folks are going nuts in record numbers. If you're in the business, you might say people are going crazy at a healthy rate.

No small amount of those seeking help has been involved with some kind of religion that drove them around the bend.

It occurred to me some time ago that there is a paradox here. The very kind of hysterical practices like tongues, miracles, healings, voices and visions of God and Angels that some churches and TV ministries encourage, are the very things a host of psychologists and psychiatrists are trying to cure! And, like the promoters of sick minds through religion, are doing quite well for themselves in the process. A symbiotic relationship if I ever saw one!

Once I stopped laughing about it, I began to look at the tragedy of it.

Watching a religious talk show where the usual religious versions of Can You Top This and You show me yours and I'll show you mine was going on, I kept expecting one of the participants to tell another: I'll bet my angel can whip your angel, he's bigger than yours!

It may have been the same show where Mickey Rooney (and I happen to like Mickey) described Jesus appearing to him as a golden-haired busboy in a restaurant. Paul Crouch was hosting the show and everybody beamed in appreciation of Mickey's description of the theophany.

Of course, when these kind of people get together to share theosophical experiences, religious show-and-tell time, you don't dare question one person's story for fear they won't cooperate in promoting your own.

Now I have nothing against the Harvey's of some people's experience. It's nice to have company if you're a little loony and enjoying it. A good big rabbit that is also a good listener can be a lot of comfort at times, especially if he's invisible. Probably saves a lot of trouble about things like food and bunny-litter.

Children have stuffed toys, dolls and it is perfectly normal for children to have conversations with these. My brother, Ronnie, and I had quite a few and they often proved far more attentive listeners than the adults around us.

But I'm not altogether sure how we would have reacted if any of these stuffed playmates or the resident pet cat had responded audibly. Dr. Doolittle aside, it is a little unusual to carry on protracted conversations with animals. Especially if the human part of the transaction claims the parakeet, dog or cat is holding its own in the dialogue.

My little pond and waterfall in the backyard is host to a number of birds and animals. A pair of Quail nested and now the baby chicks, hardly larger than bumble bees, troop behind papa and momma scratching for food and learning to be quail. These and the baby squirrels are as cute as can be and I enjoy so very much watching them through the windows where I have my desk while I write.

The granite rocks, trees, and bushes are home to my little guests and the critters are most welcome company. I never tire of watching the antics of the squirrels, especially. Like Thoreau, who found birds and animals equally good companions, I watch, enjoy and learn. Lizards are plentiful as well and have their own, peculiar and enjoyable traits.

When a lady guest happens by, I have found they don't mind the reptiles with legs too much. It's snakes most have an aversion to. But, rarely does a snake appear. In fact, I have only seen one though there are more, undoubtedly, about somewhere because of the natural habitat afforded.

I inadvertently had three small squirrels as houseguests once. They had come in through a vent in the roof. They were easily live-trapped and returned outside (I discovered they were kind of stupid about peanut butter, much like men and sex) and I put screen around the vent to keep them from getting back in the house.

But I have never struck up a two-way conversation with my small companions. Oh, I talk to them on occasion, but I'm not sure how I would handle any audible response.

There are two occasions of animals speaking in the Old Testament. The Serpent, of course, and Balaam's donkey (Numbers 22). The first chapter of Hebrews, verse one, tells us that God spoke to the prophets in various ways in the past. But in only one instance did he use an animal to communicate verbally with a man.

The story is accepted as fact in II Peter 2:15 (though the sin of Balaam is mentioned in other places like Jude and Revelation).

One may safely assume that if that angel of the Lord had really wanted to hack the prophet into doggie kibble he could have done so at any time. Then why have that poor donkey take a beating three times?

As usual with many Bible stories, especially in the Old Testament, there is more here than meets the eye. Certainly more than Bible commentators take notice of.

And while I take exception to Wellhausen and many of those who follow the so-called Higher Critical School of thought, while I may disagree with much of Niebuhr and Barth, many of the points and questions raised by these scholars have validity. You simply do not throw the baby out with the bath because of points of disagreement. I am not willing to cast good people into hell because they died un-baptized or were baptized differently than others or because they disagree about the Lord's Supper.

But a Christian does accept the Bible as the Word of God. My labored point is that being a Christian does not necessarily relieve one of the rational intelligence of a mind. God, I am certain, expects us to use our minds and in the exercise thereof, conflict arises between me and many of the brethren who expect me to swallow their personal stories of miraculous, supernatural experiences.

Then there are basically honest men who will not face the hard and legitimate questions that arise from Scripture and natural creation. There are many reasons for this.

If one of these people is a strong adherent of a particular religious persuasion, whether Baptist, Lutheran or Roman Catholic, etc., he is most inclined to follow the party line unquestioningly. Many of these will try to avoid such questions by assigning the subject to the Mystery of God!

They don't seem to realize that by mysticizing God to some nether region, no progress of doctrine can ever be achieved and the differences between professed believers will only grow wider, mysticizing God to some nether region will only acerbate the present chaos of the churches.

For example, when I have tried to discuss who the US and OUR are in Genesis 1:26 and the ONE of US in Genesis 3:22, things get a little sticky.

God could not have been conferring with angels since man was not made in their image but his. In debating the subject, the great commentators like Keil and Delitzsch, masters of the Hebrew language, conclude that the plural form of address is to be understood as the pluralis majestatis, the imperial WE.

Some have taken the passages as a proof of the Trinity, God the Father, Son and Holy Spirit in conference (no women allowed, of course).

The search for answers, my point, should be interesting, intriguing and exciting. It should not be stultified or discouraged by mysticizing it to nonsense like *You just have to take it on faith* as a mystery that will never be revealed to our merely human minds.

There are things of which our physical minds have difficulty but are understood spiritually (I Corinthians, chapter two). And I find no prohibition of our searching out and understanding the things of God apart from those methodologies described in Scripture as witchcraft.

That prohibition alone would discount seeking for answers in any but a rational manner. So much for TV evangelists.

Jesus affirmed that in our new lives, there would be no marrying because we will be as the angels in respect to neither being male nor female.

No sex, no heaven! Typical man thinking according to women. Not that women don't enjoy sex ever as much as men but let's face it; men don't suffer the aftereffects like lactating, carrying and birthing a baby. Women really get the short end on this, not to mention those monthly reminders and having to live as the prey of predatory men.

Speaking of amoebas (brainless, one-celled animals) and TV evangelists, some of you will remember the close call Oral Roberts had when God was going to kill him unless he could raise the necessary ransom. Whew! Enough suckers came to the aid of the guy who described seeing a 700-foot Jesus and good ol' Oral was snatched from the jaws of death.

I remember the place in Jimmy Swaggart's book where he needed a valve job for his car in his salad days. He describes anointing the car's hood with oil and praying over it. Presto! Instant valve job.

I've always had one problem with that story. Why did God want to cheat some poor, hard-working mechanic out of work? Oh, well, the ways of the Lord are mysterious at times, and even weird if you buy any of this guacamole!

But then I remember this is the same guy who said on his TV show that God had told him he, Jimmy Swaggart, was the only man God could use to save the world! I have always wondered how Pat, Oral, Humbard, et al. felt about that one?

I tell a story in my Weedpatcher book about an old Indian I used to go hunting with when I was a boy.

He told me he had once owned a pistol that was used to commit a murder.

He said he would sleep with that gun under his pillow but every morning, it would have blood on it. He would wipe off the blood but the next morning, more blood. He said he finally sold it. Probably good thinking.

I was raised to never show disrespect to, or question my elders. That was just good manners. It would never have crossed my mind to dispute that old Indian. It was a good story, he enjoyed telling it and I enjoyed hearing it. But I didn't believe it. A born skeptic.

That old Indian would have been crushed in his soul if he had any idea I wasn't buying it. So why hurt him unnecessarily? He wasn't trying to hurt anyone with such a fabulous tale. And, more to the point, he didn't charge anyone for listening to it!

Now I am all for a good, honest, entertaining lie. Being an inveterate fisherman, it goes with the territory. Part of my veneration of Sam Clemens is the fact that he was, undoubtedly, the most bodaciously, God-gifted, natural born liar with which this old planet has ever been blessed! May his tribe increase.

But I distinguish between Sam's and that old Indian's lies and those told by the children of the Devil, lies that are intended to take advantage and do harm to others.

I recall old lady Walker in Little Oklahoma stuffing a rag in an empty light socket when electricity came to the community to keep it from leaking out. And there was an old fellow who would never eat anything from a can that had been opened from the bottom because this poisoned the contents.

This kind of ignorance didn't harm anyone. It's good to know the difference; that electricity doesn't leak out of empty light sockets and the peaches are just as good whether the can is opened top or bottom.

But let's face it folks, if things like this are used to hurt or take advantage, that's another matter entirely.

For example, when someone in honest ignorance is doing something foolish, we try to help him or her. We even try to educate our children in schools. And not doing very well.

But a con is something else. And trying to con people with prayer, song, fabulous stories and the blessing of Scripture is reprehensible!

Now the Black Coats, as Tom Paine called them, have a notorious history of conning people. And just because the witch doctors on TV, radio and in pulpits don't wear masks, feathers (though I often want to see them in such dress with the appropriate tar undercoating) and shake rattles doesn't legitimize the scurrilous acts of these charlatans and scoundrels.

The folks in my grandad's little church didn't really expect anyone to take their having a good time with their religion too seriously. The singing was spirited and joyous, fellowship was good but no one really blamed the Lord for the performances of old Lady Walker or Mrs. Hall. It was an outlet of expression these old ladies seemed to need in their lives. And it was entertaining, especially to us children.

The multitudes in the charismatic churches flock to them to put some joy in their lives, to be noticed and they get a chance denied them in their ordinary, sometimes mean and desperate lives to perform, to be someone, to be noticed.

Whether it's an introduction to an invisible rabbit, Harvey, or someone saying they have an angel you can't see, as long as it does no one any harm and isn't meant to take advantage, let them have their rabbit or angel, I won't complain about it.

But please spare me, don't spout gibberish blaming it on the Holy Spirit and calling it an angelic language. I've never heard an angel speak but I'm sure I would understand him just as Zachariah and Mary did.

And don't try to sell me a story about some fairy tale printed on tablets of gold! The Moroni of the Mormons is aptly named for the morons who buy into such nonsense.

The whole point being that even though we may pat ourselves on the back and proudly proclaim our modern age and freedom from the superstitions and mythologies of the past, there are more than enough still around for people to go on killing each other in the name of God and saying they do God a service in the killing!

Now whether I am persecuted in the name of those calling themselves Christian, Jew or Moslem makes little difference. There is no justification for any such thing in the name of God any more than the silly, even hurtful antics of those who promote phony prosperity gospels, superstition and false guilt in the name of God and Jesus for a paycheck and their egos.

Now, a word about end-time spectators and prophets and the harm they do through their egos, superstitions and ignorance:

The study of eschatology in particular regard to the conditions that are supposed to prevail shortly before the return of The Lord in Glory is one of the obligations of The Church and her scholars.

But we have the example and caution of those early Christians who foolishly believed the Lord's return was so imminent that they left off their jobs, sold possessions and were left destitute and an embarrassment to the Gospel.

We have had groups of people in recent times that have done equally foolishly and the world, properly, has looked in derision at such foolishness. God has suffered accordingly.

One of the grave errors of this present age is making God look foolish by telling the world that since Jesus is coming soon, there is no need to confront evil and the tyranny of despotic government, there is no need, as in the case of our founding fathers, to do battle with the oppressor, no need to lay up for our children and take back the birthright which is theirs as Americans, a birthright that we, through apathy and inaction allowed them to be cheated of, allowed to be stolen from them!

The Bible teaches that if any not provide for their own, fathers and mothers working and planning for the welfare of their children, they are worse than infidels; they have, in fact, denied the faith! I Timothy 5:8.

This injunction of God would be utterly hollow, foolish if fathers and mothers take the position that a future for their children is not the will of God, that they are not to take responsibility for making such provision by the declaration that Jesus is coming soon so what's the difference if evil men and women destroy any hope of a future for my children?

This emasculating false gospel that would teach Christians that they are to sit idly by while the Devil and his servants have it their way by default, by an Abandonment Theology, is one that denies God's people have an obligation to both discern evil and take action against that evil!

Tragically, this kind of so-called teaching has resulted in many Christians not even voting! Yet these same people will acknowledge that good and faithful men and women of God gave their possessions, even their lives to secure, and insure, this precious heritage of the franchise.

A bloody war was fought, rightly or wrongly, to birth this nation. Since that time, other wars have been fought to insure that America stay free of tyranny. Good men and women gave the fullest measure of devotion, their lives, for the purpose of our liberty, a liberty that is being wrested from us by our apathy and our failure to stand up against the oppressor!

Will not their blood be required at our hands if we fail to do less, if we fail to heed the words of Jefferson and others that *The price of liberty is eternal vigilance*? And of what good is such vigilance if it does not produce the fruits of righteousness in continuing freedom for our children, our posterity?

It has been well said that any nation that fails to cherish its young, its posterity, has no future! I always add: Nor does it deserve one!

If, as our founding fathers clearly intended, government was to serve the people, we have indeed fallen on hard times. As with those ancient Hebrews in Egypt, we find ourselves under harsh taskmasters and Pharaohs who are demanding, by ruinous taxation and even confiscation of property, by perverted laws that are increasingly stealing our personal liberties and command that we make bricks without straw!

If God's people, those that are called by his name, are called to be Salt and Light can sit idly by and do nothing to confront such evil, they do so in flagrant disregard of the price that better men and women paid for the freedom and liberty that we have so taken for granted, even despised as Esau his own birthright and we certainly deserve the judgment of God against us, we deserve nothing less than the daily, encroaching enslavement by Caesar and his obvious agenda of World Government and the total confiscation of our goods, even our very lives!

Those who call themselves God's people are responsible to take action against such tyranny. If we can, in any way, justify the actions of those founding fathers that secured to us a Republican form of government, secured to us and our posterity the kind of government that emphasized personal liberty together with personal responsibility for our lives with the legal protection, the Constitutional Rights to do so, we must accept that God clearly intended his people to do what is required to insure that such a government, such rights be maintained.

Any doctrine that teaches that Christians are to sit idly by while the Devil and his servants have it their way flies in the face of both the Scriptures and the very foundations of this nation, this America!

But with so many hopping on the Prophecy Bandwagon by sensationalizing in order to gather a following and make a buck, it isn't any wonder the world looks on Christians as a bunch of kooks.

It's as though these people do not believe they must give an account to God for their actions, as though God's judgment will never be passed on them, as though God were blind to their selfish, egotistical antics!

Small wonder Sinclair Lewis in Elmer Gantry has that fellow asking Elmer why he doesn't believe in God? Gantry and his tribe, these latter-day charlatans, prove by their words and actions they truly do not believe in God! If they did, like the demons of James, they would be trembling!

Now, for that love story.

We read in the Bible that God is love, that those that love are the children of God.

The great musicals of Broadway and film that American poets and composers gave us have one theme: Love. The great plays and operas that preceded and paved the way for these have the same, prominent theme.

But these great works of art have another common element: Tragedy!

I am known as a romantic. I have written books on the subject. The stories I tell are not fiction; they have come from my experiences. And in the course of such experiences, especially in the affairs of the heart, I have learned to separate the diabolical from the divine.

I love Cinderella stories. Pretty Woman is an excellent example of such. And so, I believe, is the Bible.

A supreme example of my heterodoxy, many will call heresy, is my wondering if God wasn't lonely and created us as an act of searching for love in his own life? There are suggestions of this in stories and films where men try to create the woman of their dreams. And women who fantasize and dream of that Knight in Shining Armor.

We are absorbed in the book, play or film, vicariously living the dream and hoping all ends well, that they live happily ever after. And we usually come away saddened that such a happy ending isn't in the plan for us.

I believe the image of God (both Him and Her) in us is the capacity to dream, choose, plan, create, hope, and imagine. And above all, to love!

But, as the story goes, we became like God in knowing both good and evil. And God asked: What have you done? Have you eaten from the tree that was forbidden you?

There should be an exclamation point at the end of these questions. God did not ask these things quietly, I think he shouted! And it may have been that he was in shock from the act of betrayal confronting him.

The narrative suggests to me that these are distinct possibilities. How very common, in one respect, all of this is to the human condition. It has all the ingredients of the betrayal of love and trust, of the loss of a loved one through deception and seduction, the blasting of a family relationship because of the selfishness of others as in the act of adultery.

Pretty Woman, as with Rahab of the Old Testament, has the prostitute as a woman with a heart for faithfulness. She wants love and romance; she wants to be faithful to a man who will love her, who will cherish her. But the circumstances of her life dictated she rent her body to survive.

But that good and decent woman was there all along, she had the dream of a Knight in Shining Armor, of being chaste and pure for him but he didn't come along in time to save her from predatory men, molestation and the cruel circumstances of her life. I have known too many girls and women cast in this mold.

I submit to you that the story of the Bible is a Romance (discounting the emphasis given to war, killing and sacrifices, together with the lack of the equal value of women), a love affair between God and us. And, as with life itself, all the ingredients of love with all its hopes and dreams, and tragedy are represented.

It is no accident of language that The Church is called the Virgin Bride of Christ; that the Bible has a happy ending with a wedding, tears are wiped away, and all live happily ever after!

You will never hear a sermon preached on this theme of romance; you will never read a religious book of this nature. Oh, yes, there is a multitude of attempts, but they lack one essential ingredient to have any credibility: The Errors of Love!

Love makes mistakes. It risks betrayal because of trust and commitment. It leaves the door unlocked out of such trust; it leaves itself vulnerable to lies and thefts, even murder. Since love is never suspicious, it is easily deceived and taken advantage of. Along the way, Love learns to discriminate. It begins to evaluate and, through betrayal, the heart becomes guarded and not as easily given as it once was.

There are things that can only be truly learned by experience. I believe God learned, and is still learning about us. There is an engagement period through which a man and woman are to learn about each other. But it takes living together to have any hope of really knowing each other. And even then we take the risk of betrayal, of not thinking or suspecting that other we loved and trusted would ever be capable of such a heinous act.

Things such as God intending a man and woman to be joined as one without separation except for death or adultery have really taken a beating.

And why were men like Lamech (before the Flood. Genesis 4:19), Abraham, Jacob, David, Solomon and others allowed to multiply women to themselves without God intervening? What happens to love and romance when such things are allowed? And how does this impact on God's plans for us, on the history of humanity and the evils with which humankind has had to contend, evils that in these times seem to be escalating? So much to the story.

It doesn't help that evolving religious systems have usually proven anything but systematic. One of the lengthiest in history; that of dynastic Egypt was in flux and in many cases confused and contradictory.

In a case of mixing politics and religion, the priests of Egypt had their work cut out for them during the heretical reign of Ikhnaton. But that was nothing to what they had to do in order to justify a female Pharaoh, Hatshepsut, the daughter of Thutmose I in the Eighteenth Dynasty.

How did the priests do it? They concocted the story that Amon-Re got the queen mother pregnant resulting in the birth of Hatshepsut. Presto: A divine birth by the God. Now why am I reminded of the Immaculate Conception (the sinless birth of Mary's mother)? The Black Coats have always been resourceful.

Jews and Christians face many such things in their own systems. For example, just who is The Angel of the Lord?

While the Bible says God is a Spirit and the apostle John says no man has seen God at any time, there are instances of men like Moses seeing God.

The Angel of the Lord. Is this a ghost or spirit? An ancient concept of peoples, including the apostles, understood a ghost or spirit in this sense. When Peter was knocking at the gate, the other disciples claimed it was his angel.

Yet the angel that freed Peter struck him to awake him. And when Jesus appeared in the upper room he told the apostles to touch him and asked: Does a ghost (or spirit) have flesh and blood?

While I don't credit such a thing, it may be possible then to consider The Angel of the Lord as a physical manifestation of God Himself. He may have assumed this form in his appearance to Abraham and others.

One of the more peculiar personages of Scripture is Melchizedek. He is the ruler of Salem (Jerusalem) to whom Abraham pays tithes after rescuing Lot.

Much is made of Melchizedek in the NT comparing Jesus to him, a typological interpretation. This ruler has no Scriptural background or genealogy yet he must have been a righteous king for Abram (later Abraham) to pay him homage.

One reasonably asks just what the religion of this Melchizedek was?

Surely he was a worshiper of God, a High Priest of God according to the NT yet we know nothing of him apart from the sketchy account in Genesis and the mystical interpretation of his priesthood in the NT.

But it would follow that Yahweh, Elohim, had men like Melchizedek around that had established his worship before the covenant with Abraham that would eventually lead to the Exodus and the Law of Moses.

In any study of the evolution of the relationship between God and mankind, such things as this must necessarily be factored in. And unless they are, one is left with the kind of arbitrariness of the religions of superstitions and mythology.

The point being that God had people in the world beyond men like Abraham of whom God approved. And it isn't likely such men were circumcised, a savage, barbaric emasculation of babies, both male and female.

I think it follows that there are those in the world today that worship God in spirit and in truth that may well have never heard of Baptist or Presbyterian, etc. or theology that might make it to heaven without a systematic theology of Soteriology sanctioned by the churches.

Of course, given the confusion that reigns in the churches today, it might do as well to simply follow the Golden Rule and trust Jesus as the human representative of all those that love others and thus fulfill God's requirements of acceptable worship in the truth.

Chapter four

Some Popular Christian Superstitions

Imagine my surprise when a recent study determined that children who were exposed to good literature, music and art did much better in mathematics and language skills than those who did not have these things in the home!

Yet, there will be a number of young parents out there to whom this will come as a revelation. These parents will probably come from families that did not encourage these things themselves.

As an educator of many years' experience, I have written a great deal about the importance of such things in the lives of young people. But when a culture supports things like the idiocy of Rock Kings and Queens, when the entertainment media sells sex and violence wholesale, children, young people, the future of a nation, is the final cost.

That children are woefully ignorant of what is best for them comes with the territory. That is one of the things God invented parents for. To teach their children better.

Of course if the parents are drunkards or drug addicts, if the parents listen to the noise and trash they call music and keep the tube tuned to mindless, gratuitous sex and violence, if the reading in the home, if it exists at all, consists of pornography or comic books that are no longer comic, the outcome is easily predictable to anyone with enough sense to tie their own shoelaces.

So we have become an illiterate nation and our young people, the future generation, have little idea of their heritage of music, literature and the arts. And are, as a result due to our indifference to them, increasingly the potential victims of those who would take advantage of such ignorance.

All of which brings me to the subject of religion in America and the churches that are dedicated to ignorance, superstition, and prejudice.

Aquinas, that great theologue of the church, wrote at the end of his life: I can do no more; such things have been revealed to me that all I have written seems as straw, and I now await the end of my life. Three months later he was dead.

It is my hope, primarily for young people beginning with my own children, to dispel some of the ignorance and superstitions that led Aquinas and the churches a false path; that led to his dismal assessment of his own work.

Some superstitions are useful. For example, if you have a mouse in the house you are likely to be spared an infestation of elephants. Very useful information of no small comfort, especially if you are allergic to, or have an aversion to, elephants.

Imagine, if you will, the little woman and you are lying in bed and she says: Dear, I think I hear a mouse. You immediately reassure her with the words: Not to worry my love; just think of how many elephants it is keeping out of the house. A husband should always be an unfailing source of such helpful wisdom and encouragement.

If you soak a dead cat in stump water, the resulting potion will cure warts. Homeopathic remedies have a long and noble history. I have found it useful to hang an ex-mother-in-law's picture upside down to ward off unwanted guests, vacuum cleaner, and encyclopedia salesmen. Works. The picture of an ex-wife works well with roaches. If you're a woman, try the ex-husband's picture.

Thanks to the numerous educational books and films on the subject, most of us are able to perform your average exorcism and deal with the normal demons, ghosts and spirits that, according to TV evangelists, are in every closet, under every bed, and probably controlling or possessing your in-laws and little brother.

In the good old days, we'd be busy killing Canaanites, building altars, wringing the necks of doves and pigeons and sacrificing sheep and oxen to keep God happy and the Devil away. Gimme that Ol' Time Religion! With this brief introduction to the serious business of religion, it can readily be seen that if enough common sense is applied to the subject, it can be quite reasonable.

At a time when Jesus Seminars are bringing the traditional religious pot to a boil by voting what is Scripture with red, pink, gray and black beads, when Christological views are on the Internet and TV evangelists are trying to outdo each other with their Vaudeville versions of a religion of tongues, miracles, demons and visions of angels and making money the old fashioned way, Steal It! - it behooves me to address the issue in a different vein. And I hope to do it with a good deal of humor, my forte.

Now I have to admit that some of my comic relief from the seriousness of the subject matter might be construed as being funny as a root canal or your daughter marrying a lawyer. But hang in there and give me a chance to prove myself.

If the Bible is a Romance about a love affair between God and his creation, mankind, which I believe it is, a totally different view of Scripture is required than the churches have ever undertaken (Particularly in regard to the religious views of Jews, Christians, and Moslems that women are unclean and a sin by definition doctrines of these religions).

And if that Missing Half of Humankind: Women! about which I have written a book of that title is taken into consideration, we might even get to the root of the problem of why the history of the human race has been one of war and conflict. Bottom line: It is the relationship between a man and a woman (Adam and Eve if you will) that determines the course of a family that determines the course of a nation that determines the course of history.

I also think God needs our help and cooperation in sorting out this mess. My rationale for this is my heretical view that God is not perfect according to the dictionary definition, but much more human, for lack of a better word, than the churches give him the benefit. If we credit that earliest of all church councils in Jerusalem, we must allow of God's need of, and desire for, our cooperation. This should give all good Fundamentalists something to think about.

As I write, the sun is warmly shining through the windows where I have my desk. I notice a small bug of some kind is doing a well-executed backstroke in my coffee. Well, it is an Olympic year and he's probably in training. I think if I hear Bruce Jenner one more time I'll scream.

Superstitions are enormously interesting since they usually have a basis in fact. But for the life of me, I can't figure out why a rabbit's foot is considered lucky. That poor rabbit had four of them and where is he now?

The Phoenix. In Greek mythology, Phoenix was the son of Amyntor, king of Thessalian Hellas and became responsible for raising Achilles.

But I'm talking about the bird, not the son of Amyntor, the city in Arizona, or the movie with Jimmy Stewart. Most know something of the story of this mythological bird the history of which was known to Hesiod and Herodotus.

Supposed to be as large as an eagle with a musical cry and brilliant plumage, only one could exist at a time. The Phoenix was remarkable in its sexual orientation.

Since it obviously couldn't mate it would build a nest, set it on fire and was consumed in the pyre from which a new bird miraculously arises from the ashes. Being a proponent of old fashioned sex; I don't find this a very satisfactory method of reproduction in my opinion. But we are talking about a bird; and such a bird gives some meaning to Birdbrain.

Being such a nice and very popular story of great antiquity, it was given a lot of credence. So much so that the earliest church fathers compared it to the virgin birth of Christ and the resurrection! A Latin poem of 170 lines, The Phoenix, was inspired by this allegorical connection.

But the Phoenix, despite its popularity, even to those early church fathers, does not appear in Scripture, Old or New Testament. And neither does a hundred other popularly believed myths of antiquity. However, in defense of the Phoenix, you won't ever hear of a town or car being named Pterodactyl. And that critter was real.

A long and laborious process that weeded out many works purporting to be the words of God including many myths and superstitions fixed the Canon of Scripture. But even after the second Trullan council of 692, which may be said to have formally closed the canon, some books remained in dispute. Luther had doubts about the Apocalypse and the epistle of James.

The Dead Sea Scrolls have shown how remarkably successfully scribes throughout the centuries preserved the Old Testament. Yet, textual criticism of the Septuagint (The Greek translation of the OT) and Masoretic texts proves some liberties were taken with the OT and the results cloud some issues.

Some passages were purposely changed or paraphrased to avoid embarrassment. Some were corrupted through notes, pious attempts to harmonize certain parts, particularly the Gospels, and glosses that found their way over a period of time into the text.

There are instances where some priest or scribe must have thought a miracle or two might help honor God. Much like many so-called evangelists of today. One such instance is found in II Kings 13:21 where a dead man is resuscitated by touching the bones of Elisha. Elisha, according to the story, was a powerful prophet of God; but it's things like this that resulted in the holy relics of the church and their attendant superstitions.

But it isn't only the OT that zealots tried to help out; the NT suffers as well. For example, all those holy people that came out of their tombs at the crucifixion. The story, undoubtedly added out of holy zeal at a later time than the original autograph of Matthew, is in the same category as the end of Mark where we are assured we can drink poison and handle cobras at will.

There are known cases of fools handling snakes and drinking poison just to prove the literal Bible and the devoutness of their faith. They usually prove two things, in my opinion: They are fools and know nothing about God!

In spite of such holy tampering with the book, all in all, the Bible we have today is relatively free, notwithstanding some obvious exceptions to the contrary, of many superstitions and myths. Any reading of the apocryphal literature and so-called Lost Books of the Bible immediately shows why such things were not accepted into the Canon of Scripture.

As to the *Textus Receptus*, our present Bible, the real student must be aware that even the received text continues to be subject to textual criticism.

Honest study accepts the fact that there are corruptions of the text in places, there are irreconcilable contradictions, and that to take the position that the Bible is free of such things is to have a superstitious belief in the book rather than an honest reverence of the truth.

If, in the words of Jesus, one is to search the Scriptures for truth, they must do so honestly without prejudicial and superstitious ignorance holding sway in their minds. In other words, objectivity and real learning are the criteria. An unfailing guide to what is of God and what is not remains I Corinthians 13, that remarkable treatise on love, the Scripture that all of us would do well to keep before us.

Anyone lacking the appropriate library for Biblical studies can get a very good overview of such from any good edition of the Americana or Britannica. And I strongly recommend they do so. The study of superstitions and mythologies has a legitimate place in the study of history and the study of religion. And such a study has a place in our modern age of Christianity. In fact, it is a much-needed one.

Historically, the earliest beginnings of America from Jamestown and Plymouth Colony on are rooted in the Bible. The earliest documents of freedom and liberty such as the Magna Carta in England, the Mayflower Compact, the Declaration of Independence and Constitution of America are rooted in parts of the Bible as much as in the writings of French philosophers and others.

The Mayflower Compact, for example, contains these words: Having undertaken for the Glory of God, and the advancement of the Christian Faith ... a Voyage to plant the first colony in the northern Parts of Virginia....

In spite of the Biblical origins of America as a Christian nation, abuses of human rights and a lack of the love of God and others were abundant. There was much of superstitious ignorance and a great deal of evil practiced in the name of God.

Cotton Mather is a name synonymous with extreme Puritanism and the Salem Witch Trials. Taking his A.B. and A.M. from Harvard (His father, Increase Mather, had served as president); he was an extremely well educated man for his times. His later disaffection with Harvard led to his urging Elihu Yale to found Yale University and he was offered its presidency in 1721 though he declined.

Mather had a strong scientific bent, urging inoculation against smallpox for example. Benjamin Franklin, who one would think should have known better, regarded him warmly and credited him for his own penchant for practical schemes.

Few men wielded such influence for their times. Yet, Mather's superstitious Biblical prejudices did much harm.

An illustrious, early graduate of Yale, Jonathan Edwards, was a devout, religious philosopher given, as the Mathers, to scientific inquiry. Edwards was greatly influenced by the works of Newton and Locke. He evolved a philosophical theology of piety with an emphasis on the sovereignty of God determined intuitively by the active Spirit of God in the believer through the Bible and Creation. He also emphasized Cause and Effect in his theological writings and sermons. To Edwards, sin was a necessary corollary to grace.

The Great Awakening as it has been labeled of 1740-41 was the result of the evangelistic efforts of men like George Whitefield and Gilbert Tennent who, with Edwards, preached Terror Sermons (Edwards' Sinners in the hands of an angry God) that resulted in mass conversions.

Tragically, the excesses of religious hysteria were abundant as a direct result of such preaching and many innocent victims of these excesses paid the price for this religious fervor. Examples of the hysteria were great increases of superstitions involving witches, ghosts and demons seen and experienced on every hand. There were supernatural manifestations of visions of angels and demons; people, purportedly under the influence of the Holy Spirit, demons, or angels would act like animals; barking like dogs, rolling on the ground, going into trances, speaking in tongues, etc.

My point being that in spite of their genius, men like the Mathers and Edwards contributed greatly to ignorance and superstition because of their religious prejudices.

Thomas Paine wrote in his Age of Reason: "... lest in the general wreck of superstition we lose sight of morality, of humanity and the theology that is true." Paine was educated and experienced enough to know what he was talking about.

This man, of whom George Washington wrote: Without Paine there would have been no war for independence, was vilified by the churches of his time for his outspokenness of the superstitions and abuses of religion, of the Black Coats, priests and ministers that preached such superstitions.

Thomas Jefferson, in attempting an early attempt at demythologizing the Bible, literally took his scissors to a Bible, cutting out all those passages he thought not Scriptural.

Ignorance of our history as a nation, of the Bible and its origins, of the history of the Church is rampant among churchgoers of today.

And even in the churches and seminaries where such things are taught, religious prejudices still hold sway over the facts of history and reason, still retaining much of the superstitious ignorance of the Mathers' and Edwards'.

When Galileo tried to defend the Copernican theory of planetary motion and the position of the Sun in conflict with Rome's Ptolemaic and Aristotelian geocentric theology, he was threatened with the Inquisition.

The Roman church's position was that teachings like the Sun, and not the earth, was the center of the planetary system were in opposition to Scripture and, therefore, heretical. So convinced were the scholars of the Roman Church that they declared the error more dangerous than the teachings of Luther and Calvin!

Galileo was forced to recant but the damage had been done. Fortunately his writings were disseminated, and men like Kepler, Descartes and others prevailed for heliocentrism as opposed to geocentrism.

Looking back, we shake our heads over the ignorance and superstitions of the past. But we do so mindless of the cost of confronting these things and the price paid for the advancement of knowledge over ignorance, superstition and prejudice.

Still the advancement of knowledge is something that most agree is good. Even the most religious shake their heads in agreement. Ignorance and superstition are bad things they all say. But, of course, my beliefs are not ignorant or superstitious they are quick to add. We'll see. Let's see if you have a superstitious belief in the Bible or if it's a belief founded on the real facts of the Bible!

One of these Biblical facts is that God admits to being grieved, sorry he had ever created man and was determined to destroy him from the face of the earth! Genesis 6:6,7. God evidently felt he had made a mistake in their creation. But I contend it was a mistake that love commonly makes out of love and loneliness, out of a need to express the love of beauty and creativity as an artist.

If there be any truth to the story of Genesis, I think it was God's loneliness and his love that changed his mind in regard to Noah. But he did change his mind! And love, as it always does, took another risk of betrayal.

When, according to the narrative, the Israelites had Aaron make them a golden calf while Moses was on the mount receiving the commandments, God was going to destroy them and make a nation of Moses. Deuteronomy 9:13.

But Moses prevailed with God, arguing how He would appear foolish in the sight of the other nations, of how they would ridicule Him if he did such a thing, and even asking God to blot him out with the Israelites if he should destroy them. Exodus 32:32.

Considering the problems God has had with his creation of humankind from Adam and Eve on, one may legitimately ask why he didn't just knock off Adam and Eve at the time and start over? To have your first attempt at children wind up so bad, then to have the first child of those original parents be the murderer of his own brother did not bode well for the future.

Such obvious questions are about as popular as poison oak or ivy to the average pew-warmer. When I ask such things of the average Baptist you would think I just told him he had won a Dr. Kevorkian Gift Certificate!

Objectivity is not the forte of the average person dedicated to a particular religion. I'll never forget the reply of a couple of Afghani soldiers when a reporter asked why they had shot a Russian prisoner: Because he wasn't a Moslem! Any civilized person is appalled at the inhuman, religious fanaticism whether Catholic, Protestant, Jew or Moslem that has such an attitude toward others not of their belief.

But in objective examination of the teachings, the doctrines and traditions from which such fanaticism evolves one can only shake their heads that such ignorant superstitions hold sway in the pulpits of America! A belief system that cannot hold up under the examination of love for others, and especially love for those that do not agree with you, that refuses to engage in an exchange of ideas, needs to reevaluate itself.

I recall a Jewish judge in Tehachapi, California catching all kinds of hell for a remark he made not long ago. He said Hitler's worst crime against humanity was not the Holocaust (exaggerated in the numbers murdered or not), but that he made the legitimate study of ethnic differences anathema! That took extraordinary courage for this man to make such a statement, objectively true as it obviously is. Every liberal and Jewish organization you can name came down on him.

Personally I don't think Jews should have their own organizations directed at singling them out as a special case category! Anti-Semitic? What about anti-African, Puerto Rican, Mexican, Irish, Italian et al.? Why should one race alone have such a self-servicing device with which to blackmail the world? The judge tried to make this point but even the churches seem brain-washed to the special category status of Jews!

The whole world, I believe, is rightly fed up with this attempt to hold the world hostage to some perceived special status of God for one race alone of all the others in the world! In spite of the obvious fairness and factualness of such statements, both Jews and the churches will now call me anti-Semitic. And such ignorance and prejudice on their part will hardly promote truth.

Theology suffers enormously from this Chosen People syndrome in vain attempts to justify past crimes both against and in the name of Jews, in twisted and distorted attempts to make them something they are not.

There is no other system of religious belief so rooted in a theology of love than Christianity. Yet, it seems that chaos prevails, and while so many profess to love Christ, they sure seem to hate each other as old J. Vernon MaGee pointed out.

Having survived the Mathers' and Edwards'; America still had Moody and Sankey, DeWitt Talmadge, and even that great old orator, William Jennings Bryan to contend with. At a time when the sermons of Spurgeon and Parker were being printed in full in the London Times, evangelistic fervor was going on apace in this country leading to Billy Sunday and Amy Simple.

The Mathers and Edwards were not all wrong. They had much good that they contributed. Moody, Talmadge, Spurgeon, Parker, Sunday all had much good that they contributed. But the prejudicial ignorance and superstitions they preached mitigated against the good. And I don't credit Amy with anything but the devilish popularizing of women evangelists that led to the disasters of the Tammy Fayes.

Far too many, men and women, who could never make it in legitimate theater or other areas of entertainment, discovered a gold mine for their theatrical aspirations in religion. Why not? It has a long, if ignoble, history. And if you just have to be a song and dance man (or woman) and have the chutzpah to pull it off in the name of God, there have always been enough sheep to go around.

I'm not sure that my old friend, Gary North, was correct in his assessment that women get religion and sex all confused, but women like Amy, Mary Eddy and Tammy sure give him ammunition for his argument. Men, though, are basic and notorious for using religion for sexual ends.

Of more contemporary damage to Christianity in America was the Scopes trial of 1925 that pitted fundamentalism against evolution.

It was really no contest since it was easy for Darrow to make the literal word of the Bible appear ridiculous. The fact that Bryan was far from being a theologian didn't help matters.

The ruling went against Scopes as a matter of law, but was later overturned. But the damage to the credibility of the Bible, thanks to the sincere but ridiculous beliefs of Bryan, had been done. It still took Tennessee many years to get the state law against teaching evolution off the books. The law wasn't repealed until 1969.

But Bryan is not the only one who has believed that God is on the side of ignorance and prejudice as long as it is sincere ignorance and prejudice. It is most unfortunate that the ridiculous theory of evolution (ridiculous as usually taught in the schools because of the lack of fossil evidence of mammalian sexuality; how they became male and female) was promulgated by nothing less than a sincere, and ignorantly prejudiced, attempt to uphold the honor of God and the Bible.

Whether the Gospels or Deuteronomy, Kings and Chronicles, it should be obvious that some liberties were taken in the accounts. Some of these, like Bryan's attempt to defend God's honor, have caused no little trouble for Him.

Yet the Bible remains an essential book as a tool of understanding some things of history and myths. And while the textual problems may be worked out, it still takes an objectivity in the exchange of ideas to have any hope of answering some of the foundational questions that naturally arise from the study of God and humanity; many of which the Bible does not, directly, address.

No eye has seen, no ear has heard, no mind has conceived what

God has prepared for those who love him - but God has revealed it to us by his Spirit. I Corinthians 2:9-10.

Paul's interpretation of Isaiah 64:4 is that of the rabbinical teaching of his time. But the real point of this chapter of Corinthians is that we are to have the mind of the Spirit of God to lead us in understanding the things of God, being taught of God Himself and be able to judge righteously.

There are several instances of the way OT passages are used in the NT that make little sense. Certainly the reader of today would not understand the connections made. There were quotations by Jesus of the OT that he used and interpreted to mean something entirely different than the reading these passages convey to us without his interpretation of them. These put a new slant on Scripture in many cases that confounded the Pharisees and Sadducees of his time. The Sermon on the Mount is a good example.

Throughout this sermon, Jesus emphasized the condition of the heart rather than the letter of the law. Rabbinical teaching had taken a turn for the worse since Ezra and Nehemiah's time. Religious teaching had come to the point that Jesus claimed it had usurped the Word of God and substituted the teachings and traditions of men.

Jesus was emphasizing the Spirit of the Law as opposed to the Letter of the Law. As Paul was to point out later, the letter kills but the spirit gives life. Where Jesus emphasized love and mercy, the religious leaders of his time emphasized the keeping of ordinances; lists of rules like our latter-day Pharisees who tell us you can't smoke, chew, drink or cuss and get into heaven.

Now I don't advocate profanity, smoking or drunkenness. But a beer and cigarette in your hand doesn't consign you to the outer reaches in my opinion. And when I hit my thumb with a hammer, Golly, gee whiz doesn't quite cut it for me. A good, heartfelt Hot Damn, Sonofabitch! is worth the weight of a good, deep groan in the morning at times.

And these same Pharisees might think hell and damn are only appropriate to the pulpit but I disagree. Yet, I remain opposed to vulgarisms and sexually demeaning so-called humor. These, like drunkenness and using the name of God or Jesus as epithets, don't commend anyone in my opinion.

But there are religious professionals, like those Pharisees of old, that think their man-made rules should take precedence over God himself. And they are quick to judge, just like those infamous hypocrites of old never perceiving the beam in their eye while they poke at the mote in yours.

Jesus taught as one that had authority and the common people heard him gladly, we are told. But he put a slant on the Scriptures that he summed up by saying that to love God and your neighbor as yourself was all the law and the prophets.

This was not appealing to Pharisees, Sadducees, and Lawyers who wanted to justify themselves by a code, a list of do's and don'ts, rather than be judged by their hearts.

But this falls into Jesus' statement that he had come to fulfill the law and establish a New Covenant between humanity and God through his sacrifice and the provision of a new heart through regeneration by the Holy Spirit that would bring people into a living relationship with God and love for their neighbor.

Read Paul's epistle to the Galatians. God's children are his by faith, those who live in faith of God. But at one time, we (the human race) were under guardians and trustees until the time set by the father. And though we were joint-heirs with Christ as children of God, there were things we needed to learn before we could enter into the kind of adult responsibility that is led of the Spirit.

Now you don't have to be particularly religious to recognize the appeal of this. And it is little different than what many philosophers such as Socrates and Confucius espoused.

With such an inheritance of God, we are expected to live knowledgeably and responsibly before God and the world. The Law, as Paul explains, was to lead us to this position of responsible adulthood.

This whole exposition implies that the relationship between humankind and God was a parent/child one. And, as with all parents, God learned about us as we were learning about him. Parents, with love as the operating principle, still make mistakes but the overriding principle of love wants the best for the child.

By ignoring this basic principle of a family relationship, by insisting on some man-made definition of perfection for God, the scholars of the church have led us on a blind path for centuries.

I was not a perfect father to my children as they, now grown, can testify. But I loved them as only a father can love. And in many cases, had I known better, I would have done better.

I would ask those who presume to know Jesus better than I, of what was he ignorant that he had to learn; in what way was he imperfect that he needed training and instruction?

The Party Line: Jesus was perfect!

Ok, let's consider: Although he was a son, he learned obedience from what he suffered and once made perfect, he became the source of eternal salvation for all who obey him ... Hebrews 5:8.

If he became perfect, what was lacking before? The human experience. After all, despite superstition to the contrary, Jesus was, after all, only human.

As a result of the human experience, we are told that he is able to understand and sympathize with us. Hebrews 4:15.

Did Jesus know uncertainty; did he struggle against a decision of his father? Yes.

He had made it clear to the disciples on several occasions that he was to be crucified. Yet, in the garden as he prayed, he asked his father if it were possible to prevent this from happening! Why the discrepancy? Because he was only human.

Did Jesus ever lose his temper? Yes. Several times.

In Luke 9:41 and Mark 9:19 Jesus says, as a result of the disciple's failure to cast out a demon: O unbelieving and perverse generation, how long shall I stay with you and put up with you?

He upbraided his disciples on a number of occasions for their lack of faith, of their lack of belief and trust in him.

And, of course, we have the tossing out of the thieves in the temple, Jesus using a whip to do so; and we have the harshest and most scathing, damning language in all of Scripture in Jesus' pronouncement against the hypocrisy of the religious leaders of his day, the Scribes and Pharisees.

But in a total mysticizing of Jesus by making ridiculous claims like the Virgin Birth, miracles and the Resurrection thereby relegating him to religious nonsense, his very humanity, that humanity he learned as a mortal human being, one with us in our human condition, is obfuscated, even denied by the churches.

There are many who condemn me for pointing out some of these things in respect to God and the Bible; facts of human nature and sensible thought of which they take vehement exception. For example my contention that you don't check your brains at the door when you enter the sanctuary! Asaph didn't in Psalm 73.

The way those hypocrites treated the prophets; the way they treated God himself caused Jesus to weep over Jerusalem.

Melville rightly said: "The truth? It don't pay!" The haters of the truth are still in the business of promoting themselves rather than the truth.

Chapter five

Why not marry a whore!

Christians become experts at Complaining and Muddling Through

A reading of the Psalms shows the very kind of humanity of our ancestors of which I am writing. They criticized God; they complained to him, they argued with him and even made demands of him and accused him of not caring about them at times. How very family-like, how very human!

I contend that these ancestors, men like David and Asaph, knew more of the real nature and character of God than we do today! Why did these men of God say the things they did as though God were more like a human father than some deity far removed from the human condition? I believe it was because they knew him better than those in the churches of today!

However, the teaching of Jesus and the NT declares that we are supposed to know better than men like David and Asaph; that we have inherited the promises of God and are supposed to be able to exercise the maturity of adults.

To watch the churches in action you would think Christians have regressed to childhood status. Where do we see this maturity, this growing-up that God expects according to the Bible?

I think superstition and ignorance stultified growth, by church leadership insisting on mysticizing God to a status incomprehensible to legitimate study and legitimate, philosophical inquiry.

A primary example of the failure of the churches is their not being able or willing to cooperate with God or each other, as did that earliest of all church councils, the Council of Jerusalem.

When Paul and Barnabas had to answer the accusation of the Judaizers, those that insisted Gentile believers had to be circumcised and obey the Law of Moses to be saved, Peter pointed out what God had done through him for Gentiles and that they had been accepted of God without such requirements.

After hearing the arguments pro and con, the council decided not to impose the Jewish law on Gentiles. This was an affirmation of salvation by faith and faith alone!

However, there were four things the council decided should be imposed: Believers should abstain from food sacrificed to idols, from drinking the blood of animals, from the meat of strangled animals, and from sexual immorality.

The first three prohibitions were sensible at the time since such practices were so common to heathen, religious practices, and Christians were to be separate from such things. The last, sexual immorality, is a given for all-time and not unique to any religion or period of the ages.

But the major point to come out of this council was in the letter from James, the head of the church at this time, to be delivered to the churches.

Here it is: It seemed good to the Holy Spirit and to us not to burden you with anything beyond the following requirements: And the list of those four things follows.

Do you see the point? It seemed good to the Holy Spirit and to us! God did not hand down a verdict in the matter. According to the letter ascribed to James, God took counsel with the leaders of the church to come to a decision that was acceptable to men and God in cooperation with each other!

There comes a time when mom and dad see their children grown and making lives for themselves. The wise parents encourage this growth of their children. They thrill to the decisions of their children that lead to success. And the wise child will always hearken to the counsel of his parents.

In the best of circumstances, a family council of parents and grown children will result in the best of decisions. If they truly love one another, they want the best for each other. And there will always be decisions to be made that are better made in such a council rather than on one's own.

A child wants the approval of the parents in the case of marriage, for example. Why? Because the parents should have attained some degree of wisdom beyond the child in such matters. And the child should be able to trust the input of the parents since he knows it will be based on their love for him or her as their child.

The child, because he or she loves this other person, wants to know the parents will love them also, will find them acceptable in the family circle. Any child lacking this family relationship faces a real void in their life.

Didn't God know what was best in the case of that early church council? I presume he did. Yet, according to the narrative, he conferred with his grown children in the matter and the decision was one of a cooperative effort.

James, Peter, Paul, Barnabas and others had to know they were taking an adult step in growing up in this matter. It was God's place, as the Father, to allow, and listen to, the thoughts of his adult children before a decision was made. Now that's Family, that's good parenting!

This was an imminently sensible approach to a solution of the problem. How is it then that the leadership of the churches has fallen on such hard times that such counsel is not taking place today?

I take it that God's children were expected to grow up and take over the Family Business! And they have failed!

The advice of Jesus comes to mind: Go back and do the first works again!

If it ain't broke, don't try to fix it is a common expression. The educational establishment would do well to hearken to these words of wisdom in the teaching of school children.

In attempts to fix things that weren't broken, the leaders of the churches have done incalculable harm to the Gospel and the relationship in God's family, the human race.

Most would agree that it is extremely difficult to try to have a sensible discussion with most about religion. And most difficult of all when the conversation revolves around the Same Old Thing, the stories that have become concrete in the dogma of the churches.

Businesses fail when they lose contact with their market. Not much call for buggy whip manufacturers today. It has always been an enigma to me that people so sensible in other walks of life take sudden leave of their senses when discussing the things of God and the Bible.

It's as though some of these folks think God places a premium on ignorance and they have a license to practice!

But then I would never have thought of Abraham's nephew, Lot, as a righteous man if it didn't say this in the NT. But the narrative evidence for this is the way those Sodomites treated him; but his drunkenness and the act of his two daughters, implausible as the story is, that led to the Moabites and Ammonites leads to some interesting conjecture and speculation.

In fact, the whole story of Lot and the destruction of Sodom and Gomorrah deserve much discussion. For example, how many people know that Zoar would have been destroyed along with these two cities if Lot hadn't made a deal with the angels to go there for safety?

Nor would I have known about angels that left their home and station being bound with chains in darkness for judgment, about Satan contending with Michael the archangel over the body of Moses and the book of Enoch if I didn't read this in the epistle of Jude.

Speaking of which, in reference to the present crop of so-called evangelists, the words of Jude come prominently to mind: Yet these men speak abusively against whatever they do not understand; and what things they do understand by instinct, like unreasoning animals - these are the very things that destroy them. Woe to them! They have taken the way of Cain; they have rushed for profit into Balaam's error; they have been destroyed in Korah's rebellion.

Paul mentions two men, Jannes and Jambres, who opposed Moses. Yet we don't find these men in the OT account. Possibly the magicians of Pharaoh's court.

Does God engage in hyperbole? Read John 21:25.

Did God actually plan on such pain and suffering for the human race? And if not, what went wrong?

Many have attacked the Bible out of a sense of trying to do well. But such attacks have been the result of the abuses of the Bible by religious people who thought God would bless their prejudices and ignorance! Not going to happen.

It is believing in God that compels me to ask the hard questions with which the churches refuse to deal honestly and sensibly. This refusal only gives ammunition to the enemy and makes those purporting to speak for God, as though he couldn't speak for himself, look like fools.

It is one thing to be a fool for God in the sense of love, compassion and doing good in the face of evil. It is quite something else to be a fool through religious antics, hysteria, prejudice and superstitions.

Yet some will deceive themselves that they are being persecuted for the cause of God and Christ when, in fact, they are being treated as the fools they really are in every fleshly sense of the word!

It is against reason that the same God who gifted the worst infidel with genius isn't going to give a believer the same genius, wisdom and knowledge, isn't going to expect his own children to act sensibly and responsibly. Who's kidding whom?

Why should those who profess to love him make God to look foolish? I'm not going to fool anyone in my profession of love for my father, mother or children, and then steal from them, lie to them or shame and deceive them! Nor, in love for me, would any of them do so to me!

There is no attempt to be clever in my asking any of these questions. They would be obvious to anyone who cared to take the time to consider these things, who is an observer of people and knowledgeable of the histories and mythologies of cultures.

For example, honest Bible criticism derives from some questions like the ending of The Lord's Prayer. It is different in Matthew and Luke. There is no doubt that the ending - for yours is the kingdom and the power and the glory forever. Amen - is a gloss.

But textual criticism leaves some controversy about the ending, evil or evil one. There is a very significant difference, obviously, as to which is correct!

There is also some question concerning the prayer about the use of the words debt, trespass, or sin. The sense of the prayer is not changed by consideration of textual criticism and to ignore the legitimate questions that arise from such consideration is inexcusable.

But commentators do not want to deal with the seeming contradiction between asking God not to lead us into temptation and the passage in James 1:13 that declares God does not lead into temptation!

There is an abundance of good books like Harmonies of the Gospels, Science and the Scriptures, Bible Questions Answered, etc. Yet, the really hard questions like this are ignored or you are treated to some of the most twisted, politician and educationist-like non-answers imaginable.

It is in asking questions like this that results in your being treated to some of the real prejudices of the average churchgoer. And the worst (and most usual) response of all: I don't know, I've never thought about it but I'm sure there has to be an answer? Talk about intellectually lazy! I won't even go into the lack of real spirituality such a response exemplifies.

The point of this is that if questions do not arise from study, you are not studying! And you probably are not interested!

I was a classroom teacher for many years. If my students weren't asking questions, I knew I was failing to make the subject interesting to them.

It falls to those who would be teachers to make the subject interesting. That too many that are not called are filling pulpits (and public school classrooms and offices) where they do not belong seems obvious. And that goes for the Bible colleges and seminaries as well.

There are many times when I cry out to God, just like those Psalmists of old, but the heavens seem as brass - there is no answer from God. Yet, so many times I am full of hope in the face of hopelessness that I take it this is of God.

I frequently pray for wisdom and guidance, for some sign of God's favor and approval or even disapproval and I get ... nothing. There have been times when I considered myself a Christian that things have been so dark in my life that I have laid in bed clutching my Bible and the only prayer I could say was the single word: Help!

The psychosis of grief brought on by the loss of a child or a spouse, divorce, financial disaster, your children suffering and being unable to help or take the pain on yourself, all these Midnight's of the Soul cannot possibly have been in the mind of a loving God, could not possibly be his plan for humanity.

In the face of so much wrong, injustice, and suffering worldwide, you try to tell me that God planned such things! NO! I will not have it!

And if he did not plan such things, what went wrong?

Here goes:

David in Psalm 37:25 writes: I was young and now I am old, yet

I have never seen the righteous forsaken or their children begging bread.

I am old enough to find fault with David. Either he was wrong or I have met a lot of good people I considered righteous who failed the test of God. History is replete with examples that contradict David's optimism of God's taking care of the righteous.

If we are left with nothing but the Party Line of the churches in attempts to make sense of the evil of this world, with the seeming contradictions of men like David, we are left floundering.

Awake, O Lord! Why do you sleep? Psalm 44:23.

Go through the Psalms and mark every passage where men cry out to God as though he didn't know, didn't hear or didn't act. You will be amazed at the humanity expressed and the thoughts such men had about God. They declare the error of those who think God is omniscient, omnipresent, and omnipotent.

God can do anything. Wrong! He does not seem to be able to change a betraying heart, he does not prevent us from making injurious choices, he has not kept the suffering of untold millions from happening, and he has not prevented wars and evil rulers from gaining ascendancy.

Perhaps God chooses not to intervene, chooses not to prevent incalculable suffering of the creatures for which he is the responsible party as Creator. Perhaps we just don't see the Big Picture!

Or, perhaps, he expects us to act against evil in ways we have not; perhaps he expects us to take action against evil as God's adult children and act responsibly in the face of evil.

We face many unanswered questions in this regard. Jesus says in Matthew 10:34 "Do not suppose that I have come to bring peace to the earth. I did not come to bring peace, but a sword." Yet he is called, The Prince of Peace!

In John 9:39 we read: For judgment I have come into this world....

In John 12:47 we read: ... For I did not come to judge the world, but to save it.

Luke 22:36-38 ... if you don't have a sword, sell your cloak and buy one.... The disciples said: See, Lord, here are two swords. That is enough, he replied.

John 18:10,11 "Then Simon Peter, who had a sword, drew it and struck the high priest's servant, cutting off his right ear. (The servant's name was Malchus)". Jesus commanded Peter, "Put your sword away!"

Matthew 26:52 Put your sword back in its place, for all who draw the sword will die by the sword. And in Luke 22:51 No more of this! And he healed the servant's ear.

When a minister and very close friend of mine was going through some really deep waters he asked me, Sam, what am I to do?

I told him: You just muddle through.

We seem to be forced into becoming experts, at times, in just muddling through. My friend had to agree.

I raise these questions because I want answers to my questions. I'm like that father in Mark 9:24. I do believe, help me overcome my unbelief!

It isn't the unbelief in God with which I struggle, though there are many things about the nature of God and his (perhaps his and her) origins that keeps me wondering and asking questions; it is the unbelief of those who purport to be God's servants yet do so much evil in making him appear a fool! It is unbelief of a system of religion that denies the real nature of God as I perceive him, and that he does not expect us to grow up and study to show ourselves approved in the sight of both God and men!

Now I wonder about many things. I wonder why God had to come see for himself if things were really as bad in Sodom and Gomorrah as he had been told?

I wonder why, if God were so set on monogamy, he allowed men like Lamech, Abraham, Jacob, David, Solomon and others to multiply women to themselves? Was he really mad at these guys and trying to get even?

Speaking of sex in the Bible, and it figures prominently as well it should since the Bible deals with a lot of reality we have the story of God telling Hosea to marry a whore.

Now there are a lot of guys who might get a tad upset at such a command. Not old Hosea, he went right out and did as God told him. He married the whore, Gomer, and they even had a couple of kids; a son, Jezreel, and a daughter, Lo-Ruhamah.

What's in a name? Quite a bit in those times. Read the story and you will understand the point God was trying to make.

Now I'm not going to argue with God if he gives me an explicit command. And I'm not going to impugn Noah by saying he couldn't swim. But let's face it folks, if you read the Bible, there are bound to be questions about God's dealings with people at times.

Let's hear it for Judah! This is the guy who conspired with his brothers to sell their brother Joseph into slavery. Among his other attributes he slept with his daughter-in-law, Tamar, thinking she was a prostitute.

The purported reason for the deception of his daughter-in-law and her purpose in servicing Judah was that he had not given her his son Shelah to replace the two sons God had killed, one of which was Onan. Sound familiar?

Now pregnant by her father-in-law, though he didn't know it was Tamar he was doing because she had disguised herself and wore a veil (I'm not going to touch that one at this time. I'll save it for another chapter.) Judah wants her stoned to death for being promiscuous!

But Tamar had played it cool. She had made Judah give her his staff and seal until he had paid her in her role as prostitute. Good thinking. But she skipped, taking the staff and seal with her, before he returned with the promised payment.

Now she confronts him with those tokens of payment as the father of the baby and good old Judah is caught with his proverbial pants down. Who ever said the Bible wasn't interesting reading?

The sheer hypocrisy of Judah, and men in general, that a roll in the hay with a prostitute was ok but the women better watch out! Apocryphal or not, Jesus made a good point when those Jews only brought the woman and not the man for judgment. According to the Law, both were to be stoned to death. How typical that they only brought the woman. How Judah-like!

Judah's wife had died; God had killed his two sons so who would blame him for seeking the consolation of a warm, woman's body? I'm a proponent and devout believer of monogamy but you wouldn't find me slashing my wrists under the circumstances. However the hypocrisy of the thing is really galling!

Well, to go on.

Why didn't God intervene before David murdered Bathsheba's husband, Uriah? Then kill the baby that resulted from the adulterous union only to allow another baby of this unholy union, Solomon, to become King of Israel? And since we are told God loved this child he told the prophet, Nathan, to name him Jedidiah. II Samuel 12:25. But who ever heard of the wisdom of Jedidiah or King Jedidiah's Mine?

Just who are these sons of God and daughters of men in Genesis 6:1? Yeah, I know, the Sethites. Won't fly. Never has.

And when will Biblical expositors ever get around to admitting that the word Strive or Contend means to exert much energy, to struggle? But to admit that they would have to come up with an answer to God saying he wouldn't always Contend, Strive with men! Genesis 6:3. And that doesn't fit a theology of Perfect - Omniscient, Omnipotent, and Omnipresent.

Abraham, as I have pointed out in the past, argued with God about the destruction of Sodom and Gomorrah because he really thought God was going to make a mistake! And this Friend of God was truly attempting to keep his friend from making a mistake. I contend Abraham knew more about the real nature of God than we do!

Where, exactly, did Cain get a wife?

Now I don't know if George Washington just had a natural hatred of cherries as a boy. Maybe the tree was in his way when he wanted to use his slingshot or bean shooter from his bedroom window. Maybe he had just got the hatchet for a present and wanted to test it out. The encouraging part of the story is Washington's early penchant for veracity.

If we were to accept the story as the truth, rather than apocryphal, you can see where the study comes in.

The kid cuts down the tree. We aren't told why? But we are told that when caught with the goods, he can't tell a lie. He owns up to the despicable act.

Yet, when dad confronts him, there is only one little boy with a hatchet in the house. What good would it do to lie? Maybe George had had other experiences with a hatchet; maybe he had monogrammed the dining room table or customized the legs of the piano previously?

We could go on at some length in this vein. And it would be an interesting study.

But we have far better sources of material for determining George Washington's character and veracity than a story; interesting as the story may be and as rooted in the real character of Washington as it might be.

The textual study of the Bible is much like this. That some of the material is of the same nature as Washington and the Cherry Tree must be a factor in such study. But the over-all view is one of such integrity and truthfulness in so many instances that it deserves, demands in fact, such study.

The Battle of Monongahela on July 9, 1755 had three historians; all three of which were eyewitnesses. Washington was one of them and served under General Braddock during the battle.

Yet the three accounts of the battle differ in significant details. None of these men intentionally lied; but all three had a different view of some aspects of the battle. And these three views are in conflict in places.

We face some of this difficulty when we come to the study of the Bible, especially in a study of the Gospels. It may sound very spiritual to say: If it's in the Bible, I believe it; I don't question it! I can only say: You ignorant, pompous fool!

Still there are those who really believe they are taking a stand for God in such an attitude of ignorant prejudice. Such people will probably never know the real harm they do to the honor of God. And probably don't care.

The Bible sheds a lot of light on the history and nature of humanity. The principle of the Christian Gospel is that God is love. "Whoever lives in love lives in God, and God in him." I John 4:16, is an agreed commonality of all peoples and philosophies.

The Children of God, as Jesus pointed out, are distinguished by love.

This is why I call the Bible, at least in part, a Romance. And a part of that romance is the battle against those evil ones who would try to destroy beauty, and profane love.

The romantic monotheism of the Bible is in sharp contrast with the superstitious idolatries practiced from the earliest times of man on earth. Archaeological discoveries continue to support almost indescribably hideous, heathen practices such as the sacrificing of babies to appease bloodthirsty gods and goddesses.

But a monotheistic belief must take into account a plurality of Scripture and the denigration of women, items not satisfactorily answered by theologians and one that the recent Jesus Seminars have missed as well.

Not that attempts have not been made. Keil and Delitzch, for example, try to make a case for the pluralis majestatis, God speaking of Himself and with Himself and foundational of the Trinity in Genesis 1:26 and 3:21.

But it would serve the Truth well to keep in mind that even experts like K&D and others with an orthodox Christian or Jewish mind-set have a prejudice they are intent on proving regardless their academic qualifications. Honesty that honors God is not a prejudice or bias that dishonors honest scholarship and chooses to ignore facts.

As per Romans, the first chapter, there is little argument philosophically that the creation of God reflects his nature.

But turning to Genesis 11:7, Come, let us go down and confuse their language ... together with the plural pronouns of chapters 1 and 2 requires much examination. The pluralis majestatis is not very satisfactory in this instance of 11:7. Just who is this US?

This early use of a plurality in reference to God together with Jesus' use of Psalm 82:6 in John 10:34,35 calling us gods may shed light on the problem.

From the earliest history of the human race there has been a pronounced belief in the supernatural, of a spiritual world of beings different than man.

The corruption of pantheistic religions as opposed to the monotheism of the Bible (and its intentional disavowal of the equal value of women) may, nevertheless, have some basis in fact. The evolving religions and mythologies of the human race may have elements of truth.

From the Biblical narrative one might suppose, given the necessary degree of imagination, that Satan may very well have creative ability. If so, you might also suppose there is the possibility that the early life forms such as the dinosaurs may have been his creation. It is worth examining, though only for those given to thinking of such things, whether there was, in fact, a race of beings different than man that led to Satan's hatred of, and attack on Adam and Eve.

While such a thing might seem more suitable for an X-Files episode than legitimate speculation, it must be remembered that many myths and superstitions have some basis in facts.

An examination of this idea might help explain Genesis 6:1,2 concerning the sons of God and the daughters of men and why this led to God's painful exclamation that his spirit would not always contend with that of man's.

The Nephilim were on the earth in those days. Genesis 6:4. Some commentators have construed these as the descendants of Cain, as the Hebrew language used indicates in the case of the giants or heroes of this verse, men of reckless ferocity and without godly conscience. Non-studied readers of the Bible are certainly led astray here in most translations and versions.

Some commentators have given credence to the possibility, since the language permits, of assigning these sons of God who took wives of the daughters of men assimilation between two species.

That Cain may very well have been the progenitor of a race of beings defiant of God as exemplified in the idolatrous practices and violence that filled the earth and drove God to the decision to destroy mankind is a possibility, given the narrative. But it does not explain where Cain got his wife.

Nimrod of Genesis 10:8 is another corruption of most translations that lead astray. The name means we will revolt; and it means revolt against God! As to being a mighty hunter, this was opposed to God's intention that man would till the soil. Nimrod is credited with founding Babylon and Nineveh.

If the flood was intended to start over with Noah and his sons, it failed. If the earth was re-peopled with the progeny of Noah, sin quickly gained access through Ham resulting in Noah's cursing him and his line, and blessing Shem and Japheth.

But keep in mind that the wives of Noah's sons had to come from somewhere among those wicked people that were destroyed by the flood. Bad Seed?

The story of the building of the tower of Babel and the confusion of tongues is a fascinating one. That men thought they could build a structure to reach heaven is most improbable.

But given the story in the OT, the clear intent of these men was to consolidate and build in such a manner that, in some way, threatened God or his plans for humanity. The language used "If as one people speaking the same language they have begun to do this, then nothing they plan to do will be impossible for them!" leads to such a conclusion.

All of this is most troubling to the average pew-warmer. As well it should be.

The fact that so much of idolatry is reflected in cruelty and horrible, grotesque pictures and idols of antiquity should be a clue to the corruption of a truth. It may be that this truth is that there do exist children of God and children of the Devil by some definition and the commingling of these constituted the Bad Seed of Ham.

Did Cain take a wife of a created species of Satan? Did this ultimately lead to the eventual evil that was so prevalent that God determined to destroy all life on earth? While I do not believe in the Devil of religion, there may be an even more interesting truth at the bottom of such speculation. Such is the intrigue of studying ancient myths and superstitions.

But back to that tree in the Garden, the tree of the Knowledge of Good and Evil that led God to say the man has now become like us to know good and evil. In the context, the US has to include that very knowledge of evil and the ability to discern between good and evil which is a characteristic of God-likeness.

It is said that the ability to distinguish between good and evil, the diabolical and the divine, requires experiencing both. But I do not have to molest a child to know it is diabolically evil, that they who do such a thing are devilishly evil.

Since I do not have to practice evil in order to discern it, what makes me different than those who do such things? Am I better than they are or different? If different, what constitutes that difference in others like me who do not practice evil without conscience? Whence this conscience in some and the lack of such a thing in others? Will genetics eventually explain this?

Yet in my own consciousness there is every evil imaginable to man.

Back to that tree of the Knowledge of Good and Evil. Speculatively, its fruit may well have contained several corrupting toxins; one of which may have passed on death through an aging process. The antidote may have been in the Tree of Life.

Whatever the case, the infection of Adam and Eve resulted in both a Cain and an Able, and later, a Seth. So the heart of man is described as desperately wicked and deceitful above all things, who can know it? Jeremiah 17:9. But that potential was there in the beginning with Adam and Eve as God created them.

Still, I do not rape, torture, murder and pillage even though such things are in my consciousness. Why am I loath to do such things that come so easily to others?

Children of God and children of the Devil! An interesting parentage and demanding knowledge of the parents! If genetic, what of the progenitors of the difference in such genes? Back to trying to make sense of the Bible and other mythologies, the histories and mythologies of the human race, that part of the human race that has always been humane and, possibly, those others.

There is the potential for repentance in men. But not all men, as the Bible makes clear. Esau and Judas are examples. But even an adulterous murderer like David, while not escaping the consequences of his sins, was still a man of God according to the Bible. But unable to make restitution, a requirement of true repentance, the sword never departed David's house and his own family became a curse to him.

The story of the Bible, the main theme of literature and the history of mankind, is the struggle between good and evil. But if mankind, humankind, humanity is struggling against another race, another species disposed against all that is pure, good and beautiful, against love for one another, and set on the destruction of God's plans for such a people?

Was this forbidden tree productive of Bad Seed? Did it predispose to evil? Eve gave birth to Cain and he became a murderer.

But God had created Adam and Eve with the ability to choose. They could, evidently, make choices for evil as well as good as evidenced by their choices that led to the seduction/deception of Eve and the betrayal of God by Adam.

Cain was cast away from home and made to wander in the land

of Nod where he found a wife. There has to be an explanation for that race of beings in which he found her.

But this did not save the Sethites from the evil of Cain, and his descendants infecting them to the point that the whole world was eventually filled with wickedness and violence.

Enoch, we are told, walked with God and God removed him. Why? Obviously Enoch was different, and that difference is reflected in the book of his name mentioned by Jude. But it most certainly was not the book of that name available to us, which is an obvious fraud.

Jude had information not available to us. His mention of those angels who fell, of a race of Celestial beings including Satan, being cases in point. Perhaps those godless men who slipped into the church that Jude says were prophesied of from long ago were children of the Devil and of his race?

There has to be a rational reason for the evolution of good and evil, for so much corruption of humanity and the continual conflict of history. Within the same species to have torturers, serial killers, people with no discernible conscience, in conflict with the sacrificial love of others who exemplify the best of humanity has to have a basis that we should be able to determine.

Reputedly the earliest book of the Bible, Job, treats God's dealings with Satan and other angels in an interesting manner, particularly in respect to the interaction with mankind.

One of the most interesting parts of Jesus' ministry was the casting out of demons. He had converse with them, they knew him as the Holy One, the Son of God and even asked if he had come to torment them before their time? Matthew 8:29.

While granting the ignorance and superstitions current at the time, one is still drawn to such stories. We still want to have our UFOs and things that go bump in the night. But the human behavior and beliefs of the period are of utmost interest to the scholar.

The request of the demons possessing that poor Gadarene demoniac to be allowed to enter a herd of pigs is most interesting. Better a pig than nothing? But apparently it wasn't the usual thing for demons to infect animals; because they must not have realized it would drive the pigs insane resulting in their running into the sea and being drowned. What became of the demons as a result? Where'd they go?

Where is the Abyss of the Bible, where is the Pit, that place of Darkness, to which fallen angels were consigned? Hades has a long history in the legends of men and a prominent place in Scripture.

Despite the difficulties that plague our search for answers, the Bible does offer hope of such. One of these areas of hope is the monotheism of the Bible as opposed to the myths and multiplicity of the gods and goddesses of men's invention.

While I credit these myths with germinal truths, and I believe we have much to learn from them, we would be swimming in even murkier waters without the Bible as a guide in spite of its anti-woman bias and the contradictions and myths.

With so much in myths and legends to draw from for seminal thought, and with which to compare the Biblical record, I believe answers to our questions can be found.

But I believe the monotheism of the Bible must be studied from a different view than traditionally. One God has to be interpreted to include a family and a family relationship between the heavenly and the earthly and leave room for understanding of the US of God's use of that pronoun in reference to himself in Genesis.

I call this romantic monotheism because of the requirement of romance that there be only the two lovers. Bring in a third party and love and romance is blasted, betrayed, profaned.

In the Bible, God calls himself a jealous God. He will have no other gods before him as per the first commandment. The language of Scripture that the Israelites went whoring after other gods, committing adultery against God, is a case in point.

So God, according to the NT, as the Ultimate Romantic, looks forward to a Virgin Bride, The Church, to fulfill his own romantic dream of a love-partner in eternity. This is why I choose to call a part of the Bible a Romance.

But in this instance, you have to view God in the NT as a bachelor, as opposed to the God of Genesis where there may be a Mr. and Mrs. God cooperating in creation.

Like any real romance, the course of true love does not run smoothly. Many things intrude to disrupt the lovers; and like the reality of true love, it has many envious enemies who try to destroy the relationship.

As with Adam and Eve and romance, once a third party, the serpent, was introduced, innocence was blasted and betrayal of true love was the result. The first seduction of a woman. And the first act of a man trying to excuse his own failure by blaming a woman.

The enmity between the woman and her seed and the serpent and his seed needs much exposition because it is a part of the historical resentment of women against men, together with the fact that women, being the weaker sex, became the prey of predatory men. Also, it is a man's world; men rule and lead and women are forced to follow.

Whatever happened to alienate men and women, and I credit the story of the Garden with this no matter how it is interpreted; the result was the exclusion of women in the philosophies of men that have guided the course of nations and history.

This Missing Half of Humankind: Women! as I call it, has excluded an entire half of the human race. The result has been the history of humankind being a history of warfare. I cannot help but believe that to solve the most intractable problem of humanity, the problem between men and women, women must be included in a way they never have been.

It is a truism that men make war, not women. Not that men don't fight over women. Go to any bar; and if you wait long enough, you'll see an example. But women don't have babies to sacrifice them on the altar of the wars of men!!

Chapter six

In Refutation of Ecos Foucaults Pendulum (among other things).

There is a greatly increased surge of interest in things of the occult these days. Almost paradoxically for a modern age of such leaping advances in the sciences, the dark and mystical arts are attracting devotees in large numbers.

There are many, even legitimate, reasons for this. Thorough disenchantment with organized religions and economies are major factors. And the modern civilizations of the great powers are grossly ignorant of the superstitions and myths that still hold sway in the greater part of a demon-haunted world in which 3 billion people have never received a phone call.

Nations such as the U.S., England and France are far from being free of such ignorant myths and superstitions. You don't have to travel much in any of these countries to find that multiplied millions are given to occult beliefs and practices. A religious Atavism, for example, seems to be infecting people in untold numbers.

By strict definition, many TV and radio evangelists, the charismatic churches and itinerate healers like Mario Cerrillo, are promoters of the occult and fall into this category.

But it is almost as impossible to get the Christian community, the churches, to be honest about the inroads such teachings are making in aiding such enemies of humanity as it is to get them to be honest about sex!

One of my concerns about this growing interest in mysticism and the occult is the fact that religion of all kinds is fast losing the power to keep the poor from killing the rich. In fact, if people begin to believe in methodologies that can bring riches and power through devotion to occult deities and spells, promoters of hysteria like the charismatics;

you aren't far removed from the demands of sacrifices required by Moloch and Baal.

Humankind has never departed, for example, from the most ancient fertility religions manifested in the worship of the Queen of Heaven in one form or another, whether it be Mary, the Mother of God at the Vatican, or the Black Madonna of Salvador and Brazil.

But the most ancient history of man and the various man-like species are replete with worship of some kind. It's as though religion, by any definition, is inherent in the genes throughout.

There is a need for a certain syncretism among people. And there are commonalities to be found throughout the history of religions. It has always remained a question of which of these things draw together, and which separate, people, and why? A question of the historical paradox of good and evil that has defied our best efforts at a solution.

Being on fire for God as a young man and believing myself called to the ministry, I spared no expense of time and money in the preparation for my calling.

I had a marvelous, spiritual advisor in the person of Charles L. Feinberg (Uncle Charles), then Dean of Talbot Theological Seminary. Wilbur Smith recommended me to a book at the time: One Hundred Titles that should be in Every Minister's Library.

The number, 100, is somewhat misleading as some of these titles like the AnteNicene, Nicene and PostNicene Fathers were encyclopedic sets of books. Sets of commentaries often ran to large, and very expensive, numbers of volumes.

By the time I began to accumulate this library, many titles were scarce or out of print and I was buying books from places like England, Ireland and bookstores in cities like Boston. Before I had completed this list I had over 5,000 volumes of Bible study books.

Many were history texts. Some covered things like cultural anthropology, archaeology, comparative religions, science, languages, and the geography of Bible lands. There were books of systematic and dogmatic theology, hermeneutics, ethics, religious philosophy, and so much more.

For over twenty-years I lived in such books. And in the process, my knowledge of the Bible and its history became encyclopedic.

And I learned how very few ministers had anything approaching such a personal library. The cost alone being one of the principal reasons ministers do not have such a library.

Something else I learned. Not that many ministers were even interested in such a library or such an exhaustive and demanding study of the Bible!

During the past, ten years, I have come to realize how much of my study of the subject was misdirected by men who were exceedingly biased in their own view of the Bible. I learned how few practiced objectivity in discussing some of the questions that naturally arise from such a study.

The zeal of my youth has been replaced by a zeal for the truth and letting the chips fall where they may. My academic and experiential background has well equipped me for taking on the task of confronting the hypocrisy of the churches in their refusal to deal realistically with the hard questions of the Christian faith.

One of my academic specialties, Human Behavior, has helped enormously in gaining a degree of objectivity in Bible study. My undergraduate majors in Literature and Vocational Education have been of great benefit as well.

As a well-educated and intelligent man (the opinion of others so not to be dismissed entirely), I bring a wealth of background to the subjects I have undertaken. That they are subjects that people have very strong opinions about has resulted in the more orthodox brethren consigning me to the eternal flames.

But I have a strong compulsion (and maybe a death wish) because of my background as a teacher among other things, to confront ignorance and prejudice.

Umberto Eco writing in Foucault's Pendulum was right in respect to: The fact is that it doesn't take long for the experience of the Numinous to unhinge the mind. This Numinous is becoming a gentle partner that accompanies me as I delve deeper and deeper into the paradox of good and evil reminding me that I am fast becoming a candidate. And it is fatiguing work.

I don't fancy myself made of sterner stuff in my search into things that have driven some men mad. Some of my detractors have said I've reached that point already and advise people to keep me away from sharp instruments and dynamite. I have an interesting textbook from my graduate studies titled: Religious Systems and Psychotherapy by Dr. Richard Cox that is somewhat descriptive of the problems I will be discussing. The book covers some fourteen, major world religious systems, not counting systems of magic, exorcism or witchcraft. Mankind's absolute need to make sense of his need for standards of morality and laws, his longing for immortality and his fear of death, his belief in the supernatural, has led to great extremes of behavior; not all them promoting sound, mental health.

In fact, the worship of Satan, the practice of witchcraft, etc. is not usually taken as a sign of mental health. Yet there are equally damaging systems of belief such as those of the charismatic churches that take advantage of humankind's need of believing in the supernatural. These excesses of religious fervor have kept the supernatural potboiling.

But the mental health aspect of such beliefs can be illustrated by what happened to a close friend of mine of many years' acquaintance that is far more than merely anecdotal.

He and his wife got mixed up in a typical charismatic church. The so-called minister convinced my friend's wife that her husband was demon possessed and she was to leave him for the sake of her soul.

Not atypically, this man of the cloth soon had my friend's wife in the sack with him. Such abuses of these kinds of superstitious hysteria are a commonplace in such so-called churches. Not that good Baptists and Catholics aren't capable of the same thing, as we all know.

That sex is an absolute in one form or another in all religion is a given. Women, as Gary North stated, might confuse sex and religion, but men are not confused; they are basic. They simply use religion for sexual ends.

Whether you are a devotee of Atlantis or UFOs, sex is there. However, it may have been that our most ancient ancestors didn't understand the mechanism of sex in relationship to making babies as per Sam Clemens' parody of Adam and Eve.

But by the time of recorded history, humans seem to have made the connection that sex and making babies had something in common. Enough superstition existed, however, to bring in a fertility religion that through the ages developed rather systematically.

Still, a science of procreation was a long time coming. And even with that, the superstitions of the past remained in large part and still have advocates throughout the world today.

The point being that it is too easy to take advantage of humanity's need of religion through superstitions and myths. And there has never been any lack of Black Coats, as Paine called them, to service such superstitions.

The superstitions of our modern times, as preached and taught by our present crop of Black Coats, have a long history of great antiquity. No matter the attempts to put a new face on such doctrines, there is little new about them.

Some have described man as an inherently religious animal. I take exception to any description of man as an animal in this sense. Man has the capacity of reason and choice denied animals.

The greatest thinkers of history have bent their minds to a systematic study of humans in relationship to God or gods and goddesses. From these studies, philosophies have arisen in attempts to make sense of it all.

For most of these great thinkers, there has been a compulsion in pursuing truth. Some, like Socrates, paid the price for this search with their lives when their questions were perceived as dangerous to the status quo of religion or state.

There is a like compulsion in me to do this. But unlike Socrates, I'm not going quietly. And while there's no money in it as Melville said, the compulsion remains. If I were doing it for money or women, it would be sensible.

But I'm not so crazy (yet) that I envision beautiful women coming up to me at book signings and telling me they want to have my baby! That part of my mind, what's left of it, remains fairly rational and non-delusional. So far.

No doubt there will be those who, after reading some of the following, will consign me to the outer reaches. Some, like my old friend, Gary North, have already consigned me to the flames of hell.

And while I have reached the stage of life where warmth is more attractive to me all the time, I don't consciously seek an eternity stoking the Devil's furnace. But if heaven is the place people like Gary and most Baptists and Catholics describe, I join Huckleberry Finn in not being too sure about that place either.

In searching out a Causal Principal, a Prime Cause, an I Am and all this implies, when you have exhausted the great thinkers with all the ontological, cosmological, teleological, transcendental, and existential arguments, you are still left with the problem of the paradox of good and evil; as William James discovered for himself as per a Theistic Psychology.

Deist, Theist, Pantheist, Agnostic, Christian, Jew, Moslem, Buddhist, etc. (I do not include atheists because, by definition, none such exists), all seeking understanding of the un-understandable and their contradictions outweighing their apologetics.

Christianity and many other religions share a doctrine of Kant's moral approach to God. But Jesus did not approve, in spite of some of the history of the church that bears his name, conversion by the sword, as do many others.

But there is a Believe in Jesus or go to hell mentality in many of those who profess the name. And far too many of these know virtually nothing of the Real Jesus or the Real Bible. And that ignorance has been a literal killer among those that have called themselves Christian as well as Jew and Moslem.

With this brief introduction, let's talk about Astrology, Witchcraft, and things that go bump in the night. And lest my children misunderstand, I am not burning incense, lighting candles around my bed and muttering incantations before turning in.

If I am struck dead for sacrilege and blasphemy, as some of the more fundamental brethren are praying will happen, I want my children to know that some of the strange books they find strewn about my bachelor house were for research; not an attempt to discover the philosopher's stone, put a hex on an ex-wife or ex-in-laws, or make myself irresistibly appealing to the opposite sex (well, that might have some merit but...).

One of the commandments of the law in the Old Testament was that a witch must be killed. Exodus 22:18 and Deuteronomy 18:10. Those that sacrificed to idols were in this category as well. That such practices often included human sacrifice, even the sacrifice of babies, was a primary reason given by God for the wholesale destruction of the Canaanites by the Israelites after the Exodus.

Were witches, sorcerers, and conjurors real, could someone really consort with familiar spirits? According to the Bible, yes.

In Exodus 8, Pharaoh's magicians were able to make snakes of their staffs just as Moses did with his. The Witch of Endor in I Samuel 28 is a familiar story to many.

There is far too much evidence for the paranormal to dismiss it out of hand. The fact that God warns so vehemently against consorting with familiar spirits must have some basis in fact of danger existing in such things. But danger to who, from whom, and of what?

The entire history of the human race is tied inextricably to a belief in the supernatural. While those like H.G. Wells expressed the hope that an Age of Science would dispel these myths and superstitions (as he saw them), he would be rolling over in his grave (and may be doing so) to see our modern age so immersed in such things and the failure of science to explain it all away.

Of course, we have to give TV evangelists and the charismatic churches their due in this regard. By emphasizing the supernatural like the hysteria of tongues, visions and miracles that these kooks blame on God and the Holy Spirit, they have kept the pot boiling.

One of the greatest problems with this kind of thing is the fact that if someone has an experience, he or she cannot deny it happened. That it happened as a result of emotional hysteria is not going to be admitted; to do so would be to deny it was of God.

And if not of God, a religious person would think it had to be of Satan and no such person is about to admit they have been deceived by the Deceiver! Many, as a result, become clients of psychologists and psychiatrists. And a great many others need help.

I'll repeat something I wrote some time ago:

Now I've met a few people who didn't seem to have a full clip. They're the kind who would play Russian roulette with an automatic. They remind me of the guy that, in despair and rage because of his marriage to a nagging shrew of a wife, couldn't take it any more and decided to end it all. As he put the gun to his head, his wife came in the room and laughing, said: You idiot, what do you think you're doing now? Go ahead and laugh, he said, you're next!

Now there is dumb, and then there is terminally dumb. Realizing this, having met a few of these folks, it shouldn't be surprising there are always going to be those who are willing to support religious charlatans of every description.

UFOs might be your thing; I don't know. I don't discount them simply because I have never shaken hands with any little green men. But I draw the line at outright fraud. And especially fraud in the name of God and Jesus Christ.

The mental health industry is a booming one. Folks are going nuts in record numbers. If you're in the business, you might say people are going crazy at a healthy rate.

No small number of those seeking help has been involved with some kind of religion that drove them around the bend.

It occurred to me some time ago that there is a paradox here. The very kind of hysterical practices like tongues, miracles, healings, voices and visions of God and Angels that some churches and TV ministries encourage are the very things a host of psychologists and psychiatrists are trying to cure! And, like the promoters of sick minds through religion, are doing quite well for themselves in the process. A symbiotic relationship if I ever saw one!

Mental disorder induced by religious hysteria is nothing new. It's been around as long as the human race. In recent times, organizations like Fundamentalists Anonymous have arisen to try to help people who have been the victims of religious charlatans and delusions.

In Acts 16:16 we read of a slave girl who had a spirit of divination by which she predicted the future and earned a great deal of money for her owners by this. But Paul ruined the schtick by casting out this spirit in the name of Jesus.

The owners were so upset they had Paul and Silas, who was with him at the time, arrested and tossed in jail. But God miraculously delivered them. Interesting story.

The Apostles and those of their time had a very pronounced belief in ghosts. And Jesus did not disabuse them of such a belief.

When the Apostles saw Jesus walking on the water they thought it was a ghost. In Jesus' appearing to the disciples in the upper room after the resurrection they think he is a ghost, but he says to them: Look at my hands and feet. It is I myself! Touch me and see; a ghost does not have flesh and bones, as you see I have. Cf. Luke and John.

When the angel released Peter from prison and he went to the disciples, he was left knocking on the gate while the little servant girl went to inform the disciples Peter was there. They said it can't be; it must be his ghost!

And demons, unclean spirits? They must have reached epidemic numbers at the time of Jesus!

The belief that peculiar, even demented, people have a touch of the divine is a part of the religion of many cultures even today. The Contraries, Shamans, and Witch doctors have always been believed to have contact with spirits, and such beliefs still hold sway in many cultures.

Some believe the left side of the brain controls paranormal power. Since the right side is supposed to deal with mechanical functions, and because we live in an increasingly mechanical society that requires right function almost to the exclusion of that sensitive, artistic left side, some theorize people do not exercise the left enough to use their supernatural powers.

Left-handedness has usually been equated with evil and the sinister in past cultures. In fact, the Latin for sinister means left-handed. But if those who subscribe to right-left brain function are right, the right brain controls the left side of the body and vice versa.

This leads to left-handedness being right brain dominated. In other words, the right side of the brain is the evil side and, as mechanistic, is more inclined to materialism, robbing, cheating, stealing, and lying than asceticism or compassion. You might say if the right side dominates, the more it dominates the more the person is inclined to evil, and the theory of not trusting left-handed people has some basis in such thinking.

If the right brain dominates things like mathematics and playing chess, those that excel in these areas are usually thought to be somewhat cold and lacking much interest in people, whereas the artists and poets, creative people of great sensitivity are totally different as left-brain people. And, so it often is.

In Judges 3 we read that God gave the Israelites a Judge, Ehud, who was left-handed. He used this feature to deceive and slay Eglon, the king of Moab. This belief of the deceptive characteristic of left-handedness has a history of great antiquity long before the time of Ehud.

In Judges 16 when the Benjamites fought against Israel they had

700 chosen men who were left-handed; each of which could sling a stone at a hair and not miss, verse 16 (some exaggerations of this nature never change) A bit of hyperbole, I suspect. But the Benjamites were beaten badly, nearly decimated. It takes more than left-handed sharpshooters to win a war.

We are still learning things that impact on the superstitions and myths of the past. And some of the findings open the door to even more questions.

In studies of the paranormal, an experience fairly common among people is Deja vu. There are documented cases of things that would seem to give some credence to clairvoyance, telekinesis, poltergeists, etc. But I believe research in particle physics, brain function, and genetics will explain these things now covered under the umbrella of Psi.

Dreams are prominent in the belief systems of cultures throughout history and even today. The Bible has several stories of dreams and visions given to people. The prophet Daniel is prominent in this category.

But giving credence to superstitions is quite something else.

A superstition found in the Bible: Snails or slugs melt away as they crawl. Psalm 58:8. One can hardly blame God for this. He knows snails and slugs don't melt. Unless you pour salt on them. Literary license?

Jacob makes sure his goats turn out spotted, streaked or speckled, and the sheep dark, by placing branches from trees that have been stripped in such a fashion as to influence the animals while mating at their watering places. Genesis 30:37-39.

Mandrakes for sex, Gen. 30. But the love apples do Rachel no good and Leah has another son, praising Elohim (verse 17) for his goodness to her. I can't help remarking at this point that the whole story of Jacob in this context is a commentary on the grim reality of something that has never, and probably will never, change. Men want young and beautiful.

In all probability, Rachel was a perfect 10, 33-20-34, and Leah may have had a shape like a pear. Or maybe she needed a veil. Men, as with Jacob, will be men.

But Rachel had stolen the family gods when Jacob departed from Laban. Gen. 31:19. Whether rabbit's foot or gods, there is something comfortable about such talismans.

Jacob wrestles with an angel and becomes Israel. Gen. 32:24.

He tells his household to get rid of their foreign gods, 35:2. But this problem continues throughout the history of Jacob and will carry into Egypt with his sons.

Why, one may legitimately ask, are these stories part of the Biblical narrative? While so many of the fabulous stories and myths of antiquity are excluded, an evidence of the attempt to keep the history of the Biblical narrative in its integrity, there are still things of the paranormal from which we may learn and have a right to question; things which ancient literatures may help us to understand.

The tribes of Jacob will grow in Egypt, even becoming a threat to that nation according to the narrative. The Egyptians will make slaves of the Israelites and, in due course, they will cry out to God for deliverance.

But 400 years of indoctrination into the religion of Egypt will take its toll, as will be evident in the story of the Exodus. It doesn't help that many superstitions of Jacob and his wives and children went with them into the land of Goshen. God will have his hands full trying to disabuse these people of their superstitions and idolatry.

Yet, there are nagging questions with which even this modern, scientific generation struggles; and undoubtedly some of them formed the basis of many superstitions of antiquity.

For example, you step into a room and sense another's presence. You are with a group of people but feel someone staring at you. You look around and sure enough, there is someone staring at you.

Virtually all of us have experienced some paranormal experience that defies explanation attributing such things to a sixth sense.

The biggest problem with such things is that they do not admit of experimentation and replication in scientifically controlled environments. There are tantalizing cases, a few successes, but not nearly enough to give us understanding of the processes at work.

But the fact that such things as precognition, prescience, and dream fulfillment exist explains much of ancient religious and mythological beliefs. Lacking telescopes, microscopes, and anything of a truly technical means of explaining so many, to them, mysteries, ancient peoples turned to religion to explain such things.

Add the items that are the purview of paranormal studies today and you get an appreciation of what past generations had to face and try to explain.

But to make sense of the extremes of human sacrifice, ah, that is another matter. In nothing else does the Dark Side so well illustrate the utter depravity superstitions can engender.

And let us not forget that it wasn't that long ago world dictators such as Hitler sought magical instruments of power and tried to use things like astrology to prognosticate propitious moments of action.

Today, in today's world? Leaders throughout the world as well as the common people still think they can use charms and incantations, spells, to achieve their goals. In our own nation a short visit to Tahoe, Vegas, or Atlantic City should prove the point.

Chapter seven

The First Eternal Triangle. Pulpit Amoebae. And did the Devil or
Cain make it with the Serpent?

A reading of the so-called Lost Books of the Bible (they never
were, but the name attracts the gullible), the pseudepigrapha, and the
Apocrypha, quickly shows the reader why these are not in the canon of
Scripture. Many are worthwhile in respect to their historical value, but
they are not of the same quality of the canonical books.

Much of the Talmud, even cabalistic literature, Jewish and Christian,
provide insights to biblical study. The many translations and variations
are valuable in such study as well.

Jewish fables, as the Apostle Paul called them, and Jewish myths
as per Titus are, for the most part, excluded from the canon. But the
liberties taken by some scribes are still in evidence in places. Textual
criticism is essential to separate these, as well as some Christian fables,
from the actual manuscripts available.

For example, it is obvious, though Bible commentators have
struggled to explain it away or ignored it entirely, that when Luke tells
us in Acts 1:18 that Judas took the betrayal money and invested it
in real estate, this contradicts Matthew's account (Matt. 27:5) of his
throwing the money back in the face of the Pharisees and they went out
and bought the land. Whichever, they are agreed that Judas did hang
himself at the property.

The basic problem with exegetical attempts at reconciliation of
obvious contradictions like this is that it strains credulity and most
certainly brings no honor to God. The account in Matthew, like those
holy ones who were supposed to have popped out of their graves at the
time of the crucifixion, has an evident, religious bias.

In foolish, even superstitious, attempts to embellish the record,
the whole becomes suspect. Good, solid scholarship opposes these

attempts to help God, and is only interested in one thing: The Truth! This honors God; not fabulous stories regardless the motive.

For example, the most commonly accepted theory among Christian commentators of where Cain got his wife is that she came from the union of the children of Adam and Eve. Eventually, Bible commentators declare the two lines of Sethites and Cainites evolved.

This, of course, meant that at the earliest time brother and sister had to have children of an incestuous relationship.

One struggles with the law of the OT prohibiting such a union and making it a sin punishable by death on the one hand, and accepting God's approval of this at the time of Adam and Eve. Too much of whatever it takes in this theory.

In fact, God felt so strongly about this that he prohibited sex with any close, family member, and went into detail about how close is close. Leviticus 18 and Deuteronomy 22, which brings us to the actual creation of man:

The very first verse of Genesis tells us in the beginning, God created the heavens and the earth. The Hebrew word used here for God is Elohim, a plural noun. In other words: In the beginning, Gods created the heavens and the earth. This explains such things as Let US create man in OUR image, after OUR likeness (Genesis 1:26), The man has now become like one of US to know good and evil (Genesis 3:22), and Let US go down and confound their language (Genesis 11:7).

The word Elohim is used throughout Psalm 82 and approved of Jesus in quoting this Psalm as verification that we are gods ourselves; made in the image of Elohim.

Bible commentators give other reasons for the use of the plural in an attempt to reconcile the concept of Monotheism as One God. It is this monotheism that separated the Israelites from the other nations of their time.

A very muddy attempt. Because it leaves the Christian Trinity and the concept of a Trinitarian creation including Man at variance with the use of Elohim as a seeming contradiction to such monotheism.

However these attempts at reconciliation have not considered Satan as a creator in his own right. What a heretical, even sacrilegious and blasphemous thought! But when the door is open to speculation, and all religion is just that, speculation, why limit yourself?

But wait a minute. How long has man been around? And was he contemporary with the dinosaurs? Not Homo sapiens, modern man, as we know him. But there are other man-like creatures, hominids, which must have been.

The March 1996 issue of the National Geographic has some most interesting information on the subject. According to this issue, Homo sapiens has been on earth for 25,000 years.

However, humanoid (hominid) creatures (Australopithecus afarensis) that walked erect go back 3 to 3.4 million years according to the most recent studies and findings. There have been 320 bodies and parts discovered of this creature in Ethiopia under the auspices of the Institute for Human Origins.

But they had a brain capacity only about one-third that of Homo sapiens, the females only about three and a half feet tall, and the males about a foot taller and two-thirds heavier. Male dominance clearly revealed from the start.

The article states these earliest hominids inhabited the earth for about 900,000 years. One of the most interesting things about these creatures is the fact that during this almost 1 million years, they remained virtually unchanged! Proponents of evolution have a real problem with this.

Another point of interest, these ancient creatures evidence being vegetarians. A lack of hunting ability, a taboo against animal flesh, what? A curiosity is that these hominids co-existed with large predators that would have made them more likely to be prey than hunters.

But to have survived under the existing conditions for such an extensive period would prove great adaptability of conservation by some means. Supernatural, miraculous?

A 4.1 million-year-old bipedal species named Australopithecus anamensis has been discovered at a site called Kanapoi near Lake Turkana in Kenya. A chimp-like creature estimated at 4.4 million years has been discovered in Aramis, Ethiopia and named Ardipithecus ramidus.

An Archaic Homo sapiens is estimated to have been around 750,000 years, and Neandertal about 100,000 years. Homo erectus, as opposed to those creatures of millions of years ago with such small brain capacity, is estimated at 1.75 million years in the past. Another Early Genus Homo is estimated at 2.5 million years.

For years I have been telling church leaders there is a desperate need for a new theology to accommodate facts like these. No matter how many beautiful stories you tell, how many beautiful theories you evolve, they crumble before stubborn facts that won't simply go away.

One such fact that Bible Christians must confront is the Serpent in the Garden. This creature had the power of speech and walked erect. Christian theology has always had Satan using this creature in the temptation and deception of Eve. I think Adam was there also, not out mowing the lawn. In fact, Genesis 3:6 declares: ... She also gave some to her husband, who was with her...!

But, as I have written previously, he was probably waiting to see what happened to Eve before he took a bite. I conclude this from the fact that when confronted by God for his betrayal, he took it like a man and blamed it on his wife. And God. The resentment of women toward men has a long and legitimate history.

God's curse on the Serpent was that it would crawl on its belly and eat dust forever after. Obviously, it didn't crawl previously. Those that would try to tell us that Satan and the serpent were one and the same cannot reconcile such a thing with snakes, as we know them.

It is, therefore, much more to our advantage and for the sake of good scholarship and reason, to take the view that the Serpent God cursed was not a snake, as we know it, and was a creature much like Adam and Eve. This becomes vitally important theologically if the Christian view of Satan is a distorted one, and he is more like the accuser and adversary of Jewish theology.

It would naturally follow from the history of serpents in antiquity, the view of humanity that they represent cunning and evil, even the Dark Side of Beauty, that the story of the Serpent in the Garden should be interpreted as allegorical to the curse of God; snakes being only representative of this creature. Of course, this view may prove too sensible for fundamentalists.

Revelation 12:9 and 20:2 refers to that ancient serpent called the devil or Satan that leads the whole world astray. But the Genesis narrative leads one to believe the serpent was a distinct creation of God separate from the Devil. Especially so in the light of the fact that God would not include Satan, in either Christian or Jewish theology, among the wild animals of creation.

It isn't likely, either, that Satan entered the Serpent and used it in some anthropomorphic (Satanic version) state. God's judgment of the Serpent wouldn't make any sense in that event. An innocent animal damned because it was used of the Devil? But the Law of Moses required an animal used in Sodomy to be killed along with the person who used it. Why? The animal certainly wasn't guilty.

So we cannot discount the possibility entirely; yet the injustice of it rankles. In any event the picture of Satan and the Serpent cooperating in the downfall of Adam and Eve in some manner exists. And if the Serpent was far more than traditional theology, Jewish or Christian interprets it, some fascinating possibilities suggest themselves.

In the Temptation of Christ, Satan is an angel, not a snake. His other appearances throughout Scripture are that of an angel. So, in the Garden, the serpent is to be understood as a distinct creature from Satan.

But the serpent is among the wild animals God created. Just how wild is wild since all these animals were subject to Adam and tame enough for them to pass before him in review for naming them and seeking a companion, a suitable helpmeet from among them?

Here, as in many other places in the Bible, there is cause for caution in taking some words at face value. Just as there is a hierarchy of angels like seraphim and cherubim, Michael the Archangel and Gabriel somewhere in there, and Raphael in the deuterocanonical book of Tobit, there is a hierarchy of the wild animals of Adam's time.

The serpent was the craftiest and most cunning of the lot we are told. And, probably, the most beautiful and human-like, even homomorphic!

And it would certainly seem from the account that Eve was familiar with this creature and she and Adam had probably been visited by it before. As a result, there is no surprise expressed by them at its appearance at the time of The Fall.

Working strictly from the sparse narrative, I would guess that the serpent had already worked up a trusting relationship with Adam and Eve, laying the groundwork for cooperation with Satan's ultimate plan of causing these first parents and special creation of God to rebel.

Back to the early creations of which Satan may have been the creator:

If we take the view that God was experimenting with various creatures before he created Adam, it would mean that God (Elohim) was making a lot of mistakes in such creations like the dinosaurs, pterodactyls, and that creature 3 million-years-old with a tiny brain.

From the narrative, I would think it far more likely that Satan created such creatures and his attempts were flawed by his growing disenchantment with being number two in the Celestial hierarchy.

Perhaps this led to his mind becoming dark, malignant and malevolent, and such creatures showed this dark side of his increasing evilness. The early and long involvement of people with grotesque and hideous representations of gods, goddesses, spirits and demons like the gargoyles and goblins possibly have a basis in fact of such things.

This dark picture includes things like spirits inhabiting animals, trees, rocks, the wind, fire and water, etc.

The allegory of the Garden may put things in perspective. God's beautiful creation of Adam and Eve was in contradiction to the creations of Satan thus incurring Satan's hatred.

The Devil's creations were ugly. He isn't called a Snake, Dragon, and Beelzebub, Lord of the flies, for no reason.

But God's creations were beautiful. So Satan decided to hurt God and destroy this beautiful creation made in God's own image!

But how to go about this? He plotted carefully. And he had help, the Serpent. However, Genesis 3:1 tells us that the serpent was a creation of God! In fact, it was craftier and more cunning than any of the wild animals the Lord God had made! Paul, in II Corinthians 11:3 says: ... Eve was deceived by the serpent's cunning....

We are dealing with a creature unlike any we know. But it had to have been among those creatures Adam named in seeking a companion. Bible commentators have strained at this trying to make the serpent a dumb beast without the power of speech among other things.

But that cannot be reconciled with the actual narrative. Especially not with the plain fact that Adam was trying to find a suitable helpmeet among other creatures. Whatever the characteristics these creatures like the serpent might have had, it is thoroughly implausible that they were creatures like cows, goats, or snakes.

Not only was the serpent more cunning and crafty than any of these other creatures, it is within the bounds of speculation that it might have thought itself worthy of being Adam's choice of a companion. Having not been chosen, God creating Eve instead, the serpent may well have had a genuine hatred of Eve as a usurper. Furthermore, I would think this serpent, whatever it was, was a homomorphic female! After all, Adam wasn't looking for a Steve; he was looking for an Eve!

Unrequited love? Possible. And hell hath no fury.... If this is the line of thought, it explains a lot. Women don't trust each other. They steal the husbands and boyfriends of other women.

As a consequence, the serpent was an ideal candidate for Satan's approach to get its cooperation in causing the Fall.

It may have gone something like this:

Satan to the serpent:

Hey, Serp, you beautiful thing, you know how God has something new he calls Adam and Eve. You've met them already as neighbors when you went over to tell Eve about the Tupperware party. You know he even made them a cushy place, a beautiful garden without gophers or mosquitoes where they are living the good life not even raising a sweat! Hades! We do all the dirty work and these bland goody goodies get all the perks! It isn't fair, I tell ya!

Well, I think I know where God blew it lovely lady. He told these creatures they could pig out on anything in the garden except for the fruit of one tree. All we have to do is get them to cross God and eat from that tree and we've got'em.

I admire your thinking Dev. I've already had a few talks with these creatures and I think the woman is the one I can get to easy. She is really a curious thing. Tell her she can't have something and she wants it, tell her she can't look into a box and she can't wait to open it. And she has her sex that she uses to keep Adam shaped up and get her way. And you know how stupid males of every kind are about that!

I think you're right Serp; she has already been complaining about Adam not asking God for a raise and not standing up to him and being a real man! She really got to him on that one, and if we play our cards right, he'll probably go along just to show her he isn't afraid of God!

Now if the serpent was a female, she knew just how to get to a man. Get Eve to question Adam's manhood. Something like: If you were any kind of a man, you'd stand up to God! Here, take a bite and prove you're a man!

God condemns Adam for listening to his wife. Therefore, she had to have said something. I offer the above as a distinct possibility.

But since Adam had turned her down, the serpent had to get Eve to do the dirty work.

(One thought I have had on this subject deserves mention. I doubt Satan would have found the serpent such a willing ally if she had known she was going to become a quadriplegic in the process. But that's the chance you take when you listen to the Devil).

You'll have to forgive me a flight of fancy and whimsy. I was in a pulpit too long myself apparently. Story telling is one of my long suits.

But whatever mechanisms were at work in getting the serpent's cooperation in getting Adam and Eve to betray God, it was successful. But hasn't it ever crossed the minds of my brethren in theology that Satan and the serpent must have known God wasn't going to take this lying down, that there had to be some foreseen consequences of this action that would fall on their heads as well as Adam's and Eve's?

Satan and the serpent must have thought that causing Adam and Eve to incur the wrath and judgment of God would benefit them in some way. It is not reasonable to suppose they would take such a risk unless they saw some advantage to themselves in doing so.

Revenge? Possible. Unrequited love? Possible. There are examples enough of such self-destructive behavior. But it may have also been possible that Satan believed himself powerful enough to withstand God, that he felt threatened by God's creation of Adam and Eve and God's plans for them, plans that would supplant Satan and his hierarchy of angels.

Forced out of the Garden, it isn't surprising that the earliest religions were focused on fertility. As per God's judgment, the earth would no longer yield her strength so easily, and the battle for food became a desperate one at times.

Further, the pain and danger of childbirth put women at risk. The discovery in places like Sumer of so many figurines of pregnant women is proof of this preoccupation with fertility and goddesses like Ishtar came into vogue.

The prominence of fertility being a sign of God's approval is a repeated theme in Scripture. In Genesis, Eve thanks God for the birth of Cain. Of course, she didn't know he would be a murderer.

In Genesis 30:23 when Rachel bears Joseph, she says: God has taken away my disgrace!

Now, about the enmity God pronounced between the Serpent's seed and Eve's. Just what is the distinction between the two seeds, the seed of the woman, humanity, and the seed of the serpent ... What?

Eve is called the mother of all living. But she could not have given birth to the seed of the serpent that was a distinct seed from that of Man. The conflict between good and evil was to be a conflict between the seed of the woman, humanity, and the seed of the serpent called by Jesus in Scripture "The Children of the Devil."

These are the liars, murderers, hypocrites, Judas's, those that betray the love and trust of others like adulterers and molesters, take advantage, use and abuse, torture and maim for the fun of it, conscienceless.

A thought worthy some speculation is whether the serpent, if a female, could reproduce?

We are not told that the serpent was cast out of the garden with Adam and Eve. But why would God allow it to remain?

Engaging my proclivity for whimsy, I pose the following for consideration:

Cunning, crafty but Beautiful! The description of the serpent would support this attribute as well. God made the serpent, and all that God made, we are told, was good; that is, pure and beautiful. The serpent included.

Another point that might support the thought that the serpent, beautiful and extremely intelligent (you know, this characteristic might have put Adam off, come to think of it?) would be all the more incensed at Adam's not choosing her!

Which brings me to a very interesting conjecture; Eve, a woman, pitted against another female of a different species. Men fantasize and write stories, make films about beautiful females from the planet Playtex. Who cares if they have pointy ears or some other differences which, as long as they don't subtract from the over-all beauty (might even enhance the libido in the process) and have all the other important parts of their superstructure and plumbing in order?

Now with the Inquirer and Globe as trustworthy sources of information about alien life forms and their co-habitive conduct with earthlings.... But I digress. I wonder how many of you know Isaac Asimov wrote a Guide to the Bible?

So here we are. Adam and Eve thrown out on their ears and we have the origin of the Eternal Triangle (But with the Serpent, instead of Ingrid Bergman, playing the part of the Hypotenuse).

Interesting scenario, huh? Requests for the movie rights will be entertained.

I suspect Adam, however, was somewhat miffed at the loss of his position in the Garden, and not too likely to take up with the Serpent in spite of bestiality, sodomy, and polygamy having an ancient ancestry.

This left the serpent at odds for a mate since she couldn't make it with Adam (unless one of those ancient predecessors of Homo sap was around to comfort her).

So this beautiful creature may have waited around for a time until you know who appears on the scene. Cain!

I am assuming that at this time the curse of God against the serpent that she would crawl on her belly and eat dust was, in whatever figure, delayed, just as the death of Adam was going to take centuries. It is also possible that, snakes, as we know them, were figurative of God's judgment and have a special connection to Satan and the serpent of the Garden.

One thing is certain; snakes have always played an important part in religions throughout history; particularly in regard to fertility rites and as phallic symbols as well as symbols of evil, cunning, and deception. Wise as serpents. Ever wonder why Jesus used this description? A commonly held perception, though obviously a myth. Yet it is grounded in the reputation of that ancient story of the Garden.

Thus a possibility for two different species, the sons of God, Eve's offspring, Sethites, and the daughters of men: As Cainites!

I offer another thought just to keep us all dizzy. Suppose Satan, if he had creative power, made it with the Serpent?

In the NT, God by the Holy Spirit impregnates Mary. Did Satan, in an evil parody, impregnate the Serpent?

After all, she had a legitimate gripe with Satan: Hey, Dev, you got me into this; now be a gentleman and do the right thing. Do Me!

Her description as belonging to that class of wild animals God created comes to mind here. As with a woman scorned, Satan might have been made to see it her way rather than being subject to her wrath. Women (regardless of species, I suppose) can do that, you know.

If so, she might have gone off apart from Adam and Eve and in that land of Nod, had a daughter waiting for Cain?

This might be credible if you take the children of the Devil having their ancestry traced to this source, and still allow of daughters of men with Cain as the original Man in the scenario.

Something of this nature might explain why the oldest religions discovered emphasized the Queen of Heaven, the worship of a Goddess over the earth and mankind that depended on her to promote fertility.

A possible act of desecration of some very early churches of carvings depicting a crouching woman holding the lips of her vagina apart are indicative of this kind of Goddess worship. Discovery of stone phalli under church altars is proof of the continued beliefs of fertility worship in the Christian era.

This kind of fertility religion came into real conflict with the Father God of the Israelites. It was one of the factors in distinguishing the importance of ethical monotheism as opposed to the predominate pantheism of the surrounding nations like the Babylonian and Chaldean, especially in regard to the rebuke of human sacrifice and nature worship.

This ethical monotheism created great conflict between a Goddess of fertility, the Serpent, Queen of Heaven, and God the Father, Male dominant!

As to intercourse with the devil, this has an ancient tradition. Rosemary's Baby has its roots in such stories.

Lucifer, Greek Phosphorus, meaning Lightbearer, the morning star i.e. the planet Venus at dawn or Hebrew, shining one, has virtually no legend and is not mentioned in Scripture. Some misguided translator, in an attempt to connect the name with the apocalyptic literature intruded the name and it is found in the King James Bible, but correctly omitted in modern translations.

St. Jerome among the church fathers made an attempt, on this basis of the apocalyptic literature and Jesus' remark about Satan falling like lightening from heaven, to equate Lucifer with the Babylonian account in Revelation and Isaiah, chapter 14. Milton's Paradise Lost enhanced the propagation of this idea.

Due to this concept, the name Lucifer was held to be the name of Satan before his fall from heaven. But it has no history earlier than that of Jerome.

However, a handwritten account called the Aradia or The Gospel of the Witches by an Italian witch, Maddelena, in 1886 at the request of Charles Leland of the Gypsy Lore Society states that Lucifer, as Sun God, had an incestuous affair with Diana, his sister, the Roman moon, earth and fertility goddess. They had a daughter, Aradia (or Herodias) who was to have come to earth and teach men and women the secrets of magic.

That such stories and legends may, in fact, have a basis such as the hypothesis of Satan and the Serpent having a daughter, the possible wife of Cain, should be taken into account by theologians.

The paradox of good and evil recognized by all major religions and philosophies must have a sensible root and basis of fact. A fact remains throughout history that people without conscience have always been around. This Bad Seed must have an explanation.

Granted that genetic research holds some hope of answers will not mitigate the mystery of the origin of genes that leave an individual without conscience or the source of such a gene, or the lack of such a gene that predisposes to evil behavior.

It's at this point that I take a couple of Advil and do some light reading in Thoreau's Walden or go outside and, appropriately, commune with the nuthatches and squirrels.

The art of Cro-Magnon's in the famous cave at Lascaux in France is typical of the use of pictures to influence successful hunting. That we are talking about Homo sapiens-like creatures of some 300,000 years back is most remarkable.

The fact of hominids of such antiquity, capable of such drawings and religion, of fashioning implements with which to hunt, etc. should give theologians pause. And those creatures that pre-date even these? If Homo sapiens has only been on the scene for 25,000 years, who, in the sense of Hominidae, or what, made these paintings?

A fact that those early shamans dressed in animal skins, as the

Indians in this country, in a ritual to promote a successful hunt gave rise to a picture of Satan with horns and a tail.

The Old Religion survived Cro-Magnon times and shows up in altars and artifacts of the late, Neolithic period which gave rise to structures like Stonehenge, Aveburg and Carnac, and evidences itself in Babylonian, Chaldean and Egyptian structures.

A fascinating point is that Satan possibly had worshipers of Paleolithic times, man-like pre-Adamic creatures from great antiquity. The Scriptures put Satan at the head of those angels who kept not their first estate. Jude 6 and Revelation the twelfth chapter are interpreted to mean this.

Those early Cathars of the 1200s thought Satan, not God, created the earth. They had a little trouble with the church because of this among other things.

I haven't even gone into the potential of alien visitors, apart from God, Satan, and angels to earth, of what cultures, civilizations may lie beneath the oceans, of the Atlantis's of the mind, sands, and islands. With the progress of technology to explore these things, who can guess what may appear on such horizons of discovery?

I mentioned one time the parallel between the procreative habits of amoebas, one-celled, brainless animals and TV and radio evangelists. A few of my detractors failed, inconceivably, to see the connection.

Given the religion of most good Catholics, charismatics, and Baptists, I bow to the superior wisdom of Walt Kelly who wrote: Break out the cigars, this life is for squirrels: We're off to the Drugstore to whistle at girls. A far superior religion than these others or Satan worship. At least good, old-fashioned sex and a good cigar are enjoyable and non-existential or transcendental.

While these detractors of mine are convinced that my soul is going to wind up being stir-fried for eternity, I rather compare my thoughts on the subject of religion to that of the flight of a butterfly.

One of the most charming characteristics of a butterfly is its seemingly erratic flight path. The beauty of the fractal/symphonic pattern of the countless firings of the neurons of the brain is just such a flight path (I discount my detractor's comparison with the flight characteristics of bats rather than butterflies).

It isn't erratic at all, anymore than that flight path of the butterfly.

That butterfly knows exactly where it is going. It just, like me, wants to take the scenic route. I don't get lost; I'm just admiring the scenery. The myth that men don't ask directions is just that, a myth. We just want to enjoy the scenery. So there, ladies! (Of course I know you women aren't buying this but it makes a good story).

As Kierkegaard pointed out, it is difficult to catch one of those butterflies of thought. As soon as you have one, another immediately demands attention.

As I plowed, and continue to plow, through innumerable volumes of information, trying to make any sense of it all is the most daunting of tasks. And, it does make one a little mad. But I take heart in the fact that there is no trace of Alzheimer's; quite the contrary, I remember and know too much. And there is a lot of this worth forgetting for the sake of some peace and a quiet mind.

As a sop to my academic colleagues and as an acknowledged academic and intellectual in my own right, I understand how, without benefit of the sciences of Archaeology and Anthropology, Aquinas could lose himself in the metaphysics of a Summa Theologica and come to the end of his life counting it all as nothing but straw!

This is one of the reasons I find women and a good cigar so gratifying. There is no mysticism or metaphysics attached. I'm too basic as a man to attach such significance to something I simply enjoy. My point being that Aquinas would have been better off if he had taken the time to enjoy a woman and a good cigar. The Church would have been better off, as a result, as well.

In case my colleagues missed it, I'm talking about realities; not the purposeful, intentional obfuscating verbosity with which those that pride themselves on the ability to take 600 pages to say something that can easily be summed up in one page are heirs and practitioners.

Keep it simple stupid, KISS, is always good advice to those that think God hears them because of their much speaking. And this, of course, is that connection between the amoeba and the TV evangelist. Thought I forgot, didn't you?

Those charlatans on TV and radio, in far too many pulpits across the nation, think they can reproduce like an amoeba, brainlessly. Unhappily, there are so many other amoebae out there that pay good money for this kind of brainlessness.

But as science keeps pushing our understanding of ancient cultures and creatures from farther and farther out of the past, Christians would do well to heed my call for a theology that will accommodate these findings.

And we would do especially well to confront the ignorance and superstitions of these amoebae in pulpits and call them to account in the process.

Ah, now for my hypothesis that the trouble with humanity involves two classes of people: Men and Women! Profound, huh?

Sam Clemens, Will Rogers, and Walt Kelly were humorists. But they made a good deal of sense. It just came better to them to cast the foibles and silliness of people in a humorous way rather than drown in the morbidness of the Dark Side of realities too unpalatable to handle in a constant mood of seriousness or morbidity.

I suspect they, like myself, kept from becoming unhinged through humor. Actually, I have several defenses against total madness (hereby admitting to madness in part), not just humor; essential though that is.

I love good literature and art, good music and films and ... there is something else but I can't seem to remember ... Ah, yes, I remember now: women. Knew there was something that seemed important that I was forgetting.

When I feel myself slipping into that Dark Side of love and romance, and I am increasingly convinced of much of the Bible as a Romance, I put on a great old Broadway Musical, the last time poets worked in America, or an old classic film.

Then I have the backyard with my pond and waterfall, the birds, quail, squirrels and critters I so enjoy watching as I sit at my desk or in the yard. Quite often I have some of the great music of the past playing in the background as I write or visit with my little companions.

I even have Chip, Dale, and Alvin, small squirrels; not chipmunks though just as antic in their behavior.

There was a time in my life when the Academic ruled, when it was a sin to exercise humor, especially the kind of humor of realities. I could obfuscate with the best whether in the language of the educationist, theologian, or professional politician.

But if the goal is to communicate rather than obfuscate or cover your backside, I find it delightful to engage in whimsy and humor to make my points. And I try to keep it in good taste. I count on my children to be my best critics.

It was in finally noticing that the philosophies of men that have guided the course of nations virtually excluded women throughout recorded history that I began to ask some really hard questions of the churches and scholars.

Since the history of humankind has been a history of warfare, since women don't have babies to sacrifice them on the altar of war or the state, why should it be so?

Sam Clemens said men and women are natural born enemies. Much of history would seem to support Sam's claim. But why?

The obvious that men are bigger and stronger and will always win by force and bullying if nothing else, that it is a man's world, men lead and women are forced to follow, these are biological facts that withstand all attempts at any kind of ephemeral equality by fiat of laws that can never accomplish the real need which is equal value.

But where is the compatibility of differences, why competition and combativeness as the rule? Where the necessary melding and amalgam of the hardness of men and the softness of women resulting in a useful toughness with the resiliency to meet the needs of family, rather than the brittleness that fractures and breaks so easily?

The battle between good and evil that we face as human beings has its roots in the things that led to the allegory of the Garden with Adam and Eve.

At this point I could go browsing in any number of my dictionaries, like that of Behavioral Science Terms, and find a convenient dementia to make sense of the insensible. I could, delightedly, use my philological encyclopedia to grab hold of archaisms to expound, profoundly, on the root of the words good and evil.

I could exhaust my inventory of philosophies of every description and, finally, say: To Hell with It! and go fishing. Undoubtedly much the better course.

But if I took that easy way out, I wouldn't have a book to sell and for you to read.

So much for the easy way. Mammon rules and the wolf must

be held at bay. There is also some small chance that some Baptist or Catholic out there might yet be redeemed.

I'll comfort myself with the memories of an idyllic childhood and youth in the forest wilderness, of the girls I used to know, and my children. When it all becomes too much there is always my soul brother, Thoreau, and the easy, but hard-gained, virtue of simplicity in living.

My dear Eco, my dear brilliant Eco, methinks much learning doth make thee mad! It isn't you alone that dreams of a university dedicated to teaching the irrelevant and hair-splitting 501 as a graduate course. Like you, undoubtedly, I confess to being easily distressed by the very banality of some people's ideas of truth.

My beautiful daughter's recent words that my last essay was more readable because of the humor. Thank you, Sweetheart, I have another reason for living another day.

Gilly Duncan, poor servant girl of her master David Seaton, who, in 1590 tortured her with a rope around her neck until she confessed to intercourse with the devil. I don't know about you, but if I were tortured in such a manner I might admit of a few indiscretions; and they might multiply in scope and magnitude, as the rope grew tighter.

But she didn't stop there. By the time she was through with her true confessions, she had implicated about seventy other people; some of them highly respected citizens of Edinburgh.

One of these, Agnes Sampson, had a true devil's autograph in the area of her vagina. Funny thing how sex always found a way of being prominent in scouting out witches.

Another thing. How is it that a creature older than dirt with monikers like Old Serpent, Dragon, Old Scratch, Beelzebub, Lord of the Flies, that goes around dressed in a red union suit with a pitchfork, has horns, a tail and cloven hooves instead of feet, a face like a goat and sulfurous breath that needs a barrel of mouthwash in the mornings, that offers to show a girl his etchings in a toasty place underground furnished in brimstone and filled with snakes, toads, bats, owls, beetles, spiders and assorted goblins and gargoyles still gets the chicks? Oh, well, as the old lady said when she kissed the cow: There's no accountin' for taste!

Agnes confessed to a witch's plot against the king, James the sixth, of Scotland, later James the first of England. It may not be coincidental that the most popular Bible of all time, the Authorized Version commonly known as the King James Version, came into being under this monarch.

Seems Agnes was going to use the venom of a toad (?). This was done by hanging the hapless amphibian up by one hind leg and collecting the dripping venom (I'm not sure what kind of toad this could have been in Edinburgh. While there are poisonous toads, all the ones I have had any experience with simply peed copiously and gave you warts).

The toxin was used on some of the king's soiled linen to cast a spell making him feel like he was lying on a bed of thorns. Unable to get any rest, his majesty would die of the tired's. This method is still used by some witch doctors in Africa.

Now I'm not certain if such homeopathic remedies and practices would hold up under MediCal, but they could be missing a good thing here. In my study of the lore of witches and conjurors, it comes to my mind that in many instances they might be on a better track than a few doctors I have met. Of course I believe some doctors use similar incantations, peering into the entrails of a chicken and consorting with familiar spirits to come up with some of their ideas of healing.

But if it comes to a "Let's try this and see if it works," the party line of the AMA, or a good, confident: Eat this magic mushroom at midnight in the full moon and it'll fix you right up, I prefer confidence. Of course I'd die, but I'd die the victim of confidence rather than a Let's try this, from which I risk dying from indecision.

Back to my dream of a university dedicated to the irrelevant. If I'm going to die in any event, better to die confident I'm going to be cured. And when I'm dead, at least I'll know what I died from. You can't imagine what a comfort that will be.

Are we, in our modern age, fine-tuning religion? Are we getting any closer to the How am I here, Why am I here, and Where am I going? Not as long as the churches continue to try to do Business as Usual and charlatans like TV and radio evangelists and the charismatic scoundrels continue on their track of gulling the gullible; shaming God in the process.

If the Gospel is the Good News that we are to be redeemed through faith, if the way to eternal life is by a narrow path and few there be that find it, we have a long way to go in understanding what all this means.

I Corinthians 14:20 comes immediately to mind: Brothers, stop thinking like children. In regard to evil, be infants, but in your thinking be adults. Mighty good advice. But where do we see it being taken in the churches?

There is a spirit of the Bible that sometimes, and in some places, speaks to hearts as they read, just as some other books, textual criticism aside. No other book has had such an enormous influence on people. But it must be said, both for good and evil.

As to understanding the Gospel, it is a message of God's love for all of us. Any gospel that consigns good men and women to hell is not The Gospel no matter the church or no church, religion or no religion, of the individual!

No reconciliation of the Bible message is possible on the basis of some kind of evangelistic appeal to make a decision for Christ ala Billy Graham. There is a spirit representative of Jesus, of God and the Bible that takes precedence over all sectarian views.

That spirit, if it is of God, is a spirit of love, understanding, and compassion for others regardless their belief system. The Bible says that God is love and all those who live in love, are the children of God. If you know that he is righteous, you know that everyone who does what is right has been born of him (God). The First Epistle of John.

God has gifted some men and women with wisdom, with the power to inspire; and I clearly profit from reading their words. It is an indisputable fact that we do well to heed such words of wisdom and inspiration, especially in those things that promote love, understanding and compassion for one another.

One of the major factors in my finding myself in the camp of men like Paine, Jefferson, Clemens and Thoreau religiously is my attitude to going to church as per the following:

In a squeaky clean and sanctimonious environment with pious songs and lyrics filled with holy lying winging toward the heavens, a reading from the OT and New, a carefully guarded sermon designed to glorify God, offend no one and protect a paycheck and keep the deacons off your back, the modern shepherd of the flock takes up the collection and earns his pay. Everyone goes home glad to have done his and her duty of worship and turns on the TV.

The charismatic churches engage in their pathetic versions of Hollywood and The Exorcist accompanied with homegrown choruses written by Rock Star wannabes, the religious equivalent of 99 Bottles of Beer on the Wall. With healings of everything from gout to PMS, with tongues, visions and being slain of the spirit, the collection is taken and everyone goes home happy to have worshiped God and turns on the TV.

The Jews have a rabbi that concentrates on the practical application of the Torah, takes up the collection, and everyone goes home and turns on the TV, happy to have appeased the Deity for another week.

The Catholics go to confession, count their beads in cadence, hear a practical sermon, brief and sensible, genuflect, cross themselves with holy water, pay off the priest, and go home and turn on TV.

The Hairy Chestnuts, mullahs, priests, preachers and rabbis know a good thing. From ancient cave paintings in France to burning incense and tongues today, religion keeps pumping along with no paucity of shamans.

The difference today is the one thing that gives me hope that we will grow up in a philosophical understanding of God, the one thing that all these modern worshipers and their shamans have in common (along with the time-honored collection): TV!

Now before you accuse me of being sarcastic, a trait far-removed from such a noble soul as myself, let me explain.

Blest be the tie that binds: TV. We may all have our doubts and struggles about God and his universe. We may all have trouble with reconciling some parts of our belief system with facts of science and human nature. We may argue ethical points until it is reliably reported that ice has indeed formed in the infernal regions, but we all agree on TV!

This medium (1. Something occupying a position or having a condition midway between extremes. 2. One thought to have powers of communicating with the spirits) is the answer to our conundrum. And you thought I didn't know what I was talking about?

With the advent (1. The coming of Christ. 2. A coming or arrival) of TV, accompanied by miracles (soap that really cleans and deodorants that make women rush into your arms, tearing off your shirt and pants), signs in the sky (satellites), and virtual reality, together with the vicarious fulfillment of every dream from harems of nude, willing, nubile young women, to a woman president making men jump through the hoops, coming into the home via TV, we have it all. Like the song says: Who could ask for anything more?

Talk about worship! Just plug in and away you go. For hours on end! Oh, most holy and inscrutable Box, I am thine! And the whole world goes worshiping after the Beast! Revelation chapter 14.

Uh, oh. The Beast. Well, worship takes many forms. But at least TV brings folks together on this basis; it is one thing we all have in common in a world that is so divided on so many fronts.

The problem, however, is that we don't agree about everything on TV. Though a common focus of worship, there are still points of view that separate the brethren. So we haven't really found the perfect answer in TV after all! Drat!

While billions of people watch the flickering shadows of electrons bouncing off the phosphor (Lucifer) of a cathode tube, books fall into decline. Yet those entertaining shadows pass on into oblivion while the words engraved on a page remain. And those words, oracles, still move those who read them.

The watching of Hamlet on video will never take the place of the considered, careful reading of Shakespeare. A book allows you to lean back and contemplate what you have just read, to return to the passage and consider, turn over in your mind; it encourages that most important God-like and essential gift that separates us from the beasts of the field: Imagination. This God-like part of us as human beings enables us from the words in good books to feed our sorely impoverished souls.

In fine, it would behoove all of us to examine our beliefs in the light of our prejudices; and as the Apostle Paul had to do, reflect on those things that are surely believed, but in reality are false.

The power of the mind is awesome and largely not known or exercised. The paranormal does exist in many manifestations. Anomalies and enigmas, paradoxes, abound, resisting all efforts at rational explanation by the criteria of present, empirical science.

I am confident that in time, research into particle physics, brain function, and genetics will provide needed answers.

The long history of charlatans and Black Coats, now and in the past, notwithstanding, I have better hope of humanity finding real answers to real questions.

I don't know about you but I'm not about to have my head cut off or become cat chow for lions, or a candle for Caesar for the sake of a fairy tale! I'm a just a little mad, not plain crazy!

The true worshipers of God are those who worship him in spirit and in truth, Jesus told the Samaritan woman. I don't think Peter or Paul would have us go beyond that or try to improve on it no matter how many lists of do's and don'ts church leaders come up with.

It is in that spirit of truth that I hope we will find answers to our questions about God and his work in our lives. Skeptics will continue to have to deal with the supreme paradox of good and evil in spite of their doubts. But it will be those that seek to honor God and love one another that will find the answers.

Believers face a formidable task even so. For example, I have said that I believe if the Bible is taken at least in part as a Romance, it explains many things not otherwise understandable.

I have several reasons for this view but will have to save them for another chapter. It is quite involved.

But let's consider one aspect of the Bible that has always caused a great deal of trouble to Christians and others. Blood sacrifice.

Bloodshed and slaughter are rampant in the Bible (and in history overall). Yet to attempt to reconcile the account of God's dealings with humankind including the command of such slaughter in some cases together with the wholesale sacrificing of animals as part of his acceptable worship is, to say the least, a little difficult to reconcile with God is Love!

I believe taking some of the Bible as a Romance is part of that reconciliation. But there is a great deal more to consider.

Matthew in chapter 8 has two Gadarene demoniacs, Mark and Luke only one. Even though Matthew, Mark and Luke agree on the demons being given permission to go into a herd of pigs, the accounts are contradictory in some aspects.

As irreconcilable as such contradictions of Scripture are they are impossible to accept for those who make a book an idol of worship whether that book is the Bible, Torah or Koran. Tragically, the real lesson and heart of God is lost by the book-worshipers making more of a book than the value God places on love and humanity.

Chapter eight

Karrie and the Bear. The Duck-eating Carp. And other subjects of theological import.

It had been at least a couple of years since bears inhabited the bedroom community of Los Angeles, suburban Lancaster. So I was just a little surprised when my little four-year-old- daughter, Karrie, came in the house and announced rather matter-of-factly: Daddy, I just saw a bear outside.

There is a scene in the first Superman movie where the Man of Steel has just rescued a little girl's kitten from a tree. She goes in and tells her mother that a man in a funny costume came flying out of the air from nowhere and saved her kitty! You hear the mother tell her: How many times have I told you to stop making up stories! Whereupon mommy fetches the kid a whack alongside the head.

We lived in new housing tract close to the community college. If there were any bears about in the middle of this place in a desert community miles from any mountains or even quasi-wilderness it would have made the L.A. Times and Film at Eleven.

I knew all this, but here is my adorable little girl who was not given to distortions or fabrications telling me she had just seen a bear!

But rather than whack her (unthinkable and unforgivable) or go into a long dissertation on why she couldn't have seen a bear out on our paved streets and concrete walks in a city, I pondered her revelation.

Of course I had first gone outside to make sure bears weren't invading us. No bears. Of course, I said to myself, bears are not in suburban Lancaster.

Turns out there was a perfectly sensible answer. I learned that evening from friends that someone had a bear in a cage on a truck and was transporting it. On his way he had come through our housing tract to visit a friend and show him the animal.

In retrospect, I'm grateful I didn't react to Karrie's announcement with shouts of disbelief or well-reasoned arguments to a four-year-old why she couldn't have seen a bear! She had, and I would have been the fool. Worse, my little girl would have wondered why her daddy hadn't believed her? And even though I didn't rush outside armed with a bazooka to ward off a marauding plague of bears, I'll always be glad I pondered my little girl's statement rather than the alternatives.

An acquaintance was sharing a story about a giant, duck-eating carp when I recalled Karrie seeing the bear.

It seems, he told me, that full-grown ducks were disappearing from a pond in the area, and somehow the story of this carp gained enough credence for some people to take nets and sieve the pond searching for the leviathan, Kern County's own Nessie.

What did they get? A whole lot of small disgruntled perch, etc. But not even a record bluegill!

One would have thought that sensible people would have looked at more plausible explanations, like hungry people with a sweet tooth for duck, or people simply stealing ducks. Hey, mister! Wanna buy a duck?

This fellow and I shared a good laugh at the gullibility of the folks that led to the piscatory discomfiture of the pond's finny inhabitants. But there is a serious side to these stories.

A bear, I believe, is coming on the scene for religious people; and like the Scopes Trial, I don't believe they are going to be ready to deal with this bear.

Naturally one does not normally see bears in densely populated areas apart from Gary Larson's marvelous Far Side cartoons. Nor does one go out looking for duck-eating carp when more plausible explanations are readily at hand.

Probability. An essential and fascinating branch of mathematics. But in your factor analyses, better not miss any pertinent data.

Now what is the probability of a bear outside the house in a city? Almost nil. But do you have all the pertinent data? Isn't it possible a guy could be transporting the critter in a cage? Possible even if unlikely.

Would a little girl tell you: Daddy, I just saw a bear! or would she say: Daddy, I just saw a truck and it had a big cage and in the cage there was a bear! Here is where Probability and factor analysis becomes subtle and the best mathematicians able to use a foreign language like advanced statistics earn their pay.

A little girl isn't likely, under the circumstances of such a phenomenally strange and exciting sight, to notice a truck or cage, let alone tell you about these things. The excitement of the bear blocks out these essential details. You, as the Probability expert, have to have your wits about you to such subtleties and extrapolate to the potential, missing data. Hence: Probability, not absolute certainty.

In the case of Karrie's bear, the first possibility is that since a bear in the neighborhood of a densely populated area is highly unlikely at best, she imagined it or was making it up. Not that unlikely for a small child (or even for a lot of adults, unfortunately).

But consider the data. Is the story even remotely plausible? Is the reporting person of unimpeachable veracity? Karrie was. So, what other explanations suggest themselves?

If you start with a preconception, a prejudice, if your reporting persons or the data is suspect, a large margin of error in your probability analysis exists.

If you are a devout believer in giant, duck-eating carp, you are likely to net nothing but perch and bluegill and wind up looking like the fool you are.

But since my readers are intelligent and objective people of unimpeachable veracity, with a sincere desire for truth above all predispositions to believing in giant, duck-eating carp bear with me as I take you on a bear hunt.

An extremely difficult problem that science, the churches (and most religions) face is trying to make sense of the origin of the human race. There is a hiatus in the fossil record between Neandertal, anthropologically the creature closest to Homo sapiens, and modern man of several thousands of years.

The reported sightings of Sasquatchs, Yetis or other like creatures may have a basis in fact. These things have devoted believers and the possibility that such creatures exist should not be dismissed out of hand.

But since we lack sufficient, hard data about such things, enabling us to study them scientifically, we have this inexplicable gap of thousands of years between the utter disappearance of a man-like species and the astoundingly sharp and abrupt appearance of modern man with no possibility of evolution between the two. If this weren't a scientific fact, it would make good science fiction.

Speaking of which, fabulous stories of lost civilizations like Atlantis and Mu make fascinating conjecture and speculation. Behind these mythological fantasies there may well be a basis of fact. But investigation into such things usually reveals something quite different than the stories themselves.

In my years of study and research, I have come to the conclusion that there is indeed something else at work in our world beyond that of a comfortable and well-defined, thoroughly scientific and explicable model.

This something is the root of religious worship in all its historical diversity. For the world religions, God is the accepted something. For most of us, the whole creation, the stars, our longing for immortality shouts GOD! as per Romans, chapter one.

It is natural that legends and myths grow and change in the telling over a period of time. Many change to suit the various cultures as they travel from one place to another. It is common to find the same gods and goddesses of one culture transformed to fit another such as Greek and Roman.

Just as in the church age, the churches evolved different practices in different parts of the world, so the worship of the various deities changed in ancient times though the commonalities are there throughout.

I am going to lead the reader into some fascinating areas of exploration as we examine some of the mysteries of the origin of man, and some plausible, possible answers to our questions; especially concerning the various religious practices and beliefs and how they have impacted on civilization.

The Neandertals lasted 100,000 years, had a defined society, fashioned garments, and made shelters of animal skins; they crafted tools and spearheads of stone, drew pictures and buried their dead.

They not only buried their dead, but also buried them with stone tools, flowers, and provisions like the haunch of a deer, or bones sprinkled with red ocher to resemble blood, thereby declaring their belief in rites, magic, and some kind of after-life.

The mistaken notion that Neandertal was an apish ancestor of man was fomented by early errors like that of Marcellin Boule who, at the turn of the century, reconstructed (actually, fabricated) a brutish creature from bones and guesswork.

The preconception (devout prejudice) of Boule and so many like him that Darwin had to be right no matter what it took to prove it, led to many such grievous errors in the growing sciences of Anthropology and Paleontology. As a result, theories became facts and taught as such in the schools.

But the churches, ranting against evolution, were, for the most part, no better. The ignorant and arrogant Bryanesque attempts on the part of fundamentalists to make the Bible a science textbook made the Scriptures, together with God, look foolish.

In their haste to prove evolution untrue, religious persons and the churches engaged in a battle for the Honor of God and the Bible that did much damage. This also made it difficult for even devout and honest theologians to make compatible sense of scientific discoveries.

This preoccupation of "My view is the only correct view" has hurt honest inquiry, and made reasonable conjecture and speculation virtually impossible in too many cases. As a result, both the Bible literalist and the devout evolutionist box themselves into wholly untenable positions of error.

Neandertal was not modern man in spite of many achievements. Virtually no accomplishments of an innovative or esthetic turn of mind exist for Neandertal. There are no sculptures, carved figures or motifs chiseled in stone, no beads or bracelets, no pottery, etc.

For a creature to have been around far longer than modern man has existed and not have carried crude beginnings to the more complex is incomprehensible. Yet, such is the case.

All the sciences and arts should be brought to bear on this mystery. For example, the science of mathematics, particularly Probability, could yield some helpful data if it were accorded a high enough priority of Need to Know.

My point being that if enough known data were inputted in a discriminate program base that included facts of science, religion, the arts and social sciences, probabilities would suggest themselves that might lead to answers. The amount of material for such a database would, obviously, be enormous. And enormously costly.

With no urgent Need to Know, and no profit as a bottom line, it's not very likely to happen. That leaves a lot of educated guesswork to be done by a lot of Sherlock Holmes's with great genius powers of deduction seeking clues.

A pre-Adamic race that had the characteristics of religion and society is unthinkable in many religious circles. Yet, there it is! That it did not evolve into Homo sapiens is unthinkable to evolutionists, yet there it is!

One would think that Neandertal would have evolved, but he didn't. And one of the intriguing differences between this species and modern man was language, the greatest factor influencing the inability of Neandertal to develop much beyond an animal-like existence.

Twenty years ago, Philip Lieberman of Brown University studied the vocal capabilities of Neandertal. What he deduced goes a long way in explaining the lack of innovativeness for this species. They could not have had a spoken language like that of Homo sapiens!

The construction of Neandertal's vocal system, like that of apes and chimpanzees, precluded producing three, primary vowels: AH - EE - OO. Without these vowels, a language as we know it is impossible.

This left Neandertal without a complex language system and, logically, therefore unable to produce a written language as well. All other differences aside, it is that deficiency that doomed Neandertal to a near-animal existence regardless of the longevity of the species.

For a civilization to progress, especially scientifically, a written language is a primary and absolute essential. Many cultures during this time of Homo sapiens like those of Africa failed to advance much beyond the level of Neandertal because of this deficiency of a complex language and the consequent inability to produce a written equivalent.

Signing, facial and body expressions, guttural, clucking or clicking sounds, marks and drawings on cave walls, animal skins and bones enables a culture to go so far and no further.

An enormously important significance of language is the ability to conceptualize abstractly. We think in words and sentences. If you lack a language, no such conceptualization of any complexity is possible. This, obviously, greatly impacts imagination.

Even cultures of today that lack complex language skills make few discoveries, are given more to occult and mystical explanations of natural phenomena, and have little or nothing in the way of sophisticated science, literature and the fine arts.

If, for example, you look at the sun or a flower but have no way to describe, figuratively or specifically, what you are looking at, you are extremely limited in your perception of such things, and certainly cannot share any nuances of meaning or emotion to others. In short, you have very little imagination to exercise.

Hence, little in the way of experimentation and discovery, and virtually no way to pass such learning on to other generations. You are left, as well, with no way to relate to your environment and others apart from a belief and acceptance that there are mystical forces of the stars, animals, nature which is controlled by spirits.

So Homo sapiens, gifted with the power of speech, made enormous advances within a brief period. Early on we find numerous things lacking in Neandertal culture like well-crafted fishhooks and bone needles for sewing, the atlatl which enabled a man to hurl a spear with mechanical advantage, artistic works in flint, stone, carvings on bones and actual sculpture. Arrowheads are found announcing the development of the bow.

Hollow bones of this early period of Homo sapiens have small holes, crude recorders, one of the first musical instruments. Pictures of harp-like instruments show up very early. Music and art was almost immediately a feature of modern man as opposed to Neandertal who had none of these things.

Another intriguing difference between Neandertal and Homo sapiens is the development of boats and rafts. No artifacts of this nature are to be found in the time of Neandertal. With the advent of modern man, they began to appear.

Since it is probable that before Homo sapiens appeared, the world consisted of a single landmass, it would be understandable that earlier species had no need of transportation over water. With the land breaking up into continents, the development of the boat would be a natural result.

But even the most ancient discoveries of Neandertal shows evidence of religious practice like burying their dead with ceremony. This is not a case of anthropomorphism. Neandertal, though a different species from modern man, had religion.

Granting it was of a crude kind, probably occult; who or what did Neandertal worship? Was it totally animistic, naturistic or was there a pantheism, even a monotheism involved?

And what leftovers of Neandertal, pre-Adamic religion, carry over to Homo sapiens? Quite a bit, I imagine.

When Paul preached his sermon to the Greeks of Athens (Acts 17) he said he had found an altar of theirs with the inscription: To An Unknown God. Then he said: Now, what you worship as something unknown I am going to proclaim to you. And Paul proceeds to do so.

When your religion requires you pay homage to unknown deities just in case you might miss one you don't know about, you're in trouble!

Modern man is heir to a great number of superstitions and myths that still hold sway in the minds of untold millions of people worldwide. In this country we thrill to movies of the occult; we love our Draculas and Frankenstein's, the Mummy, Werewolf, witches and goblins and things that go bump in the night. Transylvania and the Carpathian Mountains, the Great Pyramids, Isis, Thot, etc. continue to capture the imagination of multiplied millions.

It's fairly common to find well-educated people of wealth and influence in the grip of Astrology, Freemasonry, and Rosicrucianism. The Ouija Board still has its adherents. Palm readers, Dream Analysts, and Sooth Sayers still ply their trades throughout the world. People still read Nostradamus and Cayce with belief and anticipation.

The macabre, the weird, the supernatural, from the innocuous rabbit's foot to stringing up chickens and sacrifices of every kind, to magic potions and elixirs, blessed candles and medallions, the list goes on and on.

All of which should tell us something. Paul tried to tell those Athenians: God is not in birds, animals, idols or buildings, but within us.

Well, the Divine Spark may be there but a whole lot of people searched and still searches elsewhere; worshiping the creature instead of the Creator.

Since science does not answer to the need people have for God, since so many superstitions and myths still guide millions, it would seem there should eventually be an answer to what is being searched for.

To the Christian, the answer is in Christ. But literally billions of people know little or nothing of Jesus Christ. I think it vitally important for Christians to examine their belief system in the light of the fair, sensible rationale that God is not going to send good people to hell because they never heard of Jesus.

We have to explore the evidence suggested by myths, and writings of books like the Bible. And in searching out answers to our questions about the nature of God in such writings and stories, many things come into conflict with the beliefs of many people.

As to the Bible, Adam and Eve think they can hide from God. Even Cain thinks he can get away with murder. So much for Biblical affirmation of the omnipresence of God. Later, even the prophet Jonah thinks he can run away and hide from God.

As with the story of God having to come see for himself if things were as bad in Sodom and Gomorrah as he had been told, God asking Satan where he had been and what he had been doing in the book of Job, it is highly unlikely the ancients thought of God being everywhere at the same time.

Angels as messengers. What is the need of such beings if you already know what's happening? Jacob's vision of a stairway from earth to heaven with angels going up and down and God at the top of this stairway shows the perception of messengers from and to God.

The story in Daniel 10 of one who looked like a man coming to the aid of the prophet is a fascinating one. But how, I ask myself, could this creature have been delayed for 21 days by the Prince of Persia? Bible commentators construe this prince as Satan. The angel Michael comes to this creature's aid and it is only then he is able to come to Daniel.

There is mention of a Book of Truth from which this messenger to Daniel declares certain prophecies. In chapter 12 we have the passage concerning Michael and his angels that occurs in Revelation 12 where they overcome Satan and his angels.

The angel Gabriel is described by Daniel as both a creature that looks like a man, 8:15, and as a man, 9:21. Gabriel is the announcing angel of Luke 1:19 and 26 who appears to Zachariah and Mary.

The book of Zachariah in the OT gives us a picture of Satan as the adversary and accuser of Israel, a popular theme of Hebrew theology.

In the OT we have a picture of the law being given to Moses by God. In the NT it is understood to be administered through angels, Galatians 3:19 and Hebrews 2:2.

Throughout the Bible and other literature of antiquity, angels, spirits, play a prominent role; one for which God has need of such creatures to do his bidding.

But some men, the elect, as the NT says, are to judge angels in the future. We are also told that some can actually entertain (be hospitable to) angels without knowing they are angels.

Thus the ministry of angels is made prominent in the literature of the Bible (as well as the myths and legends of other cultures), and these angels appear disguised on occasion. The angels of Satan are busy as well, Satan disguising himself as an angel of light and his servants masquerading as ministers of righteousness. II Corinthians 11:14.

Women, Paul says in I Corinthians 11:10, should not pray with their heads uncovered lest they be a scandal to their husbands and to angels. The covering of women's hair when they pray is a sign of the authority of men over them. The basis of Paul's admonition is that just as man is the image and glory of God, the woman is to be the honor and glory of the man. Interesting (I have often wondered why so many women buy into such anti-woman ignorance and propaganda?).

Satan (or a like figure) and demonology are very prominent parts of religious beliefs. The Bible, being a coherent source of such traditions and beliefs, sheds a lot of light on questions concerning these things. But it also raises a lot of questions as well.

Yet, with so little in the way of cognitive and reasonably accurate literature comparatively free of myth and legend of the biblical period of history, even secular scholars have need of frequent recourse to the Bible. It continues to stand alone as a, relatively, respected and respectable source of veracity and integrity.

While most Christians shake their heads in agreement to the sage dictum of lighting candles rather than cursing the darkness, I've found great antagonism to the lighting of candles that shed unfavorable light on comfortable dogmas like You just have to have faith and believe (no matter how ridiculous and contradictory such beliefs may be)!

For example, we have a very different picture of the attributes of God from the OT account than that of the churches. It is this flawed perception of the nature of God that the churches hold that has led to so much chaos and uncertainty; and, in the past, burning heretics at the stake!

The doctrine that God is omniscient, omnipresent, omnipotent, and perfect by a dictionary definition is the product of man's religiosity, and not a claim of the Bible. It is at this point that all good Catholics and Baptists start collecting wood in preparation for lighting my fire.

Since I have no desire to become a candle to light their darkness, in other words, no martyr complex, I can only hope such people might take a long look at the evidence of their prejudices before striking the match.

But there are a number of skeptics and scientists that ignorantly worship at the throne of Evolution who would be just as quick to do me in. Shame on all of them!

But the fact is that Neandertal suddenly, abruptly, disappears, and a few thousand years later, suddenly, abruptly, Homo sapiens appears.

What sense is to be made of this enigma? The Bible being a relatively credible history, more so than any competitors such as most of the myths and legends, gives some intriguing insights for those with enough honesty and determination to sort through it.

When we have exhausted the wisdom of men and the Pythias of Delphi, the Sibyls of Rome and Orphism, the searching's of Pythagoras, Plato, Zoroaster, the early Babylonian, Egyptian, Persian and Iranian cosmologies, we are still confronted with the paradox of good and evil, and ineffectual philosophies of dualism as attempted explanations.

The early attempts at codified law such as that of Hammurabi and, later, Moses and post-exilic redactors and scribes, reflect the most ancient consciousness of the need of law directed at morality and the stability of the family, the foundation of all cultures.

But all attempts to codify The Way of the Good, which have been in general agreement by all cultures throughout history, have met with resistance by the lawless ones; those that continue to do evil in spite of all efforts by the Good.

Will a sensible cosmology be the ultimate answer? The essence of the Gospel, to love God and love others as yourself, would seem to be a sensible answer.

Yet, men will do evil; and the very existence of evil thwarts every attempt to make the Good prevail. Clearly, we do not yet have an answer to the paradox.

Chapter nine

A Good Cigar and a Woman

As a mere man, I'm given to thinking a lot about women. Sex. What's a good discussion about religion if you don't include one of the most basic elements? A good cigar and a woman remain tangible and unchangeable. That folks is Certainty!

A good Christian is going to tell you he *Knows*! He knows he is one of the elect; that he is going to heaven when he dies; he believes the Gospel, the Bible and Jesus. He goes to church and pays tithes; he doesn't beat nuns or his wife and children, he doesn't lust after other women ... it's at that point I know he lies and quit listening.

Anyone calling themselves Christian should always tell the truth. You men, in spite of what Jesus said neither you nor I have ever seen a beautiful woman we didn't want to take to bed. That's a fact. Not all the sublimation, cold showers, workouts at the spa or Bible reading and prayers will change your nature in this regard. More to the point, that is exactly the way God made men so why apologize or try to make excuses for it?

Oh, but God gave me a new birth, a new nature, a new heart that protects me from such immoral thoughts and lust! You lie.

I was attending a social function of good church people. Now I'm unmarried and there was an attractive lady I wanted to meet. But a married friend and his wife were attending as well.

This man, married, didn't choose to sit with his wife. Guess where he grabbed a seat before I could? You guessed it. Right next to this attractive lady. I took the next seat and had to talk across him to the lady. When I asked my friend if he wouldn't rather exchange seats with me so he, rather than I, could sit next to his wife, he declined.

Now this friend would rise in righteous indignation if anyone suggested that he, a good Christian, and happily married, had any sexual interest in this lady. He lies. And I'm sure his wife, as well as myself knows he lies.

I could go on multiplying examples of this kind all day. I worked in enough churches to know whereof I speak.

We have those stubborn facts that all the preaching and religiosity in the world won't change. Monogamy and Monotheism was never popular and go counter to humanity and its history.

One of my favorite books of the Old Testament is Ecclesiastes:

For with much wisdom comes much sorrow; the more knowledge, the more grief ... I have seen the burden God has laid on men. He has made everything beautiful in its time. He has also set eternity in the hearts of men; yet they cannot fathom what God had done from beginning to end.

Maybe not but we sure 'nuff been workin' on it.

According to the Scriptures, Solomon tried it all, or nearly all. We don't know if he actually sniffed glue or snorted coke. But he did these things, in part, in order to make sense of so many things he didn't understand.

Ecclesiastes tells the result of all of Solomon's searching for meaning: Meaningless, utterly meaningless, everything is meaningless!

Pretty dismal assessment of things. Like Aquinas at the end of his life proclaiming everything he had done as nothing but straw!

Here was the man who asked wisdom of God in order to be a good king; and God said he would bless him accordingly because he had not asked anything for himself such as wealth, long life, or the death of his enemies. I Kings 3:7-14.

But few in Scripture blew it as badly as Solomon. He asks for wisdom and gets it. So what does he do with this wisdom? He builds the temple and installs the Ark of the Covenant; he builds his palace, gains a remarkable reputation in foreign relations, and he loved many foreign women, 700 wives and 300 concubines. I Kings 11. That's a lot of foreign relations.

We read that when he grew old (in a hurry, I suspect) these wives turned his heart after other gods like Ashtoreth of the Sidonians, Molech of the Ammonites, and Chemosh of the Moabites.

So God judged Solomon, causing the kingdom to be ripped from his son, Rehoboam, and only the tribes of Judah and Benjamin were left under his rule.

Through God's judgment of the wickedness of Israel, the Northern, then the Southern, tribes went into Babylonian captivity and the nation of Israel ceased to exist. God kept the tribe of Judah, a remnant, as a testimony to the faithfulness of his promises to Abraham, Moses and David, certainly not that of the Israelite's.

On the face of it, the ethical monotheism of the Israelites did not capture their hearts. They constantly went whoring after other gods. Judges were sent to deliver, prophets arose to warn, but the pattern continues to repeat itself time-after-time.

A basic flaw of human nature presents itself exemplified by Solomon and his multiplying women to himself. Monogamy, like monotheism, has a tough row to hoe when men and women like diversity and variety in sex and religion.

A virtuous woman, who can find for her price is far above rubies ... one righteous man among a thousand have I found but never a woman.

Solomon's bad-mouthing of women is an interesting study of the "Women are no damned good!" hypothesis that has a long history, long before his jaundiced statements. Apart from textual criticism of whether he said it or not, no one can question the availability to him of a sample population.

Men, like bees from flower-to-flower, certainly have no right to complain if women follow the same pattern. In fact, since men lead and women have to follow, I will always believe there would be virtuous women if they had examples in virtuous men.

Women are easily seduced and men are the responsible parties in seduction. And in that very seduction, men betray one another in the process as well as women.

Of all the characters of Scripture, few have such a checkered and fascinating history as Solomon. Talk about having it all! Yet, he departed from the God of David his father and went whoring after foreign women and gods.

A curiosity immediately presents itself, however. God had said he had sought and found a man after his own heart that would do his will. I Samuel 13:14. But this man, David, who showed such promise in killing Goliath, would not kill his enemy, king Saul, when he had a chance, feigned madness before Achish, the king of Gath to save himself, takes multiple wives, commits adultery and murders Bathsheba's husband Uriah so he can have her, is Solomon's father. And Bathsheba, his mother.

God kills the baby of this murderous-adulterous relationship but gives David and Bathsheba another son, Solomon. Ever wonder how Solomon felt about his parentage?

Now is David going to take Solomon aside and tell him about the birds and the bees? Is he going to tell Solomon: Son, women are no damned good! And is this polygamous adulterer and murderer going to be the role model Solomon is to look to for his future manhood?

Not likely. Absalom is going to take after his father. This boy is David's hope and much like him as opposed to Solomon. But Absalom doesn't want to wait till his dad kicks off to get the throne. He rebels against his father and is killed.

David mourns Absalom knowing the boy had too much of David's own dark side, knowing he had failed in bringing the boy up properly and being such a poor example to him.

David is dying and not even the sweet, young thing his buddies bring him can restore him. He is really gone!

Long-suffering Bathsheba brings Solomon to the dying king and puts it straight: David, you promised Solomon would be king. Now Absalom's brother, Adonijah, is trying to set himself up as king!

With a little help from his friends, David gets Solomon seated on his throne.

David finally had that father/son chat as the king lay dying. Better late than never I guess. He tells him to follow the Lord and keep his commandments; and, by the way, that dirty rat Shimei, when I'm gone take him out! I Kings 2:9.

The Bible is an honest book in many places, very human. God really tells it like it is; even when it embarrasses him or hurts him to tell the truth about those he loves and trusts.

With this Godfather bit of advice to Solomon, we have the last recorded words of David. I don't wonder that Solomon would not want to be like his dad in many ways.

God called David a Bloody man, a man of war when he wanted to build the temple, and he told David it would be Solomon who would build it. I Chronicles 28. So, in this chapter we have an account of David laying the groundwork for Solomon to accomplish the work.

The account in I Chronicles differs substantially from that of I Kings. But the main facts are essentially the same and corroborated elsewhere. This is why it is important to study all these books of the period together to get a composite that is a clear picture.

David wasn't exactly the perfect father or family man, and he sure let God down. But nothing can detract from his courage, and he evidenced a good heart in many respects even though The Sweet Singer of Israel was mighty handy with a blade and slingshot. There was the matter of those 100 foreskins (he delivered 200) of Philistines that king Saul had demanded as a bridal price for his daughter, Michal. I Samuel chapter 18.

But I've always been handy with a gun and I'm a musician and singer who loves good literature and art. The sword and the harp don't have to be exclusive of each other.

When it comes to failing with a family, I'm an expert on the subject. But I loved my family more than my own life. Like David, however, I made many mistakes and those mistakes caused a lot of problems for the family.

For those that like their religion neatly sanitized and packaged like meat in the supermarket, the churches have become adept at delivering the goods. But don't visit the abattoir where the cattle or sheep are slaughtered.

For those who think they can raise a family in the midst of violence, drugs, adultery and easy divorce without it impacting children, you have never visited the abattoir of slaughter and despair such things produce. And it is done under color of law in our courts!

Life is very hard at times. But rebellion and betrayal always reaps a bitter harvest. As good a man as David was in many respects, he failed his sons in not setting the example; he failed in one of the most important areas of life: One wife.

Granting he was king and could have as many wives as he wanted, polygamy jars with monotheism. Israel was to be different than the other nations in several regards. The Law of Moses clearly intended a man to have one wife and one God.

One can reasonably and legitimately ask why God didn't intervene in this area of the life of the Man after God's own heart (Acts 13:14) that God had intentionally chosen to be king.

With so many questions concerning God's dealings with David, and his even breaking the Law of Moses when he and his men took the sacred bread of the sanctuary, I Samuel chapter 21 (and his action in this case mentioned with approval by Jesus in the NT), one wonders about a lot of things going on between God and David.

In all this confusion, especially in the confusion of why God didn't judge David as he did others, there is a question in my mind of whether God the Father may have been too lenient to this special son of his, as David was toward Absalom?

But David was judged on a number of occasions. A primary instance was the case of his numbering the people, II Samuel 24. But we read that God himself incited David to do so in order to bring judgment on him.

Then God gives him three choices of punishment. David decides on a plague and the Angel of the Lord destroys 70,000 Israelites.

The sword never departed David's house because of his sins. And Solomon inherited such a house.

We read that God twice spoke to Solomon. But even this did not keep Solomon straight. Of course, God spoke often to Moses and David and that didn't keep them straight either.

With immense wealth and power come all the temptations of absolute corruption. It may well be that Solomon, like Adam and Eve, didn't believe God meant what he said.

I don't know about you folks but my children had a bad habit of not always believing I meant what I said. How many times does a parent fall into the "This is the last time I am going to tell you this is the last time I am going to tell you, how many times do I have to tell you, how many times have I told you," etc. ad nauseum?

So, many children grow up thinking their name is really NO instead of Johnny or Susie. And, in time, it takes a certain decibel level before they believe mom or dad means what they say.

Well, God has the same problem with his children. The NT says that while God spoke in many different ways in time past, he finally spoke to us by his son. Hebrews 1:1,2. Jesus Christ is presented in the

NT as the final word, the final decibel level. This was the last time God was going to tell us. It's up to us whether we believe God or not. And while I don't believe the superstitious nonsense of the Jesus religion called Christianity, there is much to this point.

But God gave the Israelites so many chances I don't wonder he does so with us as well. A legitimate question arises from this as to why God, just like any normal parent, doesn't have his word obeyed the first time? There is the childishness of rebellion to fair and just authority. If that Bad Seed predominates, we get the Cains, Hams and Nimrods.

The Gospel has always had hard going. Marcion, born around A.D.85 was a wealthy ship owner and a devout Bible scholar. He separated the Bloody God of the OT from Jesus and claimed Jesus was born of another God, a God of love and compassion and that Jesus came to free mankind from this bloodthirsty tyrant.

Marcion, like many others, undoubtedly knew that the use of the plural word Elohim, gods, in Genesis and Psalm 82 allowed for thinking of the nature of God beyond the monotheism of the Israelites.

He accepted most of the Gospel of Luke and some parts of Pauline epistles, rejecting the rest along with Genesis, Job and the prophets.

The Gnostics formed around Marcion's teachings, but took Jesus to be Spirit, an illusion, which only appeared to die. Over a period of time, Gnosticism became a system of gnosis (knowing) opposing faith in the supernatural aspects of the Gospel and taught that Jesus was the spirit of the Serpent in The Garden trying to help Adam and Eve escape the tyranny of a despotic tyrant, the God of the OT.

Mani, from whom the Manichaean heresy derived, was a member of a Christian sect in Mesopotamia in the 3rd century. He saw Jesus as tripartite, The Splendor, the Messiah, and the Sufferer (the crucifixion) who did battle with the dark forces long before creation. The yin and yang of light and dark forces in conflict was the most prominent of the Manichaean doctrines.

St. Augustine, at first, held Manichaean views but later repudiated them.

Eventually, the Manichaean teaching found its way into the Buddhist deity, Maitreya, the Boddhisatva. Maitreya believers brought down the mighty Kublai Khan giving rise to the Ming dynasty.

About 318, Arius questioned the relation of the Father and the Son in the Trinity. He taught that Christ was the most exalted of all created things, but inferior to the Father. The council of Alexandria in 320 condemned this view. The council of Nice condemned it as well. The articles of the Nicene and Athanasian creeds arose from this teaching known as Arianism and condemned it as heresy.

European scholars of the faith incorporated some of the teachings of the East in ever-evolving sects and cults calling themselves Christian.

There were common beliefs and elements in all these evolving religions. The contrast of Jesus as Light and Satan as Darkness, the Devil in one form or another, is one of these commonalities. A Good (light) force and a Bad (dark) force in a tug-of-war for mastery of the souls of humanity.

During the Crusades, crusaders, especially the Templars, picked up much of Jewish and Moslem mysticism which was taken back to Europe. Many of these ideas were inculcated into the arising factions including the Jesuit, Rosicrucian, and Masonic mysteries.

The politics and mysteries of the religions of these centuries cloud attempts to find a consensus or continuity of beliefs. Decrees, wars, plotting and treachery abound. Teachings of the various factions were constantly muddied with alchemy and sorcery of one kind or another. Superstitions and myths, many from the Old Religion, fertility worship, and greatly pre-dating the Adamic race tainted the most scientific of the great men of these centuries.

A degree of consensus held around the Bible. But since reading and scholarship was confined to the churches, the laity was left to whatever came out of the respective pulpits.

The flagrant abuses of church leaders became too much and led to the Reformation. But even this did not accomplish a consensus, and in no time factions like Calvinism and Arminianism within the Reformation split into opposing views.

Predestination versus Free Will became a bloody battleground in Protestantism. The old questions concerning the nature of God, of Christ, the sacraments, real presence or... the mode of baptism, practice of various liturgies, etc. kept the fires burning.

The Dark Ages gave way to a science of the Enlightenment that continued to be plagued by religious superstitions and myths, continued battles and controversy. The art and architecture of the Renaissance displays much of the superstitions of antiquity.

Shamans and charlatans, Black Coats, continued to abound, sowing seeds of discontent and controversy just as they continue to do today. These Christians, they might have loved God but they sure hated each other.

The Bible, finally in the hands of the laity, at least gave the common people a chance to compare church doctrines. But it still was the voice of the pulpits and academies that had to be responsible for organization and doctrine.

So, today, German Christians can drink beer and American Christian women can dress like prostitutes, each condemning the other accordingly.

As I light a good cigar, sip my coffee and think of women, I lean back and reflect on the insanity of it all. At least the cigar, coffee, and women are tangible, good things. Well, at least I can always count on the cigar and coffee. Two out of three ain't bad.

In my reflections I consider the religion, Christianity, that from the start was riddled with factions, some claiming to follow Christ, some Peter, some Paul, some Apollos, some demanding phallic sacrifice (circumcision) to be a member of the club, others saying Moses sucks!

A leading council and home church in Jerusalem helped substantially. With James at the head and others cooperating, a good degree of consensus held sway early on. Persecution of these early Christians held them together. The seed of the Church was sown in the blood of martyrs. Yes, people can believe a lie to the point of dying for it.

But too many questions of monumental import had not been dealt with. Controversy began to split early believers in the 2nd century and gained momentum resulting in men like Mani.

A basic creed of belief from the council of Nicaea in 325 helped considerably. Later councils made creeds into dogmas of the faith. Many came into conflict with each other as different factions tried to gain ascendancy.

The Nicene Creed was fairly basic and did not meet much argument. But the earlier Apostle's Creed threw in Jesus descended into hell, a sacred cow of Christendom and Mormons, a statement without Scriptural basis; solely an interpretation of I Peter 3:19 which is ambiguous at best and an early attempt to build a doctrine out of a single statement. The very thing for which orthodoxy condemns cults such as the Mormons and J.Ws.

The Athanasian Creed of the 5th century is Trinitarian in substance. Though adopted by the West, it was virtually unknown to the Eastern churches until the 12th century.

The orthodox hypostatic union, Christ was God-made-man, wholly human and wholly divine, the incarnation, was debated by Nestorius, patriarch of Constantinople, who tried to find a compatibility of perfect God and perfect man in Christ that made sense. The councils of Ephesus (431) and Chalcedon (451) condemned his teachings as heresy.

But the Theotokos (God-bearer, i.e. Mother of God) title given the Virgin Mary by the Roman synod of August, 430 under Pope Celestine I made this doctrine the official party line of acceptable Christology. This was totally unacceptable to Nestorius. It was too much like the Old Religion of fertility worship and made Mary just another Isis or Ishtar.

He was exiled and died in a monastery near Antioch around 451.

Eastern and Western orthodoxies have their problems with each other. And there are problems aplenty within these orthodoxies.

All attempts of a systematic approach to understanding God and his universe, his dealings with mankind are, basically, subjective. Given the data, creation, mankind's need of religion, paranormal evidences, the probability for the existence of God, these are things that few would argue.

Jesus said that those that worship God must do so in spirit and in truth for he seeks such to worship him. John 4:23.

I find myself often in the mode of asking just what is the truth? I pray and my prayers go unanswered. And I find that my view of things is subject to many evidential facts that stubbornly refuse to bow to wishful thinking.

I wish, for example, that there were more loving people, more honest people that I could trust, that God would sort things out and millions of children didn't have to die or go to bed hungry every night, that evil men didn't have positions of power and authority, that the superstitions and ignorance that rule in so many lives could be extinguished.

If God were what the churches and so many religions make of him, there would indeed be a reward for the righteous, good men and women who work hard and try to raise their families honestly, Thoreau's Heroes who stayed at their lasts and anvils and wouldn't be at the mercy of evil men and the evil one.

And don't try to make that pie-in-the-sky-by-and-by fly with me or any other sensible person. It won't pass. It never has. The fact of it is that the children of the devil appear to be a whole lot smarter and have their wits about them and their act together as opposed to those who think God has some magic wand and they don't have to oppose or confront evil!

As to what constitutes true worship in the churches, it is ludicrous, the most charitable word I can apply. Just ask yourself the reasonable and sensible question of just what is worship?

Worship in Spirit and Truth? Ok, if God were what the churches try to make him, you have a despotic tyrant that still demands sacrifices. You prostrate yourself and cry out for mercy, saying how unworthy you are, how grievously you have sinned against him, you would kiss his foot or the ring on his finger, you would chant, count beads endlessly, genuflect, bow, give your money and time in attempts to appease such a gracious, loving and forgiving despot!

And in spite of all this, you are still left with the uncertainty of just what exactly is going to happen to you when you die!

Uncertainty. To an Unknown God! Just in case you missed him in your worship.

I need to stress one point. Christianity is a predominantly European, Western religion.

And all the good fundamentalists out there cry: My Christianity isn't a religion, it's the TRUTH!

Oh, my. Talk about purposely obtuse. It's a hard task trying to get the brethren to get their dictionaries open and apply definitions of the heathen to their beliefs

So I try to make sense of mankind's religiosity in a context of trying to make sense of mine. That is only reasonable.

In doing so, like many before me, an examination of my own biases and prejudices is essential. The best any of us can do is to try to be honest in such an assessment.

Monogamy has proven to be a good thing; it makes for stable families and a stable culture. No one can dispute this. Acceptable standards of behavior, of morality, are absolute necessities for a civilization to survive. And nothing provides the motive force for moral absolutes like God.

History alone should teach us that one man, one woman, one family, is the ideal of a civilization. It is also sensible to me that God as a heavenly parent (or parents which is more probable) is the creator and the moral absolute against which all behaviors should be judged.

Christianity, in spite of the many flaws of the system and the way it is applied in churches, raised women to a somewhat higher status of value above that of other religions. But still left men the bosses and far from recognizing women as of equal value to men.

Unhappily, in modern times even those women claiming to be Christian go to court in droves to get rid of their husbands. And, in too many recent cases, their children as well.

Now try to tell me, in such cases, that the Love of God motivates such women! No how, no way!

But getting rid of an unwanted woman had become so easy for the Jews that even the Apostles replied to Jesus' statement in support of monogamy with horror and astonishment: If I can't ditch the old lady when I want to, better not to marry at all! Matthew 19:10. Most of these guys were obviously married.

Well, there are certainly points to be made on both sides of the Men/Women are no damned good! argument.

But God's so-called Chosen People (at least the men) weren't any hotter on monogamy than the heathen around them, either in religion or marriage. Moses might have been hot for getting rid of a wife when you consider his problems with his own. And maybe that is what Jesus had in mind when he said it was because of the hardness of men's hearts that caused Moses to include divorce as acceptable in his own brief of the Law?

I remember a lovely young lady I once knew who told me about getting her tubes tied. After the operation, the doctor told her: Ok, honey, go out there and use that for what God intended it for! Then she told me the doctor tried to put the make on her.

If I were a woman, my complaints to the Almighty would be numerous, long and loud! They might be prefaced by a few remarks like these:

Hey, God! Why'd you make me a woman? You know the Jews and Moslems thank you they weren't born women? And they're right! You have any idea how tough it is, being a woman? Of course you don't, you're a male! How'd you like to get old and wrinkled, of no value? How'd you like it if you had to look for that first gray hair and wrinkle?

If you could go one day having to look over your shoulder for potential rapists, if you had one of those funny uncles or stepfathers who liked to play with little girls, if the highlight of your adolescence was learning to wear a bra and use Kotex and Tampons, if you had to deal with boys and men who wouldn't qualify as road kill trying to make it with you, you might get some idea of what it's like down here for women!

And let's talk about breasts God! How come you made us subject to gravity in that department? And our hips? Why is it that twenty minuets after we get married our hips begin to spread out and air makes us fat?

Hey, God, how come when he turns fifty he's seasoned and mature and I get Old! He has twenty times more chance of getting a younger wife when he's fifty than I have of even getting an older man when I'm forty?

Well folks, the number one complaint of women about men is that men don't listen to them. After this little sample, God being male according to many, how much of this would you listen to? But it's True!

And guess what, she's only beginning!

Yeah, thanks, and by the way God, while you're about it, come on down here and have some freak from a different species who thinks he's a man and thinks he can take you to some cheap, greasy-choke and puke-joint for an ersatz hamburger, after which he treats you to two hours of conversation about his latest carburetor overhaul and expects you to fall all over him because it's his idea of a romantic evening!

Which brings me to another point God! This thing called Romance (this lady is just getting warmed up at this point)!

Yeah, God, I want flowers and music and he just wants to get in my pants! What kind of crazy mixed up deal is this?

At this juncture, a few million men out there cry: Lady, if it weren't for THAT there'd be a bounty on all of you!

Well, I could (and have in another book) go on at great length in this vein.

I will point out the fact that if there had been a real love relationship between God, Adam, and Eve, the Serpent wouldn't have had a chance! I don't question the love of God, but something went horribly wrong in that Garden, something I don't believe God planned, and horrible consequences followed.

It is the search into the mystery of God that has resulted in such confusion that leads to things like that inscription: To the Unknown God!

From the earliest beginnings of the Church Age, it is obvious that confusion was commonplace. In spite of church councils, many things remain unresolved; many legitimate questions remain unanswered.

Let's use a little more of that Spirit and Truth Jesus mentioned in our search for answers. In other words, let's be honest for a change.

Worship: 1. The reverent love accorded a deity, idol or sacred object. 2. Ardent devotion.

Do you genuinely love God? If so, you fulfill the requirement of worship. Would those of you who can honestly say you love God please raise your hands.

Well, fortunately for all of us, the Bible says those that live in love for others love God. That, at least, is comprehensible and sensible.

The Bible also says that to love others and keep God's rules of behavior, treating others as we want to be treated, is the essence of true and acceptable worship of God.

We can relate, understand and accept this definition of worship. Now, at least, some of you can raise your hands.

Now, once more, let's be honest. While we can easily agree on the basis of true worship of God no matter what your religious beliefs may be, there are those questions still to be dealt with that impact on our systems of religion and cultures, of how we interact with our society and that of others, of why God does not deal with some of the things we have a right to question him about. If we give any credence to those ancients, the Psalmists and others that raised reasonable legitimate questions of God, who says we do not have the same right?

In making such a search of questions of this nature, it is obvious that a phenomenal amount of data is required. Many scholars will have to give themselves to the task; especially scholars that are proficient in the knowledge of the ancient myths and legends; the religions of past and present cultures.

For example, an exercise in confusion can be had by just trying to find agreement among Jewish and Christian scholars about the giving of the Law. Not only do you find confusion and disagreement between Jew and Christian; you find confusion within the camp of both.

First, the confusion and contradictions between the accounts of Exodus and Deuteronomy have to be confronted. And they never have been to the satisfaction of either Jew or Christian.

Beginning with the names God uses for himself in the Ten Words, the use of Yahweh (or Yahvah) and Elohim is grounds for dispute. And the fact that angels figure prominently in the giving of the Law is confounding.

The Midrash and Targums have myriads of His Holiness involved with the giving of the law. An attempt at an explanation of the use of Elohim, as opposed to the legions of angels involved as per Josephus' comment on King Herod saying the law was given through angels. (Ant. 15, 5, 3, Whiston's translation).

The martyr, Stephen, says the law was given by the disposition of angels, Acts 7:53. It was ordained by angels according to Paul, Galatians 3:19. It was spoken by angels, Hebrews 2:2. There were myriad's of holy ones (not myriad's of His Holiness) at Sinai according to Deuteronomy 33:2.

Several trips up and down that mountain were made, Aaron went along sometimes; even Joshua played a part, and God spoke to all the people and sometimes to Moses alone. In short, a very confusing scenario.

But one thing is not confusing. In the Law we have a definite mechanism at work separating Israel from the rest of the world. The Law made God's attitude toward morality very clear. Idolatry, perversion, lying, cheating, stealing, adultery, murder, covetousness were not to be tolerated. Sin, as the Apostle Paul pointed out, was made exceedingly sinful by the Law.

It wasn't that other nations did not have prohibitions of the nature of The Law. But for the first time in recorded history, the narrative of the OT ascribes God codifying his own morality by an ethical system that, for the most part, was sensible and for its time, relatively free of the superstitions of the surrounding nations.

Not that the supposed Deity did not, obviously, accommodate some of the superstitions of the time; he did. This by itself is a fascinating study.

But in respect to how the Law was given, to what extent, if any, angels played a part, what the actual meaning of Elohim is in this regard, it is obvious that the resulting confusion of these things brooks no allowance of anyone pontificating on specifics of these issues, particularly in light of such things only being philosophical speculations. I hope the reader will bear this in mind when attending church or synagogue.

A paradigm is essential to any inquiry. That is the reason I have gone exploring into so many diverse elements; they are all a part of an extremely complex paradigm. Speculation concerning the nature of God isn't simple; and neither are we.

If your paradigm includes God is Love and that does not fit with a bloodthirsty tyrant who demands live sacrifices, you're not even going to get it off the ground. It simply won't fly no matter how many ways you try to justify it.

But you can try, as most commentators have done, to use the "I may be bad but he's worse" comparison.

The God of the OT wasn't requiring human sacrifice, only animals, and that was nothing to the sacrifice of babies to be burned alive in the arms of Molech of the Canaanites!

We read that God made coverings for Adam and Eve of animal skins. Noah was given permission to eat the flesh of animals. Jesus ate meat and fish. Peter, in his vision was commanded to rise, kill and eat.

Ok, so you go to the grocery store and think nothing of buying meat and fish in all good conscience. So the requirement of animal sacrifices might work if it finds no legitimate argument.

The paradigm requires inclusion of the paradox of good and evil. That is, indeed, one extremely difficult piece of data.

An essential part of the paradigm must include the errors of love and hope. Example: God is grieved that he even made man! And he says this twice! Genesis 6:5-7.

God tells his prophet Samuel: I am grieved that I have made Saul king, because he has turned away from me and has not carried out my instructions. God tells his prophet that he, God, has made a mistake! I Samuel 15:11 and 35.

Then God tells Samuel he has chosen a new king of Israel, David, a man after his own heart that will do all his will. I Samuel 14:14 and Acts 13:22. And David blows it.

In II Samuel 7:15 God tells the prophet Nathan to tell David that he will bless his heir, that his son will build him a temple and ... my love will never be taken away from him as I took it away from Saul, whom I removed from before you.

God is Love. Many people believe this. But we have great difficulty speculating on the love of God. And, as a consequence, I believe we have largely misinterpreted God's love by mysticizing it.

In the following chapter, I will undertake an examination of this thing called Love! But I would like to leave this chapter by giving the reader something to prepare the way.

While not yet prepared to join the Over-The-Hill-Gang, I have reached an age where I can begin to appreciate the feelings of those men out there who have gained a certain insight concerning women in general, which I am not yet ready to accept in my own life.

One of these things is an appreciation of frogs.

That might require a little explanation and, of course, I'll oblige.

A 90-year-old gentleman was taking a stroll when he encountered a talking frog.

Sir, sir, the frog said, I am a beautiful maiden that has suffered the spell of an evil and ugly witch. If you will but kiss me, I will be transformed, once more, as a beautiful, young woman for you!

Naturally astounded by the frog addressing him, the elderly man stooped down, and with an obvious effort, picked up the frog and placed it in his pocket.

Sir, sir, the frog said, didn't you understand what I told you?

Yes, I did, replied the old man, but at my age I'm much more interested in having a talking frog.

The above just to reassure the reader that I haven't lost track of the critical point-of-view concerning romance in the following chapters.

Chapter ten

What is this thing called Love?

I wrote a romance book titled "Birds With Broken Wings." Women loved it; men exhibited remarkable reserve. Well, maybe not so remarkable considering some of the things I had to say about men and their responsibilities in regard to romance.

For example, I wrote that God held men the responsible parties in seduction, that there would be more virtuous women if there were more virtuous men as examples. Men howled at this.

As a man I have a confession (well, several, but I'll stick to this one for now). If I had not had daughters, there are things about women I would never have learned. From this I concluded that these are things men without daughters will never, in fact cannot, learn about women. If true, this goes a long way in explaining why there are so many failed marriages.

For the most part, my little girls taught me the softer and gentler things about women that God surely intended men to know and respond to. In my relationships with women, I learned that men are the true romantics and women are the objects of that romanticism, the inspiration for it. My little angels provided the groundwork for this understanding.

Granting that their angelic natures required an occasional adjustment, my daughters worked the kind of love in my heart that any father should know. There is something of inestimable value in those little beings; but men have a hard time figuring out just what that something is?

After all, they are going to grow up to be God's most perverse creatures, Women! Typical man thinking. But they will never be Women; they will always be your little girls.

Love letters are a lost art to our modern culture. How many of you women out there have a bundle of treasured sentiments from the man in your life? Or did he ever send them? If so, did they stop shortly after marriage? If so, why? As one man told me: You got the girl so why should they? Typical.

Let's talk about the Shoulds, Shouldn'ts, Cans, Can'ts, Wills and Won'ts of love. And the prominent roles of Sex and Romance in such a discussion

If God is Love, the most basic element of our theological paradigm devoid of any soteriological demands apart from true worship of him as manifested in love for others; we need to make a careful examination of this thing called Love.

I believe the major change between Adam and those hominid species was love. There is nothing in the discovered artifacts to indicate anything like modern man's capacity to love, and express that love, among those early creatures.

This is a major reason that I believe any hope of making sense of the Bible must be grounded in taking much of it as a Romance, since it is a history of Adamic, not pre-Adamic, man.

It isn't unusual for preachers to point to the Song of Solomon and the book of Ruth as romantic. The problem is that they religionize these examples.

Look at Genesis 24 concerning Isaac; a marvelous love story. Abraham sends a servant to his relatives to get a wife for Isaac. She turns out to be Rebekah, a beautiful girl but the sister of Laban, the man who later treats her son, his nephew Jacob, in such a shameful manner.

The story of Isaac and Rebekah is a touching love story. But she is so beautiful that Isaac is in fear of his life due to her beauty and the lust of other men so, while among the Philistines during a famine, he passes her off as his sister. Strange, his father Abraham had done a similar thing with Sarah, and for the same reason.

Isaac was a good man, but I often wonder about God's requiring Abraham to sacrifice him? I don't think I would have been as compliant as Abraham under the circumstances. And why put old Abraham, and Isaac, through such a living hell? To test the old man's faith? Come on now!

It wasn't all sweetness and light with Isaac and Rebekah. There was the problem of Jacob and Esau and the duplicity and deception in getting Rebekah's favorite, Jacob, to receive the blessing.

We have another love story in regard to a most interesting character, Samson. And I'm not talking about his indiscretions with women; and one woman in particular, Delilah.

No, I'm talking about Samson's father and mother, Manoah, and...? Now why, I ask myself, isn't Samson's mother named?

Samson's mother is barren. But an angel of the Lord appears to her in the form of a man and tells her she is going to have a son. This is one of the most interesting angelic appearances in Scripture.

When Manoah asks the angel his name, the angel replies: Why do you ask my name? It is beyond your comprehension! Just like an extraterrestrial to rub it in. Ignorant earthling!

Manoah makes a sacrifice and the angel of the Lord ascends in the flames. We're doomed to die! Manoah cries to his wife, we have seen God!

Good wife that she is, she reassures her husband that if the angel had meant to knock them off he could have done so at any time. Practical woman.

Samson has a bittersweet waltz with the Lord, dependable at one time, totally erratic at others. His phenomenal strength and good looks make him a ladies favorite of which he pays due attention, and, at times, the price.

But the Lord and Samson give the Philistines (and Delilah) their comeuppance in a grand finale for which there isn't going to be an encore and Samson goes to his reward, taking a bunch of those uppity idolaters with him. Truly a most interesting, and romantic, story.

The last judge of Israel, Samuel, is another product of divine interference; pardon me, intervention, in the lives of people.

In the first book of Samuel, we have a man, Elkanah, who has two wives. Oh, not again!

Elkanah has a very special love for wife number one in his affections, Hannah. Wife number two, Pininnah, has children, but Hannah is barren.

As a result, Elkanah gives number one wife a double portion of the goodies. We aren't told how number two wife and the children respond to this favoritism.

Being a mere man, I suspect wife number one had some extra
talents she applied to her position. Maybe she was better looking, and,
not having children retained her girlish figure. Men are real suckers for
this. At least some things don't change throughout history.

But Hannah was a good girl, she was; and in spite of her husband's
extra attention, felt the disgrace of being barren very keenly. So she
prays; she prays so fervently that good old Eli, the head honcho of the
tabernacle, accuses her of being drunk. Considering Eli's experience
with his sons, good priests, he thought knew a drunk when he saw
one.

But Hannah is quick to disabuse Eli of his accusation and tells him
she is praying for a son.

Eli really is a good sort in spite of his failure as a father, and he
assures Hannah that God will grant her request. Hannah bargains with
God that if he will give her a son, he will be dedicated to the Lord. And
so it is.

Hannah gives birth to Samuel, the last, and one of the greatest, of
the OT prophets.

If you have not done so, you owe it to yourself to read these stories.
It isn't just Ruth and Canticles that are filled with love and romance.

The Pharisee in an attempt to justify himself asked Jesus: Just who is
my brother? The answer of Jesus was the story of the Good Samaritan.
In other words, the fellow who helped was brother to the one needing
help. And, correspondingly, the fellow needing help was brother to the
one helping.

But a legitimate question is: Just who am I to love? The answer,
according to Jesus, those who are your brothers and sisters; these are
the ones who need your help, the ones needing your love.

I believe God created family to teach us to love. This begins with
romance and sex. And, ideally, between one man and one woman
committed to a lifetime together.

Ideally, also, romance and sex continue to be elements of the
relationship, a husband and wife in faithfulness and mutual esteem of
each other, honoring the compatibility of differences and each other as
of equal value.

A parent's sacrificial love for a child teaches things unlearnable otherwise. As the child grows, things change; love learns other things along the way such as the love that involves discipline and chastening.

However, how do Christians reconcile love and romance with the practice of polygamy, especially the polygamy of OT times involving men like Jacob, David and Solomon?

And I have to wonder if Hosea ever gave flowers to the whore, Gomer, God commanded him to marry? Did Jacob, David or Solomon concern themselves with anniversaries, birthdays; did any of their ladies get a valentine or box of chocolates on special occasions?

I don't know about you, but if I were one of these ladies I would wonder how much my husband cared about me if he had to have a bookkeeper to keep track of all of us and when he gave what to whom?

But if the status of women was so dismally low that they felt grateful for just being given a roof over their heads; and a royal roof if possible, maybe they felt they had a pretty good deal after all. And if their sexual needs could only be met once a year, every two years, or not at all, well, that's another matter.

When Leah trades her son's mandrakes to Rachel for a night with Jacob, her complaint is that Rachel has taken her husband away from her. These are sisters. Just whose husband is Jacob? Leah has to hire him with mandrakes?

Pretty raw deal, if you ask me. How about you ladies out there, how do you feel about this? Oh, no one ever asked you? Not surprising. I doubt Jacob, David, or Solomon concerned themselves greatly about it. After all, they had all the fun.

But come to think of it, I don't recall any good Catholic, Baptist, Lutheran, Presbyterian, Episcopalian, etc. minister or priest ever asking the question of you ladies either?

Just imagine the theological revolution that might be caused by women demanding their minister, priest or rabbi call Jacob, David and Solomon to account for this?

And there is much to consider in the light of the shame attaching to women if they did not have children. Sarah giving her maid to Abraham in order to get a child, for example. But God threw a monkey wrench into the plan by making it possible for Sarah to get pregnant.

Surprise! The result being the historical hatred between Arabs and Jews. God's plan? I don't think so.

Oh, I know, you have read and heard the story that such practices was justified in the context of the times when such things occurred. Baloney! How much better for the world if there was not the historical battleground of the Middle East!

If the words of Jesus are true in regard to one man, one woman, and Christians don't hesitate to rise up in wrath at any suggestion that they are not, you can't have your cake and eat it to by claiming God thinks women of lesser value than men in this respect. Or, for that matter, in any other respect.

Jesus distinctly said that God intended the relationship to be one man, one wife for life! If you got one, you got your limit!

But maybe the Samaritan Woman at the well had some secrets that women would kill for? Five husbands, and the present man she had wasn't one of them? A very busy and obviously highly talented lady.

In the beginning, Jesus said, God intended a husband and a wife faithful to each other for life. Yet Lamech, living during the time of Adam, had two wives. He was a Cainite, opposing God, so this might explain his ignoring God's wishes in this regard.

When Eve bore Seth, she said God had given her a son to take the place of Abel. It was at this time that men began to call on (or proclaim) the name of the Lord. A change is made here from Elohim to God as Yahweh (Yahvah or Jehovah). I have always thought it odd that the opening of Genesis uses the plural for God and then changes to masculine throughout the rest of the entire Bible.

But If we take this earliest history of modern man as beginning with the creation of Adam and Eve by Elohim, there are a number of difficult concepts with which commentators have struggled and have not been thoroughly honest, neither Jewish nor Christian.

I'll temper that remark with the understanding that both have worked in honest ignorance of some things in many cases that science has brought to light. But it must be kept in mind at all times that their prejudices moved them in some instances to justify their interpretations, even textual criticisms of scholarship of the Bible when in conflict with obvious facts to the contrary.

But if we take the Bible in conjunction with science and other histories, myths and legends, even accepting the paranormal like telepathy and influences that science has not yet been able to explain, much more of it becomes comprehensible and sensible.

The potential for romance was established in the Garden. God was seeking a love in his life, a love that Adam and Eve were to fulfill.

God tells Adam and Eve that every seed-bearing plant and tree are theirs for food (with the exception of that one tree), that the green plants are food for the animals and birds; that Adam and Eve are to care for the Garden and these creatures.

No allowance for hunting or the eating of meat. Innocence, no shedding of blood, all in harmony. Why, then, one asks, did God create the animals, birds, and creatures like the Serpent? None were meant for food, no Nature red in tooth and claw.

Possible evolutionary genetics aside, the only sensible explanation is that something went horribly wrong! But what thing? After all, we are in the area of speculative philosophy and not science.

The orthodox position of the church is that Jesus was there from the beginning, the Lamb of God that takes away the sins of the world, the lamb chosen before the creation of the world. I Peter 1:20.

Blood sacrifice was initiated as expiation of sin; for without the shedding of blood, there is no forgiveness of sin. Hebrews 9:22.

We are told in I Peter that angels longed to look into the plan of God; that prophets prophesied without understanding this plan for the ages.

God had a plan. Of course. That plan consisted of the creation of Adam and Eve and all that their creation represented. Love was to be the ruling principle of this special creation.

But the love God was seeking is blasted by the betrayal of that love and trust. Sin enters into the picture and animals are killed by God to provide Adam and Eve a covering for their shame and they are cast out of the Garden.

A legitimate question: Are there other worlds in our universe, even universes, worlds that allow of Elohim (Gods) to take counsel in the creation of man? If so, is it reasonable to speculate that once rebellion to the authority of Elohim occurs, it be answered by mankind entering into a conflict between two species, the children of God and the children of the Devil?

Psalm 82 is curious in that the plural noun, Elohim, is used throughout. Jesus quotes from this Psalm to refute the Pharisees when they claim he makes himself equal to God the Father. They considered such a claim as sacrilege, blasphemy! John 10:34.

Yet Jews and Christians are confuted by this. They cannot reconcile the Scripture that cannot be broken with either the OT or NT concept of Elohim by their theologies.

Is Jehovah, Yahweh (YHWH) from the council of Elohim and the caretaker God of this world? Is this why the book of Job represents God as the head of an authority that holds kingly court and sits on a throne at the top of Jacob's stairway to heaven? Is there a council of Elohim to consider in all this? Is Satan the adversary of a plan that was formed in that early council of Elohim, a plan to which he disagreed and, as a result, was cast out of heaven together with those angels who followed him?

Is Satan the god of this age Paul speaks of in II Corinthians 4:4? The NT represents him as a roaring lion, seeking whom he may devour, masquerading as an angel of light with servants to do his bidding; he offers Jesus the kingdoms of the world if he will only worship him. Jesus heals some that are afflicted of Satan; Paul is kept humble by the torment of a thorn in the flesh, a messenger of Satan.

In the tug-of-war between Christ and Satan, you have the yin and yang of the history of the human race where some are children of God and some are children of the devil, a conflict between good and evil that has raged unabated throughout recorded history.

Love is supposed to be the motivating influence of the children of God; they are to be distinguished by this love from the children of the evil one.

If the Bible is at least in part a romance, a story of the struggle of love trying to overcome and prevail in the face of evil, a theology that understands both the diabolical and the divine is essential. Tragically, the churches, while they talk a lot about heaven and love don't seem to know much about either. But, then, how could they in all reason and logic know about such things?

It is a badly flawed theology that leads to the crimes against humanity of which the churches have been guilty. Witch-hunts, inquisitions, bloody crusades, burnings at the stake, the sexual immorality of monasteries and convents are hardly noble endeavors that represent a God of Love!

It is a badly flawed theology that disallows good scholarship in the name of some kind of spirituality and mystical nonsense that rewards foolishness and excesses of hysteria in the name of God! It is the God of the Book we are to worship and reverence, not the Book!

If Christians are to be the living letters of God, if God is manifest in his creation and his law written in all men's hearts so that no man has any excuse for not knowing the difference between good and evil, if Christ is the light of the world and men are required to follow this light, the Book is to confirm these things and give us better understanding of them; most certainly not to divide and create division and chaos!

Another view of the Bible, of its teaching, is obviously needed. To try to use it as a theological club to beat others into submission to your brand of Gospel is inexcusable!

There is no reason to believe that there are not other worlds, other civilizations in the universe. That enigmatic statement of St. Paul that men are to judge angels in the future may be an implication of this. His being caught up to the third heaven; caught up to Paradise where he heard inexpressible things man is not permitted to tell adds a degree of legitimate speculation about this. II Corinthians 12:2-4.

Ancient religions, the practice of which we can only make guesses about, may have some basis in a celestial host or hierarchy out there in the universe that left some kind of impress on the minds of early hominids. This might explain an attraction to the planets, stars, meteors and comets that resulted in astrology and the beliefs so prevalent in even our modern world that something out there has an influence on our lives.

Nor can we discount the possibility that celestial beings like angels may have manifested themselves or communicated in some manner with ancient species much in the manner of their description in the Bible and other literature.

Tarot cards, palmistry, witchcraft, astrology have never proven very successful. Yet the propensity of people to reach out to another world of the supernatural continues unabated. The belief is there. Our ability to utilize such things in any scientific way continues, likewise, to be vastly unsuccessful.

Yet dowsing, telepathy, clairvoyance, deja vu have seemingly been authenticated. The subconscious, dreams, auras, influences like spirits and untapped resources of the mind remain largely unknowns. There is a something at work in these things; we just don't know what it is.

But in what I believe to be the most unique act of Elohim in all the creation of the universe, the making of man in the image of God, processes were set in motion of which God himself did not know the outcome. But the need for creatures in his image must have existed or he (they) would not have created them.

With the Fall, Elohim had to protect the Tree of Life from Adam and Eve. The reason: The man has now become like one of us to know good and evil! He must not be allowed to take of the fruit of the tree of life and live forever! Genesis 3:22.

Why not? Because man now knew good and evil. Having become like Elohim in this respect, what danger was there in immortality for Adam and Eve? We can only suppose that they were still child-like in many respects and until they grew up, immortality would have made them loose cannons, not unlike giving children guns and bombs to play with. They had already evidenced their childishness by thinking they could disobey God without repercussion, that they could have things their way without any responsibility for their actions.

So cherubim and a flaming sword flashing back and forth were put in place to keep them from re-entering the Garden.

A curiosity: Why were the cherubim and the sword placed only at the East of the Garden? What prevented Adam and Eve, or the serpent for that matter, gaining access from the other points of the compass? Was there a gate to the Garden at the East and the rest of it walled, protected in some fashion that secured it from access in any other direction?

The evidence of the childishness of Adam and Eve by their actions is seen in their failure toward each other, a failure of love to be the guiding principle in their lives resulting in Eve listening to the Serpent and Adam blaming Eve and God for his failure. Then their failure as parents in Cain slaying Abel.

Obviously Cain did not love his brother. But if, as God said, Adam was to be a tiller of the soil, eating bread in the sweat of his brow, and seed bearing plants and the fruit of trees were to be their food, why was

Abel raising flocks? And did this mitigate Cain's hatred of Abel; was this in some way the source of his hatred of Abel?

God had to shed the first blood to provide a covering of skins for Adam and Eve. He wasn't going to kick them out of the house naked. But I wouldn't think that God would go on being the haberdasher for Adam and Eve. Not knowing what the climate might have been outside the Garden where they had to make their way, we can at least be certain it would not have been nearly as hospitable as their previous residence.

This would have necessitated the couple providing clothing for themselves to meet the exigencies of the outside world. Animal skins would have been the best choice of material. But to get them, animals had to die and Adam and Eve had to do their own killing of the innocent.

When Abel came along, he may have raised sheep to provide a continuing source of clothing and sacrifice, but not for the meat. The shedding of innocent blood, the lambs offered to God and providing shelter from the elements and clothing, could not have been a pleasant experience for Abel.

Baby animals and birds are marvelous. To hold a fluffy, baby duck, a baby bunny or squirrel in your hand is thrilling, and your heart responds to the little things. The last thing you are thinking as you hold these little creatures is butchering them.

That the innocent might have to pay the price for our own sins should give us pause before we engage in anything that might cause them harm. Beginning with our own children, we parents should always consider them first in everything we do.

Cain's heart was not right before God. But in what way? Did he have to bargain with his brother for a new lambskin suit or tent? Did he resent Abel giving God the best animals and skins? What a waste! he might have thought. Further, since he later thought God didn't know about his killing his brother he may well have thought he could fool God with less than the best he had to offer, that such sacrifices of the best were wasted.

Did Cain have a sweet tooth for veal? Did he go nuts over the aroma of bar-be-cue on an altar and he couldn't have any send him around the bend? Ever meet someone who would kill for a steak?

Did he confront Abel with some kind of plan to have a rack of lamb instead of a constant diet of bread and orange juice? Those Israelites complaining of nothing but manna and crying out for a change of diet that included meat comes readily to mind.

And let's not forget the high price Esau was willing to pay for a pot of stew! He gave away his birthright for it to Jacob. There is a certain Deja vu in that story connecting with Cain, Esau and those Israelites wanting meat. And let's not forget that, like Esau, Cain was the elder brother and, as such, was to inherit the birthright. An almost eerie similarity between Cain and Esau. I strongly suspect that Cain made some kind of demand on Abel that his younger brother refused.

When it comes to the younger, righteous brother in opposition to the elder, we recall Jacob, Joseph, Moses, David, and Solomon as examples.

I submit for your consideration that Abel tries to tell Cain that the flocks are for clothing, shelter, and sacrifice but that no matter how good lamb chops might smell on the grill, they are not to eat any.

Cain is obviously not the stuff of a good vegetarian. And he can't see wasting good meat and skins as sacrifices. As implausible as it seems on the surface, remember that God has only given the produce of the soil for food to Adam and Eve. Animal sacrifice is to be the reminder of their sin and not to be used for food, and that the innocent are made to suffer as a result of sin. I take it that this suffering included Abel, as he had to kill those innocent lambs by his own hand not sparing his own heart.

Not until the time of Noah is meat allowed of God. And that with a marked change in the relationship between men and animals. That fluffy little duck and bunny are going to grow up and go on the table.

Yet no one of a tender heart and conscience enjoys the killing of animals for food. In spite of God's allowing us eating meat, few people actually enjoy the slaughtering of animals.

Some animals and birds pose threats to agriculture, even carrying diseases harmful to mankind. This, I suppose, is one of the results of sin (by whatever definition) that includes the fear of animals for man God pronounced to Noah.

Yet the death of the innocent as in the offering of lambs and doves in propitiation for sin is to encourage a tender heart, a heart that is revulsed by the thought of doing harm to others, of the betrayal of love and trust.

These lessons were apparently lost on Cain and he murders his brother. More, he thinks he can hide his hideous sin from God just as his mother and father thought they could hide from God after their transgression.

In spite of all the fancy footwork by theologians in trying to make God omniscient and omnipresent, it is obviously not something taught in Scripture.

But there is romance as part of the character of God. A tender heart fashioned by sacrifice for others, of submitting to rules of behavior that deny your own wishes in favor of the benefit of another whether it be a husband, wife, child or friend.

The evolution of sacrificial love and romance throughout history, particularly the history of the Bible, is an intriguing subject. If it was God's intention that the hearts of men and women should be made tender through children, through the sacrifice of lambs and doves, it didn't succeed. Witness God's determination to destroy all of mankind because of the violence and evil that prevailed before the flood!

Things turned out all wrong and God admits to making a mistake in even creating man. But God's need to love and be loved, heavenly parents or no was still there. So he (they) takes a chance on love once more in the person of Noah.

However Noah's sons have married women of that very violent and evil generation that God is going to destroy! None of the fathers, mothers, brothers or sisters of the wives of Noah's sons joins them in the Ark. But the wives are!

That Bad Seed is there as evidenced by Noah's son Ham. Didn't God take that into account in saving Noah and these others? If God were going to start over with Noah, why invite the contagion on board with him?

I take the position that God did not know, but as with that most beautiful and quintessential description of love in I Corinthians 13, God's love was expressed in hope, a hope born of such love that does, indeed, hope in the face of everything contrary to such hope. Love does hope all things.

The love of God hoped things would turn out better this time around. After all, if Noah could get his sons, his family, to build an ark in the face of what had to be enormous opposition, there were grounds to believe in Noah's ability to carry through after the flood, hope that his family would continue to do right.

But there was a missing ingredient in this that caused the downfall of God's expectations: Romance!

I'm not about to castigate Noah for getting drunk. I'm sure he wasn't a drunkard or he couldn't have commanded the respect and obedience of his family, let alone God's love for him.

But he did get drunk and Ham observed his nakedness. There is much more to this than the sparse and demurring narrative tells us. Ham probably committed some perverse act with his father and tried to get his brothers in on the action.

Romantic love is not perverse. It glorifies and exalts virtue, beauty, purity and chastity. You simply cannot have Godly, divine love without that essential element of Romance!

Romance is the inspiration of love; it keeps the fire of love burning. Without it, love grows old and tiresome and, eventually, betrays.

God, as the ultimate Romantic, works in romantic love that hopes, endures, forgives, and keeps on in spite of every obstacle. It is an overcoming love that because it lives in the very ideals of romance keeps on keeping on.

But the destructiveness of the perversion of love in all its hideous manifestations showed itself in the actions of Noah's son, Ham. Thus the curse on Ham's generation, the race that would follow in his footsteps.

From this came the perversion of the worship of God, leaving off true, ideal romantic love and exchanging it for the corruption of the worship of idols and creatures rather than the Creator(s).

Ham undoubtedly knew a lot about idols and idol worship from exposure to the peoples that had been wiped out by the flood. If he were to be rejected by the God of Noah, he had other gods to turn to.

By the time of Abraham, idols and idol worship were full-blown in places like Chaldea. The Old Religion, fertility worship, was ongoing resulting in the myths and superstitions that Abraham and his descendants had to face everywhere they went.

But romantic love was still largely absent. Women, far from being an object of romantic love, suffered tremendously by being treated as chattel. Men wanted harems, not one wife for life. And the legitimate resentment of men from Eve on did not help matters.

Their sex and beauty being the only things of value they had to offer, it served the purpose of women to try to maintain some authority through the use of their sex as a weapon and by encouraging the worship of fertility goddesses.

This caused Rachel to steal the family gods, undoubtedly idols glorifying fertility worship, i.e. women, when Jacob departed from Laban.

Thus the battle of the sexes, the resentment of men and women toward each other that began in the Garden grew into the manifestation of fertility religions, witches and conjurors. Fear born in the ignorance of forsaking the true God and creator manifested itself in the many forms of idols and idol worship.

From all these things, the working of magic and sorcery as we know them began. Forsaking the truth and romantic love, men and women gave themselves to the corruption of such things and the dark arts flourished, preying on the fears and superstitions of the ignorant, and the foolish, darkened hearts of many.

A major change in magic occurred toward the end of the 13th century when the Zohar began to appear. An extensive commentary on the Pentateuch written by a Spanish rabbi, Moses de Leon, called the Kabbalah (cabala) claiming to explain the spiritual world. Cabalistic teachings were nothing new, going back many centuries before de Leon. But wide circulation of his book popularized them.

Twenty-two lines (paths) making a pattern of the Tree of Life join the ten emanations (Sephiroth).

Astrology, having an ancient history, cannot be separated from the practice of mystical arts. The original wise men of past cultures such as those magi that are mentioned in the NT were of such a background.

Many of the church fathers, and some of its greatest theologues, for example, accepted astrology as legitimate. But not in the sense of so-called *astrological forecasts* for people. Yet there was a very deep belief in a significance attached to the planets and stars beyond the merely physical and material. The star of the magi, the Wandering stars of Jude and the use of stars in Revelation for example.

Hitler and Nancy Reagan had Astrology in common. And a host of famous persons throughout history join them.

Most agree that monuments like Stonehenge were built, at least in part, to accommodate the practice of astrology. There is no doubt that the earliest religious practices involved a belief that the stars and planets had a profound effect on life and the earth.

As a result, it became vital to early cultures to be able to forecast the alignments of stars and planets, the phases of the moon, etc. Marks on bones and stones, crude calendars, appear early in man's history.

This was the earliest beginning of science. That it was a science born of mysteries is natural enough. The same is true of modern science.

The evolution of religions requiring the use of talismans, dolls, magic potions and elixirs, the search for a philosopher's stone, the Holy Grail, shape-shifting, cabalistic interpretations, all are a part of the religion of mysticism.

It took a book, Malleus Maleficarum (Hammer of Witches) in 1486 by two men, Henrich Institor and Jakob Sprenger, professors of theology of the Catholic Church to make witch hunting a science. The book, a result of Pope Innocent VIII issuing his Summis Desiderantes Affectibus in 1484 where he decried so many consorting with the devil and his demons, has been described by the scholar George Lincoln Burr to have ... caused more suffering than any other written by human pen!

But the thing that made the book the first Best Seller in history was the sexual detail it went into in describing things like examining naked women in searching for devil's marks, of sexual intercourse with the devil and demons. Talk about titillating the libido! As such, the book was the first Lady Chatterly's Lover.

People have always had a taste for the strange and macabre, for sexually stimulating literature. And humans have a perverse way of excusing aberrant, even heinous behavior under the guise of religion. In the kinky sex category, how do you top the devil appearing as a beautiful woman (the succubi) to tempt men? Or his making it with women? The devil apparently isn't discriminatory when it comes to his sexual orientation (AC/DC).

The medieval McCarthyism that followed the publishing of this book resulted in the torture and murder of multiplied thousands of men, women and children accused of being witches. Madame Blavatsky and Aleister Crowley were safe in their times, but not so their precursors of the 15th through 17th centuries.

The OT prohibition against consorting with familiar spirits. Why?

From the very earliest beginnings of Neandertals burying their dead with ceremony, shamans and cave paintings that, oddly, never included human figures, only animal, to the intricately involved Egyptian, Greek and Roman religions, there are common factors.

A profound belief in an after-life is certainly one of these factors. That a God or gods, goddesses and spirits of many different kinds, involve themselves with humanity is another.

The practice of magic, the belief in the occult, astrology and reincarnation by millions of people together with so many inexplicable occurrences of the supernatural, lends credence to some of these things. Even modern science accepts that some kind of telepathy is operational among people, and experiments in the paranormal such as dowsing are on going.

Brazil is a country given over to Spiritism. The Umbanda, an admixture of Voodoo, Catholicism and Reincarnation is given cultural and official recognition. But Quimbanda (Black Magic) has become a great social problem.

Haitian Voodoo has its snake god, Damballah, and a long tradition of mixing Catholicism, reincarnation and zombiism.

The history of religion, Spiritism and reincarnation, coupled with astrology in some form, has made many twists and turns. The ancient rites of Neandertal, the earliest evidence of religion of any kind and at which we can only guess, had to have originated with some kind of manifestation of at least what was perceived at the time to be supernatural. It is highly unlikely that such an unimaginative race of creatures manufactured any kind of religious concepts on their own.

There remains the inexplicable gap between Neandertal Stone Age hominids and modern man. This gap is made all the more intriguing because of the most unusual difference in religious practice between the two. Though some things like attention to the dead, some belief in an afterlife, seem to be there with Neandertal.

Neandertal did not make pictures or figures of people, demons, gods, or anything approaching human. He had no music, literature or art. No science of any kind. Yet, he survived a 100,000 years.

Homo sapiens comes on the scene abruptly, and just as abruptly, all the things lacking in Neandertal come into vogue. A quantum leap anthropologically.

We have a long way to go in understanding the past. Another way of looking at ancient writings and legends, myths, can help us along that path.

Chapter eleven

GOD: The Ultimate Romantic!

Probably the greatest difference between those ancient hominids and Homo sapiens (Adamic man, if you will) is romantic love. This, of course, requires some elaboration in order to explain my premise.

The lack of language by those ancient creatures made them incapable of developing romance in speaking or writing. There were no sonnets or love letters. Expressions of love may have been there, but we have no way of knowing this.

When my little granddaughter, Andrea, was a toddler, I had the inexpressible pleasure of giving her some black licorice when her mother wasn't around. This was payback. As I told my daughter Karen from the beginning "When you have a baby, I hope it's a little girl and that she turns out to be exactly like you!"

Now don't get me wrong. My daughter is the most beautiful and loving girl and little mother in the world. So extraordinarily beautiful she is the ideal of beauty, so much so that I used her as the model for the picture on my Birds book. When I talk about beauty, I want the world to know that I know what I'm talking about.

But Karen wasn't always the ideal little girl in the behavior department. Too much like her dad. She caused me a lot of difficulty on more than one occasion, like all children, and so the Just wait till you have children of your own was more than a cliche in her case.

Did I really give Andrea the licorice to get even? Of course not. It was just an expression of grandparenting is definitely better! Now I get the chance to spoil the child and let the parent clean up the mess. Fair is fair.

Expressions of love come in all varieties. Some of them quite subtle like giving your little granddaughter licorice and letting your daughter deal with the mess.

And there is what I call "the curse of beauty." My daughter has experienced this and, as her father, I suffered along with her.

But all of my children, Daniel, Diana, Karen and Michael have had to put up with their father being an incurable romantic, the poet, singer and musician that lacks common sense.

I'm able to run a lathe and mill, build a house, fix a car and fly an airplane. But given my druthers, I would find myself alone on a trout stream or in the middle of the Mojave communing with the critters, stars, rocks and trees.

But like my soul brother Thoreau, What good is nature to me if I have no one with whom to share it? I require a high degree of solitude. But loneliness is something else entirely.

My most pleasurable experiences have been in sharing the things of nature with my children. Creation has real meaning and relevance when shared with others.

Men, as with God I suppose, look for inspiration in romance. Nothing else in creation inspires the best part of the man, the child within that retains the capacity to love and imagine unfettered by the lessons of adulthood, like a woman.

She is the symbol of all that is good and pure, of virtue and all that that implies. We men write the poetry, the songs and music, paint the pictures on canvas and in words to describe her beauty and virtue, her nurturing warmth and softness, her readiness to yield her virtue to a Knight in shining armor who will cherish her and fulfill her as a woman.

How is it then, that we are more acquainted with the love is heaven but marriage is hell syndrome that afflicts us?

In a word: Romance!

I would ask all the men and women out there if they have experienced romantic love? For your consideration on the subject, I submit the story of Ann, a story I tell in a book I wrote about this thing called Romance:

I can hardly fault other men for not listening to women unless I make a conscientious effort to get their point of view myself. That this leads to some interesting things in my life comes with the territory.

Unhappily, women are not used to being asked by men for their point of view. And, when asked, are understandably reluctant to say what they really want to say or have great difficulty articulating those things for any number of legitimate reasons.

A primary reason being the fact that women have seldom been taken seriously by men when it comes to philosophy. Yet, philosophy fails by not taking women seriously.

When I express the fear of doing a solo when the music requires a duet, men like Soren Kierkegaard come immediately to mind. He, as with many like him, wrote a great deal about marriage, love and romance. But he did a solo when the music required a duet. And, lacking any real, pragmatic and empirical knowledge and experience of the subject, the music intended too often results in nothing but pontifical, egotistical noise.

My beautiful daughter, Karen, tries to help me but because she is my daughter there is an understandable reluctance, even a normal inability, to intrude into some of the areas where that significant other is needed to avoid the mistakes of a solo performance.

Now I get letters and phone calls from women, I enter into interesting discussions with many ladies I meet under a variety of circumstances. And while all of this is useful and needed, I don't pretend that any of this will take the place of that One that should be there as a constant in my life to provide the kind of insight that I know comes from more than a friendly relationship.

As a consequence, I am most reluctant to carry out some of the thoughts I have on this problem into print. Not that I am afraid to embarrass myself, I've done that often enough. Not that I fear making mistakes, I've made more than my share of those. But in preaching against hurtful ignorance I am responsible to practice what I preach in the fear that such potential ignorance and the kind of mistakes that might result from it will only be noise or, worse, actually be harmful to others.

And this leads to a major factor in the problem between men and women: Romance. I write a great deal about this obvious part of the equation. My Birds book is a romance book but it is factual, not fiction. And it is a graphic representation of that rule of writing: The difference between Reality and Fiction is that fiction has to make sense.

I was at the Club the other evening with my good friend Larry when she walked in. I'll call her Ann. She is a beautiful, vivacious, petite woman with dark hair and eyes that a man could drown in.

Seeing me at the bar, she took a seat next to me. We were delighted to see each other. We have known each other for quite some time but have never dated because she has a boyfriend. Yet, from the moment we first met there has been a something between us.

For some reason, Ann was willing to talk openly about this. The music was playing and we decided to dance. She was wonderful to hold. Soft, warm, and sweet scented, as a woman should be, so small the top of her head barely reaching my chin, she moved closer into my arms as we danced. Magic!

Then, a remarkable thing. She looks up at me and it seems right that we kiss for the first time. As we move slowly and gently to the music in a warm embrace, she says: Don, I can't give you what you want. But we can have this half as a compromise, can't we?

It hit me full-blown! I knew what was missing between Ann and her boyfriend, what that something was between us: Romance!

Ann has read some of my writing; she knows of my music, she knows me as a quiet, gentle, romantic man. And she knows I care for her.

But Ann has a need, as do all men and women, for romance in her life. She is an honest woman and would never betray. In that honesty she says: Don, I'm sorry for using you. She is trying to tell me that she intends to be faithful to the boyfriend and, yet, want's and desperately needs that romance in her life, the romance that he is failing to provide in the relationship.

It is such a tragic, familiar story. It is the reason for the phenomenal growth of romance novels among women as they seek to feed their impoverished hearts and souls.

We continued to dance, holding each other tightly; both needing someone to fill that void in our lives that sex alone will never satisfy.

Ann, like all women, was made to be the music, poetry and inspiration in the right man's life. And that right man should fill her need for the romance she deserves in her life, that romance that is the responsibility of such a man.

I ask myself the all too familiar question of why the right man and woman have always had such a seemingly impossible task in finding each other? But I have to remind myself that it takes two artists working together to make it happen and keep it alive.

I know Ann needs the music in her life, I tell her she has the music in her and I feel it as we move together in an embrace. Her whole body responds to the music and it is magic, a magic that we both realize is working in us together in each other's arms.

The music has stopped. But we can't let go of each other. We wrap our arms around each other tightly and continue to move slowly to the music we can still hear in our hearts.

Ann finally has to leave. But it is hard for her to go, leaving such magic and go home to what? If I could only get the message to her boyfriend (and all the men out there of whom he is all too typical) that he better get his priorities straight, he better start showing his appreciation for the undiscovered treasure of such a wonderful woman like Ann!

That graveyard of shattered dreams of love and romance seems never to be satisfied. Yet women like Ann, with so much love to give, wanting and needing to give that love, seem never to have this love nourished and tended like the garden of delight she represents. Let her breasts satisfy thee at all times and be thou ravished always with her love (Proverbs 5:19) is a message lost to the majority of men.

In Ann's case, as with so many women I know, the music, the love letters and flowers are probably missing in her present relationship. The growing hurt of this loss, a loss such women as Ann recognize in their lives, may follow a course of growing resentment and, finally, the death of the relationship, a senseless tragedy for the both of them.

I tried to explain to Ann that I did not feel used of her; it was an honor and privilege to provide her some hope that there was nothing wrong in her need for a man to respond to her with the kind of things I represent to her. For myself, as a romantic and poet, I find a ministry, if you will, in assuring people like Ann that if they value themselves they will not settle for less than being cherished as a woman. And I never minimize the responsibility of women in encouraging that virtue in men.

In many cases, it requires women to pay attention to things like weight control, to their appearance and mannerisms, their language and the showing of their appreciation for things like fixing the car or washing machine. It is just too easy for both men and women to begin to take such things for granted and, consequently, taking each other for granted.

I will not be the hypocrite in denying my own so very human need for such things Ann, as a beautiful and desirable woman, has to offer in my own life. And while Ann and I share a common belief and faith in God, we are normal human beings in respect to her honest comment concerning her not being able to give me what I want of her.

But she knows me well enough to know that she can trust me, that I would not seduce her; that I am known as an honorable man who will not use or betray a woman. Not because of anything noble in my own character, which is all too human but because I will not betray a woman or my children and others to whom, I must remain accountable for such things. And there is the matter of my own belief that I must, ultimately, stand before the judgment seat of God Himself to give an account for my life.

It is in relationship with women like Ann that I maintain the hope that I will find that woman who will be able to abide the poet. As I've said many times, while I have met many women who love poetry, I have yet to find that exceptional woman who can live with a poet. And I thank you, Ann, for wishing that for me.

It is February and Valentine's Day is nearly here. How many women will receive the attention they should get on this day? How many relationships will be encouraged by this day in honor of real lovers? I wonder. I hope women like Ann will find their desires fulfilled by such acknowledgment from the men in their lives.

But women like Ann know that in spite of the commercialism of the day, in spite of the flowery cards and letters, nothing will take the place of genuine love and romance, of that cherishing that is proved by living it the other 364 days of the year.

I cannot express the gratitude I have for the phone calls and letters you women provide me as I try to help us, men and women, to find answers and attempt to contribute a degree of understanding, compassion among us regarding the problems in our relationships. Please, I implore you; keep those calls and letters coming.

But, as Only a Man, and a very normal, human man in most aspects of normal, human needs, I confess to my weaknesses and failures without that significant other in my own life. But the wrong one would be a catastrophe. It might be that I have become too fearful of such a thing.

Part of that fear results from the fact that it cannot be denied that women need, desperately, to be the softness and gentleness, the virtuousness men need to inspire romance. But we live in a violent world and society that is the antithesis of such things and women are made to be hard and tough in areas where women were never intended to be so.

I am so indebted to women like Ann for letting me hold her and share the music that is intended for us, the music and the poetry she inspires as a woman.

It will be difficult for most religious people to relate to the story of Ann. There are a host of religious taboos involved. One being the abhorrence of going to bars. Another, the fact that Ann is living with a man without the benefit of legal marriage and that she danced with and kissed a man not even her boyfriend.

In condemning things like this, religious people miss the point. The point being that they should look at what is missing, probably in their own lives, in the relationships between men and women. That such an essential thing like romance is missing in their lives is an on-going source of resentment, an itch that cannot be scratched.

The loss of romance accounts for the bulk of divorces, even among those that call themselves Christian. It is also the basis for the history of humankind being a history of warfare and conflict. As goes the relationship between a man and a woman, so goes a family and so goes a society, a culture.

The greatest inspiration in a man's life is a woman. She inspires the music and poetry, the best of the literature that glorifies the purity of a chaste, virtuous woman.

Enter the paradox of good and evil.

How is it that instead of the compatibility of differences, instead of honoring what is good and noble in each, the relationship between men and women is most often competition and combativeness?

The devil of the OT was a peculiarly Hebrew description of an accusing and adversarial angel that had it in for Israelites. Hebrew theology does not have a devil in the Garden, only a snake.

Now I do not believe in the devil. But my remarks will treat him in many ways as an actual being. Why? Because he is the ideal foil for the personification of evil. In other words, a literary convenience. More than that, he gives us insights into the thinking of many people concerning human behavior. As the invention of men, he is, as I said in a previous chapter, a very successful one.

Taking all the literature together concerning Satan it would seem that his blind side is sacrificial love. If he was an object of worship by those ancient, pre-Adamic creatures, it might explain why there is no evidence of any love or art in those cultures.

Yet they buried their dead with ceremony, expressing a belief in an afterlife of some kind.

Spiritism in many forms has had many notable adherents through the ages. In modern times we note men like William James of Harvard and Thomas Edison. Sir Arthur Conan Doyle was an enthusiastic believer in Spiritism. Houdini spent much time, labor and money to disprove it, but he left his wife a secret code that if she received it after his death, would prove spirits could contact the living. She said toward the end of her life she had never received the message in spite of efforts to do so.

Imagination, language and the creative arts may have been denied Neandertal, but Homo sapiens has them in abundance. The brilliant William James died troubled and undecided about the spirit world, but felt there was a world beyond our universe more real than ours with an ocean of consciousness.

Psychical researchers have discovered paranormal occurrences; ESP (PSI) is fairly commonly acknowledged, but most certainly not understood. A transmitter/receiver with messages through the ether suggests a mechanism is involved of which we have no knowledge, but I believe research in particle physics will provide answers. The most recent research suggests a particle that travels at 300 times the speed of light. The tachyon seems immune to time and distance with instantaneous communication over the distance of the universe, something Einstein referred to as "spooky communication at a distance."

In my imagination at the instantaneous speed of thought I can travel to the stars. And I'm there in an instant, not subject to the limitation of the speed of light or any other limiting factors of speed.

And when I find a star I like, I can make it as beautiful as I want, with forests, trout streams, oceans and mountains, clear, unpolluted air and water, and filled with beautiful and adorable animals and birds that do not fear me. In short, in my imagination I can create a world.

In my imagination I converse with loved ones now departed, I can visit the favorite places and friends of my childhood. I can even have an affair with the lovely lady sitting next to me in church or a harem of beautiful women ... but that's another and dangerous subject.

The power of imagination is truly awesome. In our minds we can be anything, do anything, and go anywhere. But there is the dark side.

We can go mad. We can be demented, we can imagine all kinds of fears, and we can actually convince ourselves of things that never happened, believe we heard things never said, we can become neurotically or even psychotically delusional. Our minds can construct fairy tales and enchanted lands or horrors.

Love is the most intangible and real thing of the mind. It motivates to actions that are indeed tangible. Yet that intangible element is the motivating influence. It cannot be measured except by the tangible evidence of the actions of love.

Of all the emotions of humanity, love is the one that everyone needs and seeks; it is the ultimate happiness and fulfillment of life! One legitimately asks: Then why is it that so few ever realize the full potential of love in their lives? My own research into this has led into some very interesting areas, some of which would seem to have no bearing on the problem.

In 1921, Sigmund Freud wrote: If I had my life to live over again, I should devote myself to psychical research rather than to psychoanalysis.

Motivated by a lecture on spiritualism by Sir Arthur Conan Doyle, J.B. Rhine of Duke University introduced the legitimate study of ESP, later named PSI (the 23rd letter of the Greek alphabet often used to stand for an unknown quantity in science) and with an acquaintance, Karl Zener, came up with five cards, now known as Zener cards, to test PSI.

The Zener cards have five symbols, and used under controlled environments test for Telepathy, Clairvoyance and Precognition. Rhine's experiments beginning in the late 20s had enough positive results to encourage him and many others. By the 30s, departments to study the paranormal began to appear in universities. Men of creative genius like Doyle and James will never accept death as annihilation of being. And most believe in a life after death, of a reality beyond the veil that is immortal, with a potential far beyond anything we experience in our physical world.

The biggest problem of PSI research, whether in the controlled environments of science, the Umbanda of Brazil or the Voodoo of Haiti is that so little results of a substantive and replicative nature occurs. That PSI to some degree is common to the majority of people worldwide is a given, even among animals to a great extent.

But trying to find any degree of consistency in this research has been extremely difficult; something seems to elude discovery through controlled experiments. But research in particle physics and brain function may explain what this something is.

When it comes to PSI in animals, they seem to possess it to an extraordinary degree. Documented cases of cats and dogs traveling long distances to find their owners, for example. One journey of 3,000 miles by a dog to find its owner is such a case. This dog, Bobbie, did not take the route of its owner. The only thing that could explain such extraordinary occurrences is telepathy.

Somehow, animals like Bobbie are tuned in to their owners. There are many documented cases of animals responding to wordless, mental commands of people.

Who of us has not looked into the eyes of an animal like a cat or dog and not had the distinct impression of intelligent understanding in those eyes? And what of people who seem to have a distinct gift of communicating with animals?

The ancient myths are replete with stories of people communicating with animals, of animals like the serpent in the Garden with the power of speech.

I pose for your consideration my previous speculation, philosophically and treating with a myth, that the serpent of the Garden was the head of the animal kingdom at that time, that it may not have been the only animal with the power of speech.

Beautiful and intelligent as she was, the serpent being rejected by Adam as a suitable companion retaliated and brought God's judgment on the whole animal kingdom. So much so that God killed the first animals to make coverings for Adam and Eve.

It may be that part of God's judgment of the serpent that impacted on animals was the loss of speech or other characteristics they may have had that now show up in animal PSI.

Studies of the brain involving particle physics, particularly subatomic particles, neutrinos and tachyons, may have a relationship to psychical studies. There may be a connection between these particles and what are being called psitrons in effects like telepathy and psychokinesis.

It is well known that warts can be made to disappear through hypnosis. This is a power of the brain that has been well established scientifically, yet we have no explanation as to what processes are really at work in such things.

Scientists and Psi researchers alike are studying different wave patterns and cycles of the brain like Alpha waves. And many scientists are involved with the paranormal that would never have given it any credence scant years ago.

I believe that when these things are understood they will confirm some of the possibilities I have suggested, mythologies aside. I also believe scientists should take a careful look at some of the hints of such things from some of the stories of the Bible as well as many other myths.

But unlike all other creatures, God made Adam a living soul, according to the Bible, made in his own image distinct from animals. Given the historical record, man is unique in all creation and it cannot be implied that animals have anything like the soul or spirit of humans. And they do not possess the God-like characteristics of imagination and creativity we, as humans, have.

It may also be that only the serpent had the power of speech, this together with beauty and intelligence setting her apart and telepathic communication of some form existed among animals much as they seem to have this characteristic today.

The story in Numbers 22 of Balaam's donkey is a case in point. Apart from the serpent, this is the only time in Scripture that an animal has the power of speech. Yet the donkey's speaking raised no surprise in Balaam. Putting myself in the prophet's place, I would at least be looking for a psychiatrist, hopefully one that wasn't as nuts as I would assume I was. But the Apostle Peter repeats the account, giving credence to it. II Peter 2:16.

Fact: The most ancient histories and legends of humankind include communication between the animal kingdom and man. In some manner God's judgment of the serpent impacted on the animal kingdom resulting, in the very least, God killing animals to provide covering for Adam and Eve.

The continued use and killing of animals for sacrifice, clothing and shelter by Adam, Eve, and Abel (and perhaps Cain had to bargain with his younger brother for such things, breeding resentment) had to be a part of the judgment of God that made the animals suffer as part of the transgression of Adam, Eve and the Serpent.

When God starts over with Noah, he plainly, according to the narrative, makes animals fearful of humans. Not only will animals provide sacrifice; their flesh will be eaten. Repugnant on the face of it.

Things might have been peaceful on the Ark, but nature becomes red in tooth and claw thereafter. And animals pay the price in many ways.

But animals like dogs and cats are peculiar in that most cultures did not and still do not, kill and eat them. There is a kind of revulsion that most cultures have to doing so.

Part of this revulsion is in that seemingly telepathic communication between these animals and man. A pet dog or cat seems to be compatible with human company, even desiring and seeking it.

There are other animals, birds and even mammals like Dolphins, which display such compatibility.

My daughter, Karen, has an extraordinary gift with animals. As a child, she could catch animals like cottontails and kangaroo rats. I would ask her how she managed to do so. She could only say it was easy.

She turned out to be such a successful horse trainer that she could have written her own ticket in this profession. But she chose motherhood and I applaud her in this.

Karen raises Rottweilers, a breed that is much misunderstood. To watch her training these animals is a marvel in human/animal communication. As she could with horses, she can make these dogs literally dance for her.

PSI is evident to a mystical extent between my daughter and animals. I have always had a great love of birds and animals. As a boy growing up in a wilderness environment, I had many a conversation with birds and animals. I detail a prolonged talk with a red-tailed hawk in another book about my adventures with the critters in my wilderness wanderings.

It may be evidence of my Cherokee blood that I have always had the sense of communication with birds and animals. My eldest son, Daniel, has this trait as well. My daughter, Diana, and my youngest son, Michael, evidence it as well.

But the fullest extent of this shows in Karen. For her, it is such a pronounced gift that it is, indeed, supernatural.

Karen sees that intelligence and desire for communication in the eyes of animals and they respond to her willingness and desire to communicate.

Yet all of my children, like myself, have hunted and fished. Perhaps these wild creatures know the difference between the blood lust that enjoys the killing of animals as opposed to the way I was raised that you only killed for food or protection, not so-called sport.

I recall the time as a boy that I did not shoot a deer. It had jumped out of the trees and just as I threw down on it with my rifle, I spotted a fawn in the brush. I simply could not shoot this momma deer much as we would have appreciated the venison for the family pot.

Now I count it among the blessings of life that I can simply watch and enjoy the quail, deer, squirrels, and not see them as necessary food. And while I am not a vegetarian, I kind of wish that humanity had maintained such a status.

People love animals. At least the Good Seed among people love animals. Civilized people cannot stand to see an animal mistreated and we have laws against such mistreatment.

It is a part of people's history and traditions that animals are under our rule and should not be subjected to inhumane conditions or abuse.

Old people will hold a puppy or kitten and find great comfort in these little animals. They are therapeutic, if you will. But what is it, exactly, that is going on between human and animal that brings such satisfaction to both? And why, in some instances, have there been times in people's lives when a pet has been more solace and seemed to have exhibited more compassionate understanding than another person?

One of God's promises in the Bible is that some day the lion will lay down with the lamb and the baby will play without fear at the burrow of the viper. Peace between animals and humankind. Though the sentiment is not peculiar to the Bible alone, this helps in believing that all comes right in the end when the relationship is restored to what God intended it to be; what, in fact, it once was. Love will prevail. But God, I believe, needs our help to bring this to pass.

So it is that I try to understand the judgment God was forced to pronounce on the Serpent and the animal kingdom.

I don't believe God, by whatever definition, any more than we, enjoys the suffering of animals. That the innocent pay the price of rebellion and betrayal of love and trust should be at the forefront of our thoughts and cause us to do better, be better.

If animals suffer as a result of the Serpent's role in the Garden, so do we and our children as a result of our sin and rebellion, our lack of love for one another.

I believe romantic love is encouraged by our relationship with nature, birds, and animals. For example, you simply cannot look at the moon, the stars resplendent against that velvet canopy, without a degree of romance being encouraged in your soul. You cannot hold that baby chick, duck or bunny without strong feelings of wonder and love for such little reminders of how things should be in a perfect world.

And babies? They should bring out the very best in us. This fails when the relationship between mother and father is not right. It fails due to a nation's indifference toward children and families.

You cannot love someone without developing a kind of telepathy. Ideally, where romance continues in a marriage, the husband and wife exhibit this phenomenon to an extraordinary degree. One of the failures of scientific research into this is the lack of romantic love in the life of those being tested (Heath's Hypothesis). If you accept this, you can readily understand the rarity of such a thing. Why? Because there is so little of romance in the world today.

And maybe animals like Bobbie, who seem to be able to give their devotion so unreservedly, are able, as a consequence, to exercise their PSI capabilities far better than most humans. Love, romantic love especially, is the key to understanding these things. Heath's Hypothesis.

For me, as I take my excursions to wilderness places in the desert or mountains, I find these places mind-expanding, like looking into that starry heaven at night. As I lose myself in the total absorption of contemplating a night sky in the desert or mountains, I feel a very real kinship with such environments.

In my imagination I can travel throughout God's marvelous creation undisturbed and unpolluted by man's intervention. I am at one, once more, with the way things ought to be, the way I know in my bones things once were.

That inspiring, romantic poet within me responds to the sights and sounds of natural creation, whether the moon at night in the desert so clear I can tell each grain of sand, or winding my way alongside a wilderness trout stream, enjoying the scent and sound of the water, critters, and trees, stopping to look with wonder at some old, lichen-painted, granite boulder.

And plant PSI? We all wonder about this relationship with humankind. Do plants have peculiar characteristics that respond to voice and music for example? Many studies point to such a thing. Kirlian photography is still on going as are many experiments in plant PSI.

This morning, I was given an early morning wakeup call by a large pinecone bouncing off my roof. The beautiful gray squirrel that decided to take up residence in the old pine had done her job of gnawing the thing off and bombarding me.

Now, as I write, she is busily at work on my roof gnawing the nuts out of the cone, and I listen to her as she fusses with the thing and makes her "charming" invective-filled chatter to warn the jays away.

I do wonder about jays. The other morning I watched a papa quail chase one away while his mate and chicks were pecking away in my backyard. There is a line in To Kill a Mockingbird, one of my all-time favorite books and movies, where Atticus is telling the children a story.

He said that when his father gave him a gun, he told him that it was all right to kill as many blue jays as he wanted, but it was a sin to kill a mockingbird. I'm tempted to agree when it comes to jays. Aggressive, bullying, noxious birds. But very intelligent.

In trying to put all these pieces together, a paradigm begins to take shape. It is certain that the animal kingdom and humankind exhibits elements of the good and bad seed, that there is a conflict that results in weeds in our patch of the earth that we seem not to be able to eradicate.

This is, undoubtedly to my mind, the point of Jesus' parable of the tares. The enemy has planted weeds in our garden and it is the responsibility of God's children to do the job of cultivating and overcome evil. The story ends with the angels of God separating the good and the bad at the end of the age.

It may well be that God alone is capable of the task. But I'm not willing to just sit back and give the world to the devil by default, by some kind of abandonment theology that makes God's people impotent eunuchs.

If romantic love is the missing piece of the puzzle, I believe I find abundant facts to support the hypothesis.

For example, the dream of that genius philosopher, William James. He tells of bolting awake in the night with the belief that he had been given the answer to the riddle of the universe! An astounding concept.

What was this key of the most monumental importance? That women are monogamous and men are polygamous!

Perhaps not the best example of the genius of the man. And, admittedly, not exactly original thinking. Though a recent book claiming all men are rapists at heart ignored this revelation of James and didn't credit him.

But James was a man and thought like a man. He fully realized that men want harems and it doesn't take dreams to figure this out. He undoubtedly indulged his own imagination and fantasies in this regard as most men do.

The resentment of women, as a consequence, is thoroughly understandable. The paradox of good and evil has many of its roots in this moral dichotomy between the sexes, a dichotomy of which only romantic love is the solution.

My book, The Missing Half of Humankind: Women! addresses the problem of the exclusion of women throughout history in the areas of philosophy and theology, of why these great thinkers, exclusively men, don't even talk about their wives and children let alone give them a voice in their vaunted systems of thought?

It would be well to provide the reader the following from my Missing Half book here for a fuller understanding of my point:

I will state unequivocally, that, as a man, the only real joy and happiness I have experienced in my own life, the motivation to write, sing and make music of the softer and gentler things, the things of real beauty and romance, the things of eternal value has come from women and children.

When Thoreau wrote, for example, that as the spider in a garret, he could be happy in a prison as long as he had his thoughts to sustain him, he was wrong. HDT, as Soren Kierkegaard and so many others, placed too much emphasis on the meditative, contemplative aspect of intellectualism. And, lacking that all-important dimension of a complete life experience, wife and children, such men were blind to the joy and happiness, the understanding and compassion these bring to a man.

As a writer and poet, I know, as these men would freely admit, that Truth can only be found through the experiences of life, not academic disciplines and empirical facts alone.

As philosophers both of these men, and so many like them, failed miserably in many of their attempts at addressing the real issues of life, the things of eternal value. They never were able to present the full picture of life and living.

These worthy thinkers would never say they knew what it was like to be pregnant or give birth. Only a man-fool would do so. But the world is full of fools.

It is in the philosophies of such men, philosophies that fail so miserably to account for the real basis of strife in humanity, that they too often fall into the camp of those fools that would tell us they know, as men, what it feels like to give birth.

Ladies of the world, your fight is against incomplete philosophies of men that fail to consider or cannot understand you as the other half of the human equation, who will never credit you as being of equal value!

Now I would be the last to decry the poetic glorification of God's most beautiful, if often inconvenient, Creation. The stars, a sunrise or sunset, the trees and grass washed and scented by a recent rain, the enchantment of a wild, native trout stream, the grandeur of the Tetons and Rockies, so much to excite the artistic exultation of the artist and poet!

But even Thoreau admitted: What is Nature to me if I have no one with whom to share it? He spoke better than he knew.

The greatest intrigue and mystery of a man's life should be that other half of humankind, a woman. In contemplation of that compatibility of differences I mention so often, I find whole worlds to explore.

A woman at her best is all the intrigue and excitement the best of pioneers and explorers could wish for. I never tire of talking with these mysterious creatures, of learning the differences in their thought processes from my own as a man.

But in most cases, the great thinkers of civilization have done solos when the music required a duet with a woman. My hope in addressing this problem is to get men and women together in making real music.

The purest poetry is rightly defined as an actual recounting of life, of real lives of ordinary people. A part of the poetry of real life is the literature of a culture.

As television and videos began to supplant books, I witnessed the decline of literature and the consequent loss to our young people of virtue and romantic ideals, of a plunge into illiteracy and ignorance of our heritage. This has cheated our children of the American Dream.

As a teacher of many years' experience, I realized the truth of Robert M. Hutchins' warning that the failure to propagate the heritage of Western Civilization through the great literature of the past would lead to the situation we face today.

Hutchins, Editor-in-Chief for The Great Books of the Western World, made the valid point in 1951 that unless the ideas expressed in the best of our literature of the past was taught to our children, the results would be catastrophic! He was right.

Another point of Hutchins is one I take to heart in my own writing. This has to do with the failure of our schools to blend science and the arts, which has led to over-specialization. Dante's Divine Comedy and Newton's Principia should be studied together.

You will find that I intrude mathematics in my writing. Far from being out of place, it is essential to real learning to bridge the gap between the hard sciences and the arts and social sciences.

This need has resulted in my sprinkling anecdotes throughout my writings, stories that relate to the reality of life. But it is a truism that the difference between reality and fiction is that fiction has to make sense. And while the words of Henry James that life is mostly a splendid waste rings often true, I contend that it needn't be.

A butterfly is a thing of beauty. But part of the charm of the butterfly is its seeming erratic flight. Far from being erratic, that butterfly knows exactly what it is doing.

While I would never make such an outrageous claim of always knowing exactly what I am doing, my writing often takes on the flight pattern of the butterfly, combining diverse elements like poetry and mathematics. But this is in the tradition of poetry and philosophy, of those writers of the past who saw life as multi-dimensional rather than a narrow specific.

The reader will find the essentials of love, music and laughter incorporated in this book. The solutions to the problems of humanity must include these elements. And as with the reality of life itself, these things have a seemingly erratic flight path.

The Missing Half of Humankind: Women! incorporates many diverse elements to make a point. The point being that women have been excluded from the philosophies of men, philosophies that have determined the destiny of nations. By excluding an entire one-half of the human race, the history of humankind has been a history of conflict without resolution, what I have come to call a six-thousand-year-old problem (though undoubtedly of much longer duration than a mere six thousand years).

Much as I admire the great thinkers and writers of the past, much as they need to be studied, I have come to accept the fact that the exclusion of women in The Great Conversation, as Hutchins called philosophy, has resulted in much harm to humanity.

This book (The Missing Half) is not intended to be definitive. It is intended to call attention to the problem and seek a forum where women will be listened to by men, a most uncommon thing. One point alone, a point made by me, a man, should be of great interest to women: There can be no hope of world peace and harmony unless the problem of the historical conflict between men and women is resolved!

God had his work cut out for him in inventing sex. In the corruption of the ideal of one man, one woman for life, romantic love had to be there for it to work. Where this failed men and women looked for diversity in love and religion. Monogamy was up against it in trying to cut out those convenient religions that encouraged sexual license and immorality.

This caused the giving of law to try to enforce moral standards. This failed, of course. A new heart was needed that wants to do what is right. So Paul struggled with the good and the bad in his own soul, a struggle the demands of the law only acerbated.

That basic conflict rages unabated as men and women seek that for which only virtue will answer.

My earlier story of Ann should have a wide reading. I wish everyone would read my books about the relationships between men and women and take what I have discovered to their own hearts in searching for this elusive thing called Romance.

A continuing part of the dilemma, a part that separates the diabolical from the divine, is the fact that only men with daughters can truly understand romantic love, and only those fathers who had the kind of relationship with their daughters that promoted the purest love in the universe, the love of a father for his little girl, will ever understand women, let alone listen and learn from their points of view.

This obviously leaves a very small number of men with the necessary tools of intelligence, experience, and training who can even hope to qualify as workers in this area. And they are going to find many enemies among those who don't fit the job description, or feel they are the exceptions much like the experts in child behavior who have no children and the experts on marriage who remain single!

Chapter twelve

Don't tell me the truth; I want comfortable lies!

The anecdotal record of witches, poltergeists, things that go bump in the night, of ghosts and spirits, of haunted castles, houses and places is enormous. Human history is a continuum of such stories. And like our Draculas, Werewolves and Mummies there is a part of our imagination that responds to such things.

People, for example, love apocalyptic scenarios. Hal Lindsay made a bundle on his Late, Great Planet Earth. The fact that he was full of it and did his level best to make the Bible and the Lord look foolish didn't keep people from buying the book in droves. And Lindsay laughed all the way to the bank.

Alethiological thinking is not the strong suite of most churchgoers, however. In too many cases they might as well be using, like Mr. Lindsay, I suspect, some form of aleuromancy or peering into chicken entrails or examining the kidneys of sheep to come to some of their conclusions.

If the shadow of Peter could heal (Acts 5:15), if the talismans of handkerchiefs and aprons that had touched Paul could effect cures and cast out demons (Acts 9:12) then I wish fervently that this same spirit that mowed down Ananias and Sapphira (Acts 5:1-10) were at work in the churches. But that would require a full-time mortician in every church! Might improve the credibility of TV evangelists, if there were any left.

The book of Ezekiel and his wheels, etc. is a typical example of the misuse of Scripture. Whatever the prophet's visions mean, and not accusing him of indulging a taste for magic mushrooms, they are far more likely to be descriptive of ancient myths and legends, even things Paul referred to in his heavenly visions he couldn't talk about, than any precognition of future events.

Some, like Hal Lindsay, make much of such things in order to stir people up and make money for themselves. Their egos are the major problem, not concern for the honor of God or the truth.

Erich Von Daniken of Chariots of God fame hit on a real winner. He had a nice beginning thesis: Between 10,000 and 40,000 years ago, super-intelligent astronauts arrived on earth and mated with creatures here and produced Homo sapiens. They returned at various times to see how things were going and to introduce high tech things like metallurgy, mathematics and language.

Researchers, tired of the outright fraud of the man, finally took his writings apart citing literally hundreds of mistakes and intentional distortions. But people by the millions paid homage to his vivid imagination and fraud.

It reminds me of the old joke that one of the proofs of intelligent life elsewhere in the universe is that they leave us alone.

Not that such an initial hypothesis as proposed by Daniken is impossible. But there is no real evidence of such a thing in spite of the tantalizing desire to make such of the things he used as supposed proofs.

An alignment of the planets was supposed to have wreaked havoc on the earth not long ago and a lot of people bought into this. Didn't happen of course but they still think it's going to. Like the return of Jesus being prophesied so many times, there are always the charlatans like Harold Camping who make fools of themselves and others by the sensational. We have never had any shortage of false prophets.

Yes, there are UFOs, things that are seen and cannot be explained. But a UFO is just that, an Unidentified or Unexplained Flying Object. Rather prosaic and far from descriptive of flying saucers and little green men.

All joking aside, I won't discount the reports of some people who are intelligent and responsible who give some alarming eyewitness accounts of seeing such things as objects on the ground with creatures that take off when spotted.

Admittedly I am a Show Me kind of person. And am likely to remain so until someone presents irrefutable evidence of such things, Area 51 notwithstanding. And I sure enjoy good science fiction, always have.

But the studies involved with some of the most esoteric branches of mathematics and the physics of light and subatomic particles gives some tantalizing insights to the possibilities of space travel. For example, it has been postulated that Black Holes or Wormholes may serve as a network through space that might enable spacecraft to avoid the limitations of the speed of light in such travels. Entrancing idea.

If I can visit Venus, Altair or Ursa Major in an instant in my imagination, if I warp time and go forward or backward in my mind to future or past, this might be proof that such instantaneous transportation can actually have some basis in reality.

The studies in particle physics offer some exciting ideas about such things. Hypothetical particles like tachyons might travel faster than light. Theoretically, such a particle could arrive at a point before it left in a time warp. A Dr. Lijun Wang of the NEC research institute of Princeton has demonstrated a pulse of light toward a chamber filled with specially treated caesium gas that in effect reached such a speed it existed in two places at the same time.

His article will appear in the definitive science journal Nature. The fact that a pulse of light can arrive at a point very nearly before it left opens the door to legitimate speculation about star travel at nearly the speed of thought being made possible.

Quarks may be just the tip of the iceberg in particle physics; opening whole new worlds of exploration that might help explain brain functions that so far have eluded science.

The Einstein-Podolsky-Rosen paradox proposes two particles move from each other at the speed of light. If the course of particle A is deflected in some manner, particle B reacts as well. Yet there is no known connection between the two particles. How does particle B know what happened to particle A?

This would suppose an unknown consciousness between even the smallest bits of matter, matter that does not behave in the orderly fashion of our present framework of physics. An energy that is not subject to our present knowledge and understanding of the laws of physics does exist, and while such energy might explain anomalies of various kinds we lack an explanation of that energy.

We still have no understanding of what, exactly, constitutes life. At death, a something leaves the body. The area of particle phenomena like hypothesized tachyons could be that something, an energy that has consciousness yet does not fit the defined laws of physical science.

A Cloud of Consciousness composed of particles like tachyons could, in fact, connect all living life forms and, being immortal, survives death. Death, in fact, may be the transition to a full awareness and a state of being in a world more real than the one we leave. This fits the Biblical description of immortality.

Something of this nature could explain the fact of coincidences that otherwise remain inexplicable. Many do not know of the scientific studies in the esoteric field of coincidence. Along with Psi, it is one of those fascinating areas of facts that remain mysteries.

Psi research, in conjunction with particle research, may be the area that leads into an explanation of things that have been mysteries of inexplicable phenomena. Such things like telepathy do exist, but it will likely be an amalgam of particle physics and Psi that will lead to solving these mysteries and open new frontiers of exploration almost beyond imagination.

As a classroom teacher, I often told my students that ignorance is a real killer. It's what you don't know that can hurt you. So the emphasis on education is the pathway to light and understanding, not just the mechanism of supporting yourself, as important as this is.

But because there remains so much hurtful ignorance, charlatans still abound, the shamans and snake oil salesmen in pulpits that prey on the gullibility of the ignorant and superstitious.

In my years of study and my work in the churches, I came to accept the unpalatable fact that people want a religion that does not tax their minds, that offers a comfortable belief system. The fact that such systems do not make sense, are in fact riddled with contradictions and superstitions, does not dissuade them of holding on to their comfortable systems.

People are notorious for not accepting change. A comfortable rut is vastly preferable to making waves, rocking the boat or questioning the status quo. And people intuit that if they question their religious beliefs, something is going to change. And rather than subject themselves to such change, they will believe the comfortable lies.

If it were not for my responsibility to my children as their father, I suppose I could have settled into such a comfortable position myself. I did so for years and it wasn't until God took me to the woodshed, so to speak, on the subject that I finally faced up to this responsibility.

The bottom line was that I knew better, and if I knew better I ought to do better. Leaving a legacy of ignorance to my children was inexcusable.

This became the motivating influence for this book, something that in conscience I was compelled to undertake. It is my fervent hope that others besides my children will profit from it.

In confessing my own shortcomings, I became acutely aware of the damage being done in the name of God by so many that purports to preach the truth for a paycheck. My crusade against hurtful ignorance compels me to point out such things and such people, these enemies of the truth.

The prophecy bandwagon has always netted charlatans and doomsayers a goodly profit from the gullible. Let me make what I want of Isaiah, Daniel and Revelation and I'll have a following committed to selling the ranch and waiting on a mountaintop for Jesus before the Great Tribulation!

But I think I would prefer a tidy little racket in séances; which reminds me of something a lady friend shared with me recently.

Seems the ex-husband's mother had passed away and he called the lady with a request to make a casket-liner. The man was going to build a custom casket for his mother and thought it would be a nice touch if his ex-wife would contribute the liner.

When she told me about this somewhat unusual request, it reminded me of something I had written some time ago about the high cost of dying. I had a story going about my idea for home embalming kits. There were the beginning kits for the family goldfish or hamster to the more elaborate to take care of the favorite pooch or cat. But the big seller, I imagined, would be the Mother-in-law special. Of course, I encouraged buyers to check local health codes concerning such things.

I also wondered about offering these kits and a nice line of do-it-yourself caskets through chain stores? Probably be real winners.

But let's face it folks, our fascination with death and an after-life, of the attempts throughout history to find verification and certainty of things beyond the grave, has been unrelenting.

The thing that prompted Freud's strange comment about choosing psychic research as a life's work, the thing that drove his disciple, Jung, into the analysis of dreams and spiritualism, is the refusal to accept death as the end. The fact that the mind is capable of enormous power provides an impetus to explore and try to find evidence of PSI and a continuum of existence. But how to understand and direct this power? That is the on-going challenge.

My own approach to understanding is to focus on the power of romantic love, to probe those things that promote good and evil, search their origins and make sense of these things.

Much of what has already been determined is enlightening. The use of drugs, for example, to enhance the subconscious has a long history. The scientific experimentation of such substances and studies of things like hypnosis may yet prove very useful to our understanding.

The medical application of touching and speaking in caring confidence to the injured while setting fractured bones without anesthetic is a curious phenomenon that actually works. And Acupuncture? It used to be viewed as superstition but is now widely accepted.

I theorize that the success of such things depends largely on the power of the mind, but how is this power transmitted? Ah, that is the elusive question.

But hallucinatory or delusional enhancing substances have very little merit. If modern man, for example, has lost some ability of brain function in the area of PSI due to the practical constraints of day-to-day living rather than having, or taking, time to meditate and commune with creation, it is unlikely that any kind of drug will enhance this ability. On the contrary, much as shamans may decry this, such substances are more likely to dull the senses or lead astray through delusions or hallucinations.

Like Thoreau, I will visit a favorite tree or rock and commune with nature. I don't engage in attributing spirits to such things, but they help in my meditations and contemplation of creation. I gaze at the stars, the only real measure we have of eternity and wonder at their creation, of what lies out there for our benefit?

The throne of God, in some manner, may be out there, a celestial hierarchy of which we will be a part. When I visit the old mining claim where my great-grandmother and grandmother both died in their sleep in the old cabin, I commune with them. I find comfort in doing so. I find comfort in talking to my daughters Diana and Karen, my grandson Justin, my mother, grandparents, and my brother Ronnie who have already gone ahead of me. Do they hear me? I don't know. I only know that they are the experts in knowing the things about which I can only guess; that there is great comfort in my own heart and mind believing that I will see them again, that they will be there to welcome me.

It is the love we share that makes such things a reality to me. I firmly believe that such a precious thing cannot be lost and, as a result, has a continuum in my own life, that it has a bearing on how I live my life as though these precious ones can see and hear me.

But I am not holding séances or trying to make Faustian deals to communicate. Yet, if I should hear from them or have some indication they were communicating with me in some fashion, I wouldn't reject it out of hand. That, I believe, is part of the power of love.

While James, Freud, Jung and others recognized the power of the mind to engage in hallucinations, accepting such things as reality, there is enough evidence of the supernatural to prevent such men of genius from totally discounting it.

I believe in the overcoming power of love. I believe this is the preeminent Gospel of humankind. If there is a failure to understand the driving force of our minds, of imagination, of the dichotomy of love and hate, the paradox of good and evil, it is a failure of encouraging the power of love to rule in our lives.

To write love letters, to give flowers to a woman, sing and make music derive from that power of love. To truly love a friend, as with the relationship between David and Jonathan, Jesus and his disciples, parents for each other and for their children, should be the driving force for world peace.

A friend in Slovenia, a professed atheist and professor at the university wrote me an interesting letter concerning one of my essays on love and romance, responding especially to my story about Ann.

He commented on the fact that romance does, indeed, weaken with the years in a marriage, that it is substituted by the habit of simply living together. He agreed with me that this is an enormously complex thing and trying to simplify it as per the innumerable books and talk shows on the subject does no good, in fact, only obfuscates legitimate attempts at answers.

He calls romance a kind of attraction energy input. If the selection of a mate is right, this energy continues to work in strengthening the ties between the two.

But as I pointed out in my story of Ann, why is it that the right man and woman have so much difficulty finding one another? Perhaps the Bible has an answer for us, if it is studied and read wherever appropriate as a Romance.

The Blood Atonement! Why were men so fixated on this as to make it a part of the nature of God?

The bloodthirsty, mercurial tyrant of the OT can hardly be construed as a God of love. Unless the Bible is a romance.

To understand the longing and need of men and women for love and romance, one must take this view of the Bible. Otherwise it makes no sense.

All of the errors and mistakes of love are replete in the Scriptures. The Bible description of God by men shows the constancy of love that always lives in hope that next time it will work out and risks it all in love and trust of another; believing in that next time, and takes the chance with all the potential of the risk of betrayal.

Our longing for immortality is grounded in love; any real understanding of the work of God in creation, his on-going struggle with evil in humanity, the twists and turns of betrayal of love and trust, the enemies of truth and beauty, all are there in men's attempts to describe them in the Bible.

Also included are the things of imagination that promote both good and evil, the dark side of love and romance.

Will I take knife in hand to cut off the arm of my child to save his life? It seems the surgery required to save the human race has forced the love of God to draconian measures at times. Mistakes are made. God, the heavenly father and mother, is learning about us just as we, the children of their love, are learning about them. Parenting is filled with pitfalls.

There is the immense problem of that Bad Seed that seems too often to prevail. What to do about it?

There is the immense problem of the relationships between men and women. What to do about it? There is the problem of millions of children throughout the world suffering because of humankind's refusal of love to be the operating principle in ordering world affairs. What to do about it? There is the refusal of good men and women to actively confront evil. What to do about it?

Wise as serpents and harmless as doves. To watch the churches in (in) action, you would think they believe Jesus was making a bad joke! Study to show yourselves approved? Another bad joke.

When I was a working minister, my daughter Karen asked me if it was true that God made us out of dirt? I told her, No sweetheart; God made us out of the stuff of the stars.

But I believe that is one of the reasons we look at the stars in longing, wonder and contemplation. Somehow we intuit that is where we belong; the stars are our inheritance and we were meant to colonize them.

It may be a long reach, but I do believe God intends to make us the caretakers of stars, of our being able to continue to love, live, dream, hope, and even cooperate with God as participants in the on-going process of creation in eternity. The stars are our inheritance.

But there is a lot of evil that must be confronted and overcome. A good place to start would be our own ignorance and prejudices.

If, in searching for truth, you are prevented by the enemies of truth, for whatever reason, be it to protect some cherished and sacred cow of science, religion or race, the truth suffers. In the search for truth nothing, especially bias or prejudice of whatever persuasion, should be held of more importance.

The story of Moses is fascinating. He is portrayed as one of the most courageous and honest men of history. In spite of his fleeing Egypt in fear of Pharaoh, he went back in response to God's command.

But one charming aspect of the Bible is that of the writers often telling it like it is, not whitewashing mistakes or the failure of heroes. Moses is a good example of how things can fall apart in spite of a good beginning.

Many legitimate questions arise from a study of the story of Moses and the Exodus. And I realize the story is somewhat muddied by people's perception of it through watching the Ten Commandments rather than a reading of the Bible.

But why, for example, did the saving of Egypt through Joseph degenerate into a condition that brought forth a Pharaoh that knew not Joseph? And why was Joseph so concerned that his bones not be left in Egypt?

What was the peculiar characteristic of Moses as an infant that resulted in his being saved? He was a goodly, fine child doesn't tell us much.

When Moses is called of God to lead the people out of Egypt, he tells God, Please send someone else! Moses isn't stupid. But God's anger burned against him for this! The burning bush should have been a warning to Moses. The Lord is ticked. But he accommodates him by sending his brother, Aaron with him. Exodus 4:13,14.

It helped, I'm sure; that God had assured Moses that those who wanted to kill him when he left Egypt had died during his sojourn in Midian. Even so, he was going back to face a Pharaoh that didn't seem particularly fond of Hebrew braceros.

Moses gets off to a rocky start. God is going to kill him while he and his wife and son are resting at the local Big 6 Motel because he hasn't circumcised his son. But Zipporah does the job and calls him a bloody bridegroom because of it. I have wondered if any of the other guests were disturbed while this brouhaha was going on. Surely the boy must have had some little objection?

But Moses and Aaron get there (Moses apparently sends the family back to Midian after the little set-to at the motel) and God hardens Pharaoh's heart in the wheeling and dealing to free the slaves, and destroys Egypt in the process. The gods of Egypt prove no match for I AM and the people start the long march to the Promised Land, a land flowing with milk and honey (and, incidentally, Canaanites).

But there's a catch. Having drowned the Egyptian Army, God requires the people make a slight detour to Mount Sinai to get the Law. It's at this point that things really start to unravel for the newly freedmen.

God gives them manna, quail, and water when they complain and want to go back to Egypt.

Moses makes several trips up and down the mountain with the Lord's instructions to the people. Aaron goes with him at first. Exodus 19:24. A lot of Sunday school Dropouts don't know this.

In many parts of the law and commandments, the Lord is obviously dealing with a lot of superstitions. Of all the strange ways he deals with the people in the various offerings, diet, etc., I find it especially intriguing to read about the test for an unfaithful wife in Numbers, chapter five.

Involving offerings of grain and holy water, the woman is to drink the water after the appropriate curses and warnings by the priest. If her thighs waste away and her belly swells up, she's guilty as charged. Not a little psychology may be involved with such things.

Leviticus 20:10 states that adultery is to be punished by death to both the man and the woman. But what was a wife to do if she suspected her husband of adultery? No holy water? No thin thighs or a bloated beer belly without even the excuse of football season and innumerable six-packs?

It has to be understood that without a microscope and DNA testing, the priest's job was going to be a delicate one, and to a large degree, one of a psychologist. Science was not exactly state of the art when the commandments were being given.

While God and Moses are burning the midnight oil hammering out the Commandments, the people get a tad restless and under the leadership of Aaron make a golden calf to lead them back to Egypt. His story to Moses: ... they gave me gold and I threw it into the fire and out came this calf! Always wondered if Moses bought this.

The book of Numbers provides some additional information. How many of you know that the people of the Exodus considered Egypt a land flowing with milk and honey? Numbers 15:13.

The people become proficient in bitching, moaning and complaining and burn the Lord up. In fair's fair, the Lord burns some of them up. Numbers 11:1.

Nadab and Abihu offer strange fire before the Lord and he burns them up. Leviticus 10:1-3. God evidently gets hot at times.

A rebellion by Korah and Company results in their being swallowed up by the earth. Out of sight, out of mind. Numbers 16:31.32.

Moses' sister and brother think he's getting too uppity and start bad-mouthing him. But God tells them: With him (Moses) I speak face to face ... why weren't you afraid to speak against him?

When God leaves the complaining pair, Sister Miriam has leprosy and Aaron cries out to Moses. Moses, good brother that he is, implores the mercy of God and the leprosy only lasts seven days.

Exodus 33:11 reads: "The Lord would speak to Moses face to face." Yet, further on we read "... you cannot see my face for no one may see me and live." 33:20.

Nothing daunted, we grab our commentaries, Jewish and Christian, and are treated to some dazzling theological terpsichorean footwork carefully choreographed to totally obfuscate the obvious contradiction.

In spite of holy whittling of the square peg, it doesn't quite fit this round hole. So I go back to my suggestion that the nature of God isn't understood as a result of man's attempts in the Bible and theology to make him something he is not.

The many faces of God might make a good book. Every child knows mom and dad don't always behave in a rational manner, displaying several different faces. How could I know mom would be upset to find me using her toothbrush to clean the toilet? Very irrational behavior (Mom's, not the kid's).

If my own understanding were complete, I wouldn't be asking questions. But I think a more honest appraisal of Scripture would lead to better questions and answers.

It may well be that God, like a parent, has a face that shines and one that clouds, full of storm and fury. Any child knows the difference. When Moses asks to see the glory of God, he tells him he will cause his goodness to pass before Moses, as he stands secure on a rock. Moses, we read, sees God's backside. Exodus 33:18-23.

There is a good deal more, I believe, than a poetic use of Burning Light connected with the nature of God. The Lord, your God is a consuming fire, a jealous God (Deuteronomy 4:24 and Hebrews 12:29) may be more than poetic phraseology.

For Moses to only be able to see the backside of God in all his glory in righteousness may have been appropriate while at other times, God may well have restrained himself in speaking to him face to face.

The Apostle John writes in his first epistle: No one has ever seen God; but if we love each other, God lives in us and his love is made complete in us. I John 4:12.

Didn't John know Moses had seen God? We assume the Apostle

knew the Scriptures. So how could he say no man has ever seen God? We are left with few choices in trying to reconcile such contradictions.

But I can accept the comparison that we can look at the sun from a distance where it would consume us close up. In this sense, we see the sun and we don't see it. It is a consuming fire on the one hand and a beneficial, warm and life giving light on the other. If we can reconcile the contradiction in this way, it becomes sensible. It may, in fact, have been in the mind of the author of the Bible story. Our difficulty is often the literal word without explanation. And much of Scripture falls into this category.

That God lives in those who love is sensible. After all, God is love is our primary thesis. That this love has a great number of different expressions is also sensible, from tough love to the most romantic.

In view of the fact that there were so many superstitions involved with the giving of the law and commandments, that the people were coming out of a land steeped in idolatry, it shouldn't be surprising that God had to meet some of these things with rites and ceremonies to accommodate such ignorance.

Eventually though, these accommodations had to give way to enlightenment. As the Apostle Paul points out, such things were tools of instruction to prepare people for the passing away of these things leading to a better understanding that was fulfilled by Christ.

So there is a need to emphasize the fact that circumcision, the keeping of holy days and ceremonies are, indeed, passed away and the children of God are to live in the fulfillment of the law as exemplified in Christ in love for one another.

The Bible is filled with the supernatural, which, given the timeframe is only to be expected. As such, there are things that we are not going to understand in an age of science, and, as such, must be taken on faith. And it may well be that the progress of scientific understanding and finding answers in areas like particle physics will promote such understanding of some Bible stories as well as other literatures of the times.

The superstitions of Jews and Christians must be overcome; however, to have any hope of making sense of what God truly wants us to learn. Nowhere is such superstition as obvious as in the names given God by translators of the Scriptures.

The Tetragrammaton, YHWH, is an example. Lacking vowels, it has been translated Yahweh, Yahvah, Jehovah, LORD, etc. I have a book titled Restoration of the Original Name Bible, an entire "Bible" written with the sole purpose of correcting the mis-translations of the names of God.

A study of how the various names of God throughout Scripture have been used is a study in confusion. But unless one makes such a study, much ignorance surrounds the use of God's name in Scripture.

The El and Yh designations alone are a study to themselves, many OT names of prophets including them. The Ten Commandments, for example, use the form Yahweh, thy Elohim. Jesus used this form when quoting the commandments.

Jewish superstition prevailed to the point where The Name was only supposed to be used once a year by the High Priest, scribes began to obfuscate The Name through substitutions and transliterations and these errors were carried over into the Septuagint, Vulgate, and later English translations.

The translators of the American Standard Version in 1901 decided to disregard the Jewish superstitions and transliterations of previous versions and attempted to translate The Name correctly. But the best efforts of translators have been hampered continuously by the corruption of manuscripts.

The point being that unless one understands the myths, legends and superstitions of ancient peoples, especially the Israelites and early Christian writers and theologians, one is easily led into error. The overwhelming ignorant status of most churchgoers leaves one with an, understandably, uneasy mind in regard to the basis of their orthodoxy, a confused orthodoxy that is based as much on superstitions as academic study.

Another, and just as sober, point being that you are not likely to make much progress of a scientific investigation into the basis of superstitions if you are dealing with the kind of beliefs that are rooted in ignorant prejudices, prejudices that hold beliefs in spite of all the legitimate evidence against them. And most especially when such superstitious prejudices are self-justified in the name of Faith!

It should readily be seen that academic honesty is hard to come by when confronted by deeply held prejudice. Nor is this kind of prejudice the purview of the religious mind only. Unhappily it is all too often found in the minds of the academic community as well.

When I face the kind of dishonesty in the classrooms of universities that perpetuate myths of evolution, etc. I recall Sam Clemens' burlesque of the paleontologists of his time. I would laugh with Sam about this if the results weren't so deadly to real science.

My objection to most commentators, religious and non-religious, is that they have a mind-set that precludes legitimate questions and, as a result, make a barrier to a search for answers. And too many times, you just have to take it on faith is such a barrier.

The story of Moses and the Exodus is intriguing, fascinating. God goes back and forth with these people and Moses. They keep finding fault, God keeps taking them to the woodshed, God and Moses keep trying to keep things in line, but, finally, only Joshua and Caleb, of all that company, get to cross over Jordan. Moses can't go because of his disobedience to God, dishonoring him before the people by angrily striking the rock for water. Numbers 20.

An honest appraisal of the story of Moses and the Exodus has yet to be made. Why? Because it would bring into question too many of the shibboleths, sacred cows of religion, both Jewish and Christian. You can readily see that if I should ever write such a commentary, it would be, to say the least, quite different. Not necessarily more correct, but definitely different.

If, for example, Hitler's Germany could be studied honestly, we would discover many things that would promote understanding. No era of modern history offers so much in analyzing an entire, modern nation devoted to the Old Religion, to the myths and legends of race, astrology, of Phallic worship in its ideas, literature, art and architecture as Germany during this period of time.

But if you are hindered from looking at such a culture in seeking what may be learned from it, if you are branded anti-Semitic because you find things of value from this most unique time in history in a most unique setting (just as you would undoubtedly be accused in an honest appraisal of the study of Abraham or the Exodus), you may miss the truths that might be discovered no matter how dark and evil some of them may be.

As with the devil, there is an attraction and fascination with him and all he represents. And as with the Glory of Evil like Hitler's Germany, the understanding of the attraction to such must be studied and understood.

The Apostle Paul said: We are not ignorant of his (the devil's) devices. And I say, maybe we are not supposed to be, but that is the present status of Christians.

How else to make sense of the utter chaos and confusion of the churches? How else to make sense of the prevailing evil in the world where evil men and seducers wax ever worse, iniquity abounds and the love of many grows ever colder?

Keeping in mind at all times the words of John Scott Haldane, that great scientist and philosopher: The universe may be not only queerer than we suppose, but queerer than we can suppose.

In the following chapter we are going to look at some aspects of subatomic particle physics. Why? Because they may play a major role in understanding some of these queer things.

For example, not many people consider the study of angels and demons in scientific terms. And while I have no belief in such, it may be appropriate to do so as a study in human behavior if nothing else.

The evolving philosophies of supernatural beings have not been very systematic. Lacking hard data this is not surprising.

But there has always been a concept of such beings. That they are thought of in different ways as portrayed in the Bible and other writings lead to much confusion on the subject.

If some have entertained angels unawares as the Bible states, such angels must have a corporeal form and able to perform normal, physical functions. That the spirit or ghost of the departed is portrayed as representing the shade or double of the person, his angel, is another aspect of angelology.

But any legitimate study of the subject proves that there has never been a hard and fast consensus of opinion about angels and demons. The New Testament comes closer than any, but even here it is often confusing.

As to an after-life? Confusion really reigns throughout history. At no time has there ever been a systematic belief concerning this subject apart from one thing, and this is that there is such a belief inherent throughout the cultures of humanity from the earliest beginnings.

Again, however, it was not until the NT was written that a comparatively systematic theology of an afterlife was codified. But even this comparatively systematic organization is often confusing and contradictory, leaving many questions unanswered like that of the status of infants who die and at what point a person becomes accountable for sin and judgment? A reading of the Old Testament and other writings concerning life after death is a study in conflicting ideas of the subject.

And this is typical of the earliest records of humankind. Most ancient philosophies and mythologies agree that life began in some similar manner to the OT account. Virtually all agree that some events occurred like The Fall and the Deluge. But when it comes to the subjects of heaven and hell, of judgment and reward and the disposition of the person after death, confusion, contradictions and chaos are the norm in all ancient cultures.

Even dynastic Egypt, the single, longest reign of a civilization of relative continuity, suffered continual change, confusion and contradictions concerning the subject.

As to the Genesis account of creation, it is thought that it may have been put together by a post-exilic priestly school of redactors and patterned, to some extent, on earlier cosmologies like the Babylonian Enuma elish.

There are definite comparisons between the Hebrew and Mesopotamian stories and scholarly works of early cosmologies are readily available to those who have an interest in pursuing the question.

But a reading of things like the Ugaritic Baal epic, the Rash Shamra texts concerning the position of El in the theognomy of these ancient peoples bear no comparison to the ethical monotheism of the Bible.

The Bible alone of all such stories of creation, the Deluge and God's dealings with people, is relatively free of the superstitions and mythologies of these early accounts. If you will, it represents a far more enlightened account of creation by God, Elohim, than any of these others.

But in pursuit of true scholarship, it becomes ever more critical to examine all the material available to make sense of even the Biblical account of creation, and at all times keeping an open mind to what scholars themselves may be exercising of their own prejudices in their conclusions, Christian and non-Christian.

Keep in mind also that it does God no honor to believe in fairy tales or to hold on to cherished prejudices. The Christian who is not interested in pursuing truth is no better than the dishonest evolutionist who holds on to his own cherished deceptions in spite of the facts to the contrary of his theories.

Jesus said he came into the world to bear witness to the truth. Pilate replied: What is truth? Given the confusion of so many claims to truth, one readily understands his statement. Hopefully, we will do better than Pilate.

Chapter thirteen

The Metaphysics of Subatomic Particles and Christian Philosophy

Metaphysics: *The systematic investigation of the nature of the first principles and problems of ultimate reality.*

I start this chapter with a needed definition of the subject of metaphysics because most people, especially church people, have a gross misconception of this area of study. Far too many include it in some kind of occult category. Not so.

When we speak of ultimate reality, we invariably find ourselves talking about God as such. And there is no end of human suffering and confusion resulting from people's perception of the nature of God.

Subatomic particle research has a legitimate metaphysical side to it as brought out in the previous chapter. In this research, you enter a world totally unlike the perceived, physical universe.

It would help to consider the fact that the band of visible light that enables us to see things is an extremely narrow one. We do not see things in the enormously wide areas of ultraviolet and infrared, for example.

Yet these other forms of light exist. And some of the colors to be seen in these other areas of light are magnificent. I well remember the first time I was prospecting for tungsten using an ultraviolet light and discovered that scorpions fluoresced a brilliant blue.

A number of factors influencing light, as we perceive it, cause the stars to appear as a fairly uniform color to our unaided eyes. But stars vary in colors that we do not see.

The worlds of exploration in the area of particle research should promote an understanding of much of what resulted in religious mysticism surrounding inexplicable phenomena.

Try to put yourself in the mind of Moses at Sinai. He sees a bush that seems to be burning yet is not consumed in the flames. What kind of fire, light did he see?

Now Stephen Spielberg wouldn't have any difficulty creating such a fire that didn't burn. But what do you suppose Moses' description of a computer or shuttle launch might be?

The latent beauty of the universe, the part we do not see, is mind-boggling. The colors in rocks and living things of which visible light shows so little are magnificent.

So it is in that universe of subatomic particles, a universe that is controlled by a seemingly conscious energy that defies the mind's ability to deal with it sensibly.

For example, if a particle can arrive at point B before leaving point A, does this have a bearing on prophetic capability? If we take it as a sensible given, God is future oriented, as are we human beings. He plans, just as we do, and those plans, as all plans, are for the future.

We may fanaticize about going back into the past, but it does not seem possible in view of particle research. Yet, this very research does indicate the potential of looking, even going, into the future.

Let us suppose that if a particle, as is presently hypothesized, can arrive at point B before leaving point A, this particle can come back to point A with what is learned at point B.

Since point A, in this sense, is not the past, prophecy of the future is possible. Yet going into the past is impossible. In other words, things that have already happened cannot be altered, but with prescience things yet to take place might be. The possible flaw here is that while some particles presently show the property of being "nearly" in two places at the same time that "nearly" may be enough to preclude time travel.

I have come to the supposition that immortality does not, consequently, have a reverse gear that goes backward into the past. But it may have a forward gear to the future. It is probable that things cannot be altered physically in that future except by the knowledge brought back to a physical, in some sense, present.

With future oriented planning, the present is ordered to meet that future event and future hopes.

Parents exercise a high degree of clairvoyance and the gift of prophecy, of being able to see the future. *Johnny, if you stick your finger in that light socket, you'll get hurt.* Johnny does, and Johnny is. Parental Clairvoyance.

Sweetheart, if you marry that no good bum, you'll regret it! She does and she does. Parental Clairvoyance.

All growth, planning and learning is future oriented, even that, I believe, of God. With our learned ability to forecast the future in regard to our work in the present, we don't usually think of such things as prophetic. Yet, the farmer plants with this hope, this future sight. We try to raise our children with that kind of foresight (clairvoyance) operating in what we teach our children.

The mystery religions attempt to affect the future, to use sorcery, etc. to predict and influence future events. Astrology, crystal balls, readings of animal livers and entrails, card or palm readings, potions, elixirs and incantations, spells, are designed for this purpose.

Undeniably there are powers, energies at work that result in inexplicable phenomena. Religion, mysticism, these are attempts to accommodate mankind regarding such phenomena together with the need to satisfy the belief in an afterlife with some kind of hope.

Particle research holds promise of making such hope explicable. It holds promise of understanding the nature of God and his supreme creation, human life.

What if our very emotions are dictated by the kind of consciousness that seems to bond two particles where the effect on one is responded to by another totally separated and comparatively light years away? Yet in a subatomic universe where, crudely speaking, the period at the end of this sentence has the weight of an elephant, where the speed of light is exceeded by an enormous magnitude, things stranger than we have the capacity to imagine are the rule.

If, by the exercise of the will, we choose to love rather than hate, what is the mechanism at work? In fact, is it a choice; is it really an exercise of the will?

I meet someone and a mechanism goes to work to like, dislike, love or hate another. Just what is working in the mind to accomplish this?

Rather than popping Advil and turning on a Roadrunner or Bugs Bunny cartoon, I can gird up my loins and try to think this thing through. Probably an overt act of masochism.

This does remind me of the time a lady friend was visiting me and had to use my bathroom. When she came out she asked why I had a weedeater in there. I explained to her that I had gotten tired of seeing it in my bedroom.

As with those two particles where an effect on one effects the other, is something like this at work when a man and woman meet and the chemistry goes to work between them and bonding begins to take place?

When you consider the fact that men and women seem light years apart in the different ways in which their brains function (a weedeater in the bathroom), one might not think this too far fetched.

When Yahweh, thy Elohim gave the law he had to face the superstitions of a world, of those Israelites, with some kind of mechanism to which they could relate. Even at that, those people still turned to idol worship and in their hearts they never left Egypt.

An ontological, metaphysical frame of mind and reference is needed to make sense of God's early dealings with humanity. Further understanding can be promoted by adhering to a rule that God is, as well as a God of love, a God of reason and understanding rather than what religion tries to make of him and her from superstitions and myths of the past, including Jewish and Christian.

If God had to resort to instituting a kind of legal system based in part on superstitions and mythologies, it should be kept in mind just who he was dealing with; those Israelites who were steeped in idolatry and ignorance.

Faced with a history of the worship and supplications to gods and goddesses answering to the many diverse needs of life and living, a systematic theology of the Egyptians developed through millennia, it is no wonder the people in the story of the Exodus had a hard time dealing with the demands of a new theology of monotheism and monogamy.

Virtually all people would agree that education is important, vital to the advancement of any civilization. Say what you will, the Egyptians had been enormously successful in developing a religion that worked and was responsible for maintaining a civilization far in excess of many nations.

Unlike conditions in Mesopotamia, the Nile Valley afforded a constancy of agriculture and animal husbandry lacking in other areas. This provided the basis of the nation having food while famine struck the lands about, motivating Jacob and his family emigrating to Egypt where they prospered to the extent that they became a threat to the Egyptians, as the story goes.

God, through an educative process, tried to instill an advance in religious understanding by separating the Israelites to monotheism (excluding any idea of a Mrs. God in the process) and monogamy.

The Gospel of Jesus Christ was to be the fulfillment of the law in its most succinct form, according to the NT narrative. The Just shall live by his faith, and this faith was to be exemplified by love for others.

The failure of the churches has been their failure to go on in the educative process, a failure of preparing people to do battle against the forces of evil, the Bad Seed, the Cainites of the world.

By majoring in religious superstitions like those of those early Israelites, the churches are temples of continuing ignorance rather than the teaching institutions they were intended them to be. The churches no longer produce the Galleleos and Newton's who would prevent the darkness of religiosity holding sway in people's lives.

The complexities of life, the lack of scientific understanding of so many things in ancient times, led to religious systems that tried to answer the needs of the people. Unfortunately, there were always shamans, priests, Black Coats who preyed on the religious needs and superstitions of the people, and resulted in our own Dark Ages and medievalism. This much has never changed in spite of the advances of science.

While it may be true that the children of Abraham, Isaac and Jacob should have known better, a more charitable view of things can be had if you consider their circumstances.

Astrology and mysticism of various sorts have an attraction beyond the rational mind. Such examples make it all the more imperative that we work to understand the mechanisms involved by encouraging a more thorough study of such things.

The churches would do well to consider their responsibility in promoting such understanding, and rather than fight against science, start producing the scientists like Newton who are dedicated to both the honor of God and good science.

But if the leadership of the churches continue to hide behind priestly vestments, making long their tassels and blaspheming God in song and sermon for a paycheck, if they continue to promise pie-in-the-sky-by-and-by promoting an ignorant gospel of God's people being doormats for the Evil One and his servants, they will continue to be ineffectual, impotent eunuchs in the warfare for how can anyone of any rational mind take them seriously?

Paul well said that unless the trumpet gives a certain sound, how can the people heed the call to battle? A united church? Hardly. Look what it has degenerated into!

Discipline in the churches? We were to have gone on in understanding, the educative process, and be men! What do we have? Impotence!

And if the churches were producing good behavioral scientists, perhaps they could help bring the churches out of their present Dark Age by an intelligent and informed view of the questions I have raised, especially in respect to the relationship between men and women.

For example, what is to be made of the attitude toward women in the OT in regard to the double standard of men having more than one wife but women not allowed to have more than one husband? Are men polygamous and women monogamous as per the revelation of William James?

It might do to argue the lesser equality of women in an age where the strength of the man was needed as protector and provider. In such circumstances several women might seek the protection of one man rather than risk single status. It must be kept in mind as well that the prevailing attitude was that a woman who did not bear children was considered cursed of God (or gods).

Economics dictated as well. A girl was good for a dowry or bride payment. But not much else.

Throughout history, women have had, essentially, a single predominant value: Their sex. If beautiful, they have more to trade. But beauty fades and grim reality sets in. The mirror doesn't lie.

And the history of women like Eve, Delilah, and Jezebel hasn't exactly promoted the best interests of women. How many girls are named Delilah or Jezebel? But then how many boys are named Judas or Nero?

When it comes to youth and beauty, that much, at least, has never changed, and there is no changing it. Men want young and beautiful.

Women have to strive for security. Children were to be that security and to be childless was, indeed, a curse.

There is a clinker. Jesus says that in the beginning God intended it to be one man, one woman, for life. What changed?

An examination of what makes a man or woman satisfied with a single mate for life is challenging. But there is one essential element of this relationship that brooks no disagreement: Romance! Once that is gone, the wandering eye and mind is the norm.

Any inquiry into the primal beginnings of humankind is fraught with speculation. But why, I ask myself, is it that women have been so totally excluded from philosophy and theology? Yet there is a difference that may well be biologically relevant that results in differences of brain function, that makes men more meditative and reflective ontologically, cosmologically, more interested in thought and speculation of these things.

But it remains insane to exclude women, the other half of humankind, from philosophy.

Granted that women, historically, have been the servants of men, have had to live their lives caring for children and making a home has not been conducive to contemplation of the universe and cosmology.

While considerations of this nature must be factored into any equation of making sense of the disparity of women in philosophy or leadership in any capacity, the differences of actual brain function, even biologically limiting physical characteristics, cannot be disregarded. I fully realize this.

The judgment of God that the man would rule over the woman and her desire would be to her husband cannot be set aside either and has had a profound effect throughout history on excluding women from being of equal value to men.

But as I have pointed out in other writings, the male dominated religion of Christianity, as well as of other religions, makes man in the form of Christ in the NT to be the head over the church just as the husband is to be head over his family.

Christ is the head for the good of the church, and the man for the good of the family. Neither Jesus nor men are despots, tyrants, in the capacity of good ruler-ship. It is the abuse of such by treating women of lesser value than men that is the problem.

When a family works in cooperation of the leadership process, you have the best of all possible worlds. When any party tries to gain the ascendancy through ego, threats and bullying, whether inquisitions or a woman using her sex as a control mechanism or a man through his superior physical strength or the mechanism of religion, the result is disastrous.

It may be that studies in astronomy, particle physics, brain function, Psi may yield the reasons for men and women being so different in the way they think and act.

Of one thing I am certain; a New Systematic Theology is needed. Religious people must have a more open mind to their established orthodoxies. I hope I have succeeded in getting some of you to have such an open mind to new ways of thinking about old problems.

As to the relations between men and women, a problem of such historical insolvency should prove it is enormously complicated. Simplistic attitudes only make the matter worse.

I have a distinct advantage in speaking of these things in my children. They are bright, intelligent and have enough regard for their father that they listen. Of great importance to me is the insight they provide about these things. The fact that they are, like dad, voracious readers helps tremendously. I can posit an idea and they can take off with it and run. Intelligently.

I don't intend to minimize what so many others offer by their help. But your children are usually handy. So my kids get the brunt of dad's heretical musings and meanderings.

My children and others give me continued hope that there must be multiplied millions out there who are just as willing to confront their own prejudices in search of the truth, who want honest answers to honest questions.

And my children, among their other virtues, do not hold it against their father that while he decants on such academic esoterica as philosophical and theoretical physics, he can still fix a car, build a house and run a lathe or mill. They have never held my university training against me either, recognizing this as a necessary adjunct to the practical arts in order to make any sense at all.

However, we are all in this thing together, sink or swim.

And when the subject matter becomes too heavy it is good to return to butterfly status and engage in a little whimsy.

I fervently wish the churches that talk so much about personal responsibility, about patriotism, about good citizenship, would take a hard look at the man without whom George Washington said there would have been no War for Independence: Tom Paine! While I believe there is a legitimate argument to be had against The Revolution, perhaps such people would learn somewhat from Paine what it would take to do battle with the Evil One and his servants.

If I were ever to preach again, I would take my sermons from Tom Paine, Thomas Jefferson, Sam Clemens and the great Broadway Musicals.

I recall being raised not to hit girls. Now we boys enjoyed hitting. We were always hitting one another. Somehow it seemed imminently unfair that girls weren't allowed to indulge in this popular pastime.

We boys could wrestle and hit, rolling in the dust and dirt, bleed on each other and, in general, just have a good time. Girls? No way! Unfair.

Yet it may be just as well that girls aren't raised hitting and wrestling like boys. Girls really are different in some respects, and there just seems to be something about them that makes them look better in dresses having tea parties rather than cussing, spitting and hitting.

And boys might smell like an open graveyard or having eaten something unmentionable, but girls are supposed to smell nice at all times.

Girls should never aspire to be preachers. I have to agree with Spurgeon who, when asked about this said: I once saw a dog that had been trained to walk upright on its hind legs. I didn't wonder that the dog did it badly; the wonder was that it did it at all?

My real point is that if such damage to society is done in the name of religion, why should girls want to be a party to such a thing?

I can more readily understand women wanting to join the army or air force where they can legitimately shoot at men, but, ladies, take my advice and stay out of the pulpits. They are no place for a decent woman with any self-respect.

Sam had a way with words. Few people know of his talents as Theologian and Political Philosopher. Who but Sam could sum up Congress as succinctly as calling Judas Iscariot a premature congressman?

In respect to championing the virtue and purity of fair maidenhood, it was Sam who said he was against giving women the franchise because it would reduce them to the level of men and Negroes. Making allowance for his time in history, how far-sighted his assessment of the situation.

I believe Sam recognized the ploy of spineless men at the time whose solitary goal in supporting the franchise for women was to be able to make them equally guilty for the mess in government, and further the cause of numberless husbands who, like old Adam, could take the resulting chaos like men and blame it on their wives.

So if the reader should misconstrue Sam's and my words concerning the franchise in the hands of women by trying to make us say: *We should never have given them the vote!* please keep our pure and selfless motives in mind.

And as a champion of the Gospel, who but Sam could sum up the role of the churches in America with such a straightforward assessment as his observation: *He was as happy as if he had just gotten out of church!*

I recall reading of Sam making a point concerning an Episcopal minister, a Reverend Sabine, who refused the offices of the church in properly burying a play actor, one George Holland. The good reverend did not hold with the corrupting influence of the stage and theater.

Sam's reaction to this was somewhat volatile with his more uncharitable remarks concerning the good priest of the church describing this noble man of the cloth as a … *crawling, slimy, sanctimonious, self-righteous reptile.*

In meditating on Sam's letter and the changes in our society, I recalled the prominent role the churches always played and their continuing influence.

I ask the reader to forgive me for my self-indulgence in castigating those who would lead by superstition and ignorance, preying on the gullibility of the sheep, the great unwashed. I write in hope that those that know better will do better; that there may yet come forth those who believe God needs our help and will apply themselves to the task of confronting ignorance and evil.

In doing battle with the forces of evil, I take the position that the

Devil and his children are capable of learning. The tactics of the Evil One have changed with the times.

Both God and the Devil did things to meet the superstitions and ignorance of the past. While God confronted these things, the Devil learned to use them to the detriment of humanity.

Much of humankind is still steeped in ignorance, following false religious concepts. It is my contention that the children of God should apply themselves to learning.

When Jesus criticized the children of the Light by saying the children of this world were smarter than they in regard to applying themselves to the material goals and objectives of life than the children of God, we would do well to heed his words.

If the churches could unite, for example, in just getting a constitutional amendment banning molestation, it would tell the children of the Devil we were serious about the warfare.

But if we cannot unite in common cause against evil at such a fundamental level, where does that leave us?

I will second-guess here. The many attempts to do battle at even this level is beset with the petty egos of men and women who want to make a name for themselves, who want to build personal empires and make money for themselves, rather than do what is right in the name of God and for the benefit of children, of posterity.

Virtue and integrity are not terms usually applied to the churches any longer. And in the words of old J. Vernon McGee: These Christians may love God but they sure hate each other! As long as this holds true, there isn't much hope of things changing for the better in the churches.

Learning has increased. If the Devil, as a metaphor, knows how to use advanced knowledge to his purpose, isn't it about time religious people got used to the idea that they better do the same?

Almost two-thousand-years ago, the Apostle Paul wrote: For this world in its present form is passing away. I Corinthians 7:31.

The Gospel of Jesus Christ was a New Covenant for humanity, a chance to break free of the prevailing superstition and ignorance that had held people in bondage to darkness.

But Jesus meant it to be a Covenant of love, a Gospel of Good News that would manifest itself through God's love in us. A life dedicated to Christ was to be exemplified by that love.

On this basis, who can say the churches have not failed to honestly represent Christ? What do we see? A list of do's and don'ts without Scriptural foundation, clannish, cliquish organizations that still practice the superstitions of religion rather than leading in teaching, education and tolerance, and, most certainly, not organizations recognized either for their love of God or the peoples of the world!

As for myself, I refuse to be represented by the charlatans of pulpit, TV, radio and trashy books espousing superstitious ignorance and hysteria in the name of God and Jesus and the tired, same old thing Sunday after Sunday that does nothing in preparing God's people to do battle against the forces of evil!

If we have a leadership in the churches, schools and government that is filled with those whose hearts are as dark, self-serving and phony, as the Devil's or a politician's, who is to blame? Certainly not God!

I have a TV antenna on my stove. Someone walks in and sees it and, naturally, asks why I have a TV antenna on my stove?

Now every natural-born human being that has ever been in such a position knows a well-contrived lie is worth the weight of a good groan in the morning. But caught short my usual reply would be: Don't you?

There is a natural tendency in me to feel tenderhearted toward those who don't have a TV antenna on their stove. Especially if I lack an acceptable explanation of things like TV antennas on my stove. People who don't have things like this are deprived, poor souls.

Modesty forbids that I claim anything like the God-given gift of Sam Clemens, the most gifted natural-born liar that ever blessed and graced the planet. But I try harder.

A perfectly natural explanation is that this antenna is to be used, eventually, for FM reception in the canyon where I live. Lacking cable, I have to improvise. A friend gave me this item and told me I could get good FM reception with a few modifications to it.

Naturally I couldn't let on that I had put the blamed thing on the stove so I wouldn't have to feel guilty when I saw it. That meant putting it somewhere unobtrusive; somewhere it wouldn't intrude its presence. The stove, an implement of infrequent use, seemed ideal.

Well, I have a habit of putting things that have some kind of priority in a more or less conspicuous place. In this case, I put the thing where it would be obvious just in case I ever lit off the stove and yet not interfere with the daily needs of living.

I would have put it in the bathroom but the weedeater is still there. As a bachelor, what better place than my stove where, once I cleaned off the cobwebs, it would remind me to get the job done? After all, I may eventually want to fry an egg or some okra.

In reality, the writing is my priority in life. As a consequence, there are some things that I have difficulty just getting around to. And isn't that just like human nature?

But folks, there are some things we are just going to have to get around to if there is to be any hope of things changing for the better. These things demand change, they demand our attention before it's too late!

I am often asked by people what they can do to change things? I would suggest they start asking the hard questions for which the churches claim expertise and leadership. The deplorable state of our political leadership is the result of the people not exercising the franchise responsibly, of asking things of government as though the hard-working, tax-paying middle class will always make the payment for such things. You may be a good person, but if you are not politically active, you are not a good citizen.

There is no free lunch. The bills always come due. And when there are no more cookies in the jar? No one in his or her right mind wants a French Revolution. But we certainly seem to be asking for one!

Yet, unless responsible people come together in common cause to *Cleanse the Temple*, religiously and politically, things will only get progressively worse.

However, only those who are responsible, who have a dedication to our posterity and who pay the price of accountability in their own lives have any right to demand answers and an accounting of others.

For all those pew-warmers and Sunday school dropouts, stop behaving as though God has some magic wand that he is going to wave and make everything all right in spite of the inaction of his people. It isn't going to happen! There comes a time when parents have a right to expect their children to grow up and behave responsibly.

I believe all that love are born of God for the love of God dwells in them.

But I will never believe in the kind of love of God that the churches espouse that fails to grow in knowledge, fails to lead in the search for truth, fails to discriminate, fails to confront evil, or fails to love those who simply disagree with their own theology.

Too many times we are left questioning the Providence that seems to delight in blessing the wicked, those scurrilous reptiles that gain the ascendancy. Folks, it isn't the fault of the snakes if they prove smarter than we are. If we find ourselves, like old Asaph, wondering why the wicked prosper, we have only ourselves to blame.

I hope you will join me in a New Reformation, a New Systematic Theology that acknowledges God has more sense than the churches have given him credit, and insist on the leadership doing the job for which they hold the position.

Whether in government, the schools or the churches, nothing changes for the better until people who know better, do better.

Now I get the distinct impression, looking at that statement that virtually every head out there is nodding in the affirmative. And, just perhaps, there is the answer to the question of the paradox of good and evil.

I cannot accept that a God of love intended evil to prevail; I cannot accept a God of love intended such misery and suffering of children worldwide. Since dualistic philosophies have failed to come up with a sensible answer to this paradox, we must look elsewhere.

The problem with this is the fact that that *elsewhere* is an area of such unthinkable responsibility that people shrink from even considering it!

Is God responsible for evil? Since dualism, since none of the philosophies of humankind, offers an answer to the paradox, this is the only rational and sensible conclusion.

Next, if God is a God of love, how can he be responsible for evil? Only one way: He made a mistake!

That God is capable of error is the only sensible answer to the problem. And that is virtually unthinkable to all orthodox religions and, for that matter, to the non-religious as well.

But I maintain that the mistake was one of love. And love, as I have already pointed out, takes risks and in taking those risks, the potential for betrayal is always there.

Once love is betrayed, the hopes, dreams and plans of the lover go out the window. Love is not prepared for betrayal because it trusts implicitly and lacking suspicion, it cannot consider the What If? of betrayal.

So I suggest that God could not have been prepared for the betrayal of his love and trust and humankind was blasted by sin, by the betrayal of that council of the gods by their creation, to make man in their image. Once this happened, God had to accept responsibility for his creation with the potential of evil, but also had to meet this betrayal with love, forgiveness, judgment and discipline.

Did God truly understand what would happen in the creation of humankind? No. Did things get better after God's judgment? No. Why? Because humankind still, in the image of God, had the capacity to choose.

The bad choices of people resulted in the ascendancy of evil and the story of the Deluge. And good people still seem not to have learned to do battle with evil!

God(s) may have created humankind in their image out of loneliness, out of love. And that love was betrayed resulting in God's decision to wipe out humanity.

But he risked it again on Noah. He, or they, risked loving others that failed or betrayed his, or their, love.

Where does that leave us, the human race? It leaves us with the responsibility to meet evil and overcome it. This cannot be done as long as internecine rivalry exists among the religions of the world, as long as people hate one another on the basis of ideological differences and prejudicial hatreds.

I have said that God needs our help. He does.

God did not intend evil. But that was the chance he took and it was the failure of good men and women to fight the battle that grieved God to the point he said he had made an error in creating man; that plunged the world into conflict, a conflict that evil dominates because good men and women won't fight!

Though filled with allegory and myths, such Biblical examples of

God and humanity and the course of human history present many lessons yet to be learned.

Perhaps you thought I was being extreme, for example, in suggesting a Constitutional Amendment against molestation? Yet, if good men and women know this most heinous act against the most innocent of victims is evil, why not?

And such a monstrous act against children should not be opposed for the evil it is on the basis of being a Christian, Jew or Moslem; it should be opposed because it is evil, because it is destructive of morality and a morally healthy civilization!

Murderers should be put to death expeditiously, not because of religious conviction but because morality and justice demands it, because the evil will always prevail when not confronted and dealt with decisively and with determination to win over the evil!

Adultery and divorce should not be a joke, but dealt with as the evil things they are, the betrayal of love and trust to the destruction of family and the maiming of children, the erosion of the moral foundation of a society!

Until justice prevails, there can be no hope of confronting evil! And God does not have some magic wand to bring such a thing to pass; he depends of his people to accomplish this!

God will not prevent my committing murder, from rape, adultery, lying, cheating, and stealing. I make the choice not to do such things because, as a god myself, if you will, I have the capacity to choose between the good and the evil.

But that murderer, rapist, seducer, adulterer, liar, cheat and thief has the same capacity of choice. Am I, who choose the good, to continually be the helpless victim, or do I do battle against wickedness? That, too, is a choice. And let's face it; if the wicked prevail, just whose fault is that? God's? I don't think so!

These are the hard, unpalatable, irrevocable and immutable facts. Don't think for a moment that something that calls itself a church is going to fight the kind of battle needed, it isn't!

The situation calls for good people taking action knowing it is wrong for children to go to bed hungry, it is wrong to bring children into a situation where they cannot be taken care of, it is wrong for the irresponsible to be supported by the responsible, it is wrong to have laws that pervert the cause of Justice and rewards irresponsibility, corruption and evil!

If leadership in government and education is corrupt and failing, why do good men and women abide it? Where is the holy steel in the righteous backbones of God's people?

Yes, I believe God made a mistake in love. But having done so, having paid the price of his error, are we who know better and don't do better going to leave it to God to bail us out of things that are our responsibility? Are we going to keep taking it from evil men and women, the Bad Seed of Cain, and sit waiting for an apocalyptic deliverance?

There is untold suffering worldwide because the children of God are letting evil win by default!

If a mad dog threatens my child, I shoot the dog. How long are so-called good people going to let the mad dogs run and threaten at will! And then get angry with God because they cheat, maim and kill our children!

God needs our help. But he needs the help of people who are willing to honestly examine their hearts and minds, who are willing to admit they have failed to stand up to the evil and do battle, not in the name of some orthodoxy or ideology, not because they are religious, but simply because it is the right thing to do!

Chapter fourteen

THE AMERICAN POET

This chapter will be somewhat different because it's time for me to emphasize the importance of God and the spiritual element in our lives.

I am no longer a religious man. My remarks throughout this book should be understood and taken in the light of this. But my background in religion, my experience and education, cause me to realize that there are very important things that I have learned along the way of life that have to be couched in the kind of writing that people can relate to.

So it is, in many instances, that I use religion as a kind of metaphor of the human condition. It is true that humankind is a religious species and always has been. And much is to be learned by keeping this in mind. So the reader is asked to make allowance for this in my following remarks.

Also, I repeat the cautionary words that many of my remarks are of philosophical speculation and should be understood in this context. In no case should such remarks be taken as facts rather than opinion. It is never my intention to represent as fact, what is only philosophical speculation, whether of a religious or sectarian nature.

I was once asked to assist in establishing a college and seminary that would be quite different. The reason being that America is falling into moral decay, and doing business as usual in the churches isn't going to save us.

When asked who the first two Apostles were, Tom Sawyer replied in desperation, "Adam and Eve?" We may laugh at Tom's desperate answer but it reminds me of many a similar answer to Bible questions. My great-grandma was fond of showing off my Bible knowledge as a child. For example, she would ask me in front of others: What was Noah's Ark made of and I would dutifully reply: "Gopher wood."

Now my grandparents, my great-grandma and I had no idea that the Hebrew word translated Gopher wood was an uncertain translation. In the NIV it is given as Cypress. But we knew our King James Bible was God's Word and would defend Gopher wood to the death.

I don't think anyone in Little Oklahoma as Southeast Bakersfield was called in those days, knew there were any other versions or translations of the Bible and we would have branded anyone a heretic and blasphemer who suggested such a thing. The Old Time Religion was good for Paul and Silas and it was good enough for all of us. And anyone that had a lick of sense knew Paul and Silas used the King James Bible!

But while ignorance and superstitions were rampant among us dumb Okies, we did have one advantage over many educated people, and we believed what God said. We didn't understand a lot of it, but we believed it. If God said He destroyed the world by a flood, we didn't doubt it. If He said the sun stood still for Joshua that was that. Jesus was virgin born and cast out demons and no one better say otherwise. There are some plain advantages in just simply believing and taking God at His Word (that His Word was only a book written by men was something I had to learn much later in life).

As I, often, reach back in my memory to that simple time of my childhood among simple and honest folks, the women in flour sack dresses and us boys in our bib overhalls and barefoot, I long for the plainness and openness of our dirt-poor community of a simple time of simple virtues. A time before drugs and a collapse of morality were destroying our nation.

It was a time when the bad guys really did wear black and the good guys wore white and, sensibly, kissed the horse instead of the girl (I know, but the aberration of Hopalong Cassidy didn't count. Maybe he was the forerunner of the anti-hero, in attire at least. But I'd hate to hang that on Hopalong. In any event, there was never any question about his being a good guy and our hero).

But, by the end of WWII, there was a quick change of culture in our nation. The boys came back from overseas where so many had gained a cosmopolitan out-look and that, together with the nation having become the preeminent world power, an industrial giant with the Atomic Bomb, women working at men's jobs, the abandoning of the simple, agricultural way of life, so many, many changes. Gone forever, the way of life we knew as children.

I have lived long enough to look back far enough. I grieve for the loss of so much for our children. In my simple way, it seems a tragedy that young people know more about the local Mall than an animal trail along some shimmering, singing, mountain stream or a clear, night sky bejeweled by countless stars, that their ears are accustomed to the noise of Metallica as opposed to the hoot of an owl.

It does bring to mind the statement in the Bible that He uses the foolish (Read: Simple) things of this world to confound the wise.

I just got back from a hike in Fay Canyon. The recent snow and rain has been sufficient to cause the streams in the area to be running nicely.

This is a particularly beautiful area and while walking through the forest, I lived again some of the fun my children and I have had here and similar places in forest and desert.

As I walked along one of the streams, my eye caught a glimpse of a piece of obsidian. Sure enough, it was part of an arrowhead. This area has a lot of game and, judging from the shape and size of the fragment, I'm sure some Indian had shot at something, probably a deer or maybe a rabbit and this was the remains of his attempt at dinner.

A couple of hours later when I was returning to my car I came across a place where it was obvious some folks had been cutting trees for firewood. I spied some shell casings, .45 auto. Being a re-loader from many years' back, I have a habit of picking up brass.

Someone must have emptied a clip judging from the number I found. As I was gathering the cases, I found a 1985-penny. I'm growing gray-haired and my eyes aren't as sharp as they once were but I still see obsidian, shell casings and money on the ground.

I sat on a granite boulder beneath a big, old Digger pine beside the stream and examined my artifacts.

It must be my Cherokee blood that responds so to such an environment. I could well imagine the Indian and what he had to contend with in living off the land. My thoughts ran to what it must have been like here before the intrusion of the White-Eyes. Then I looked at the .45 casings and the penny. The Indian could never have imagined the culture that would produce such marvels. What a difference between that arrowhead and the .45 and his wampum and the penny with the technology that produced such things.

And I thought about a simple man like myself that has taken it upon himself to question the teachings of the great scholars of the Bible. But I also thought about what that Indian understood in his own culture and environment. His knowledge was certainly extremely limited compared with what European nations possessed.

He functioned well enough in the world he knew. And, as in the allegory of the cave, thought he knew a great deal.

But the Indian's knowledge and expertise were to prove no match for the superior learning and technology of more advanced cultures. An arrow is no match for a .45 auto. But imagine, if you will, the tremendous difference between the time and the world that existed for both the Indian that shot his arrow and the person that stood in the same place firing that .45! Who do you suppose God holds more accountable?

While I long for a simpler way I once knew as a child, while I know that much with which I was blessed as a child was denied my own children, I, like the Indian, will learn and adapt or perish.

The Indian may well have had a profound belief in The Great Spirit but it did not save him or his way of life when opposed by a greater power. That he was ignorant of things like systematic theology, having his own equivalent in his own system of superstitions and beliefs, was to prove no match for the great learning and *better ways* of his conquerors.

I was impressed once more by the seeming accident of birth that made me the beneficiary of being a citizen of the United States; that I was born in a time of such vast advances in the sciences.

And so it is that so many things twist and turn through our lives that bring us to moments of decision that can so thoroughly change things for good or evil. So it is that I began to question so many of the things that I had simply accepted as Articles of Faith that had no sound basis in Scripture or the realities of life.

I do not have any longer the excuse of the Indian or, even, a simple product of Little Oklahoma for my ignorance. I got educated. More, I have a wealth of experience for which I am both responsible before

God and, from which I am to draw for examples of my own blind orthodoxy and childishness.

I can envy my Indian ancestor for his freedom from technology, for his escaping having to pay a mortgage and fight traffic. But I cannot envy his ignorance and superstitions. I loved my grandparents dearly but I cannot envy their own ignorance and superstitions.

I do believe, however, that, as with the Indian, had they known better they would have done better. They did the best they could on the basis of what they had and they were honest in those things. I hope I can do as well.

The following remarks are not intended to be the work of the kind of Biblical Scholarship of which the field has been, and is still being, covered in respect to the languages and manuscripts, archaeological discoveries, etc. More books have been written about the Bible because of such studies than about any other single subject.

It brooks no contradiction to say, categorically, that no one has any right to think themselves truly educated who has not read The Bible from cover-to-cover. The single book, the Bible, which has had more influence on the world than any other, intelligently prevents such a contention by anyone.

But in spite of the exhaustive work by scholars for centuries, legitimate questions about God, the Bible and his works have been ignored or, entirely missed.

Some of these questions have caused great persecution, even the death, of those who have asked them. Some, as mentioned, have been missed entirely.

My primary purpose for this study is my children. I want them to understand the importance of Bible study. More, I want them to come to The Bible with open and receptive minds, unprejudiced by the teachings of men.

The study calls into question some of the doctrines and interpretations of the churches and their scholars. It is hoped that my remarks will cause others to take another look at some of their hard-held tenets of the faith and reconsider them.

Before I begin with some of the questions concerning this kind of Bible study, let me use an example to which most parents can relate.

The Bible tells us to discipline our children, that to spare the rod is to hate your child and not let your heart spare for his crying.

While I have come to whole-heartedly disagree with any physical abuse of children for whatever reason, I do use the following by way of example:

Any parent who has had to deal with rebellion and lack of obedience in a child knows the pain and anguish of doing such a thing out of love for that child.

But imagine if you will, this scenario:

Little Johnny or Susie: Why are you whaling the tar out of me?

The parent: Because I love you so much!

Johnny or Susie definitely isn't buying this at the time. Ah, but when they have children of their own! Those immortal words of parenthood.

This is not an all-too-repeated sermon lead where the minister, using such an example, tells us, tiresomely, God has to take us to the woodshed on occasion and we ought to be grateful he loves us so much. Most of us, like Johnny or Susie, will wish he didn't love us so much at times like these.

No, I have a different spin here. I would like to honor God. And too much to allow of shoddy work being done in his name. It will appear, and justifiably so, that I approach some of the questions of the faith once for all delivered to the saints in the manner of whaling the tar out of the way the churches do business, of the way church scholars have avoided, ignored or purposely obfuscated legitimate questions we have a right to ask of God and others who say they speak for him.

Among these questions are those of historical significance. The Crusades, the Inquisition, the Reformation, the battles fought (and still being fought) between nations claiming they had (and have) God on their side, etc.

Of special interest to me are the War for Independence and the Civil War in this nation.

The proponents of the Revolutionary War, our Founding Fathers, claimed God was on their side. The Crown claimed to have God's special ordination to rule. The question of slavery rears its ugly head here as well as the question of taxation without representation, really a spurious argument.

Napoleon, who said that God was on the side with the most cannon, was a pragmatist and didn't blame God one way or the other.

The churches on both sides of the ocean argued their points of view during the 1700s. But we won and God was on our side. Of course.

During Civil War times, preachers North and South of the Mason-Dixon Line pleaded the righteousness of the causes of both. Now I have always had difficulty with trying to see God on both sides of the issue, arguing with himself. It's like he couldn't make up his mind that was right, if you were to listen to the churches of that time.

This attempt by our ancestors at national suicide, this internecine bloodletting of brother against brother, nearly did us in. And we are still, today, paying the price for that lack of agreement among those who claim God is on their side.

God does say in Isaiah 1:18 *Come now and let us reason together.* But somehow this message seems lost to the majority of churches throughout history.

My somewhat labored point being that if reason did prevail, we wouldn't be in the mess we're in.

But wishful thinking won't take the place of action. And where evil is discerned, action is required.

There is an evil at work in the Devil's (to continue to use the Devil as a metaphor) mostly successful attempts to turn the churches into impotent eunuchs. This emasculating work of Satan has resulted in the churches no longer being a moral force for good in this nation.

I guess God isn't a shouter. Children are notorious for being able to discern decibel levels. When dad or mom's voice reaches a certain pitch, then they know the parent is serious.

When Satan called God's Word into question: Has God said...? Adam and Eve, like children, must have thought, Well God didn't really mean what he said. Wrong! Maybe God should have shouted. But Adam took it like a man and blamed it on his wife. And God.

Well, if God winds up shouting at us it will be because he couldn't get our attention any other way.

I'm going to suggest an alternative. Suppose we start asking the hard questions, in all honesty, and searching, honestly, for answers?

While there are many, many questions that we have a legitimate right to ask of God, there are some that have defied attempts to answer.

Theologians through the ages have tried, without success, to answer, for example, the problem of the death of babies. What does God do, or have planed for, these little ones? Did God, in fact, make such provision in the case of Adam's failure?

One idea I have had has to do with the work God has for us in eternity. It is possible that God has taken these little ones for us to work with, to raise and instruct in a pure atmosphere of love when He calls an end to this age.

A similar question arises about the age of accountability. At what point does a person become responsible before God for sin in their lives? At what age does the individual face the prospect of hell, according to the Christian religion, for refusing to accept Christ as their Savior?

I am certain that what I have come to call Blind Orthodoxy is one of the greatest impediments to finding answers to these questions. As long as theologians presume that God is omniscient, omnipresent, and omnipotent, characteristics men have assigned Him that He does not claim for Himself, I do not believe we can find satisfactory answers to such questions.

Just a couple of examples of several I could give:

When the Lord and those angels appeared to Abraham the Lord told him he was on his way to Sodom and Gomorrah to see if all he had heard about conditions there were as told him. The words of the Lord: *... I will go down and see if what they have done is as bad as the outcry that has reached me. If not, I will know.* Genesis 18.

Why did God have to come see for himself?

There is another part of this story I find intensely interesting.

Abraham bargains with God. This man is called in Scripture a Friend of God (II Chronicles 20:7 and James 2:23).

From the narrative in Genesis, Abraham expresses the fear that God is going to do something out of character for the righteous judge of all the earth! Will God, the righteous judge of all be unjust and kill the righteous along with the unrighteous? he asks. "Far be that from you Lord!" he exclaims.

If we are to honestly accept the incredulity of Abraham that God could do such a thing this raises several interesting possibilities about the nature of God, his relationship with humankind and his relationship with Abraham in particular.

Was Abraham, out of love and concern for the honor and integrity of his friend, God, fearful that his friend would do something out of character, that God would make a mistake? If so, what was the basis of his fear for his friend?

So Abraham bargains with his friend out of fear that his friend will make a mistake. And God does not argue with his friend. What a very human scenario. Too human for the churches to admit of.

I definitely believe in the perfection of God. But I believe he is perfect by his definition, not that of men! As children of God, we are commanded to be perfect just as God is perfect. If that perfection must conform to a dictionary definition or the several churches' definition of God's perfection, none of us has a chance!

For an answer, when we turn to the churches, to scholars and the abundant commentaries on the subject, we come up empty. Or, worse, are treated to some of the most obfuscating linguistic fancy dancing of which men are capable. It takes some of these people several pages to express their ignorance and plead a label in lieu of understanding!

God asks Satan in the book of Job: Where have you come from?

Satan tells God he has been sightseeing on earth.

God asks if Satan has knowledge of Job. It seems Satan is well acquainted with poor, old Job.

We know the deal that was cut and Satan loses. But I can't help but feel sorry for Job's wife.

Apart from the general interest of the story itself, and it is an intensely interesting story that I could discuss for hours, I draw your attention to the fact that God asks questions and enters into a situation that has very human attributes and elements. Like asking questions. If I knew it all, and I once did, I wouldn't have to ask anybody anything. And that would be deadly boring.

Conservative, Jewish and Christian scholars have shied away from the wisdom of the philosophies of men for fear (or in ignorance) of being branded liberal or heterodox. While it is very true that the wisdom of great thinkers is no substitute for the wisdom of God, while it is true that many have become puffed up by worldly knowledge, it is a grave mistake to lightly dismiss the thoughts of the great, secular men of history. In spite of their never asking women to join them in The Great Conversation.

I believe it is abundantly clear that, throughout the ages, God has shown that He has been learning about us as well as us about Him. The fact that He has dealt with men throughout history in different ways, much as a parent with a child, at least indicates strongly that there is a Parent-child relationship where God, as our Heavenly Father (and mother), is learning how to deal with His children and that this is evidenced by the childishness of the ancients and God's various ways of working, teaching, and commanding.

A word about exegesis. There are two mentions of men named Lazarus in association with Jesus. One a beggar in a parable by Jesus told in the Gospel of Luke, and another, a friend of Jesus, the story found in the Gospel of John.

The bottom line of the parable in Luke is Jesus' pronouncement that "If they believe not Moses and the prophets, neither will they believe though one rose from the dead!"

Ok, Jesus says people are not going to believe God through signs and miracles.

Then we have the story of the raising of Jesus' friend Lazarus in John and we read: Therefore many of the Jews who had come to visit Mary, and had seen what Jesus did, put their faith in him.

A contradiction may be seen between the two stories. But, wait a moment. The just shall live by faith! (Habakkuk 2:4). This was the battle cry of the Reformation, the call Luther got as he was kissing his way up those stone stairs.

There were some that saw Lazarus raised and ran off to tattletale to the Pharisees. They didn't believe in spite of one raised from the dead. While the story is undoubtedly apocryphal, the writer certainly knew a great deal about human nature.

Imagine if you will the frontier of the mind. Now, I have a Ph. D. in Human Behavior from one of the most, if not the most, humanistic universities in the world. It is a prestigious school with very high academic standing. The university prides itself on its research, its work in the various fields of psychology, its originality and the quality of its graduates.

I had tough going in this school. Its basis of understanding was in direct opposition to Biblical thought. And at the time I still held to many religious beliefs of Christianity. But as my dear and old friend,

Dr. Charles L. Feinberg, pointed out, I would just have to *jump through the hoops* as he did at Johns Hopkins, if I were to make it.

The education I have received through various colleges and universities has at least equipped me to deal knowledgeably with the best in this world's wisdom. And I do not treat it lightly or ignorantly.

I credit the best works of history and theology for my education in these areas. The melding of all these things, together with a host of skills learned by getting grease under my fingernails, gives me a decided edge over those that attempt to give answers but have a great deal of presumed knowledge, i.e. opinion expressed as fact, which is derived from bias and prejudice.

It's easy to dismiss the ignorant nonsense of the charismatics and Pentecostals, the superstitions of the Roman Church, Mormons and J.Ws but it is not as easy to deal with some of the Dogmatic Theology that has had the imprimatur of church councils through ages past.

If I am correct in my assessment of the situation, that The Church was to grow in understanding through its infancy, childhood, adolescence and, now, adulthood, I Cor.13: 8-12, then much of the Dogma of its earlier periods should have passed away and given place to maturity. To go on to perfection in the sense of Hebrews 6:1-3 seems perfectly clear in this regard.

The sincere milk of The Word that we should grow thereby should give place to the meat which belongs to those who are ... mature, who by constant use have trained themselves to distinguish good from evil. (Heb. 5:14).

Having studied the ancient creeds and scholars of The Church together with secular history and literature, it seems abundantly clear that God expects us to grow up and leave behind Jewish fables as Paul called them. I include the fables of those that hold to their blind orthodoxy in spite of all the evidence that their belief systems are riddled with superstitious nonsense.

Now, I believe it is well past time that those professing themselves Christian do some growing up as well.

God hath not given us a spirit of fear, but of power, love and a SOUND MIND! I place my own emphasis in this regard on that sound mind. In an age when so many religious practitioners make God to look ridiculous, I think it needs to be affirmed that God is not the author of confusion. He is not some mythological idol. He is not the character the charismatics and Pentecostals make of Him, but neither is He hard at work trying to create mysteries of religious nonsense, accessible to only the privileged few that know the secret handshakes, rites and formulas of some elite coterie of priests.

These priests specialize in pious, religious phraseology devoid of any common sense or rational thought. In this regard, they are no different in plying their trade than the politician who speaks much without saying anything, or the education specialist who is accomplished in the same manner.

The Priest-practitioner will say something like: *The mystery of the majesty of The Most High* and actually believe he has said something of consequence, that he actually has communicated something of understanding and value to the hearer, when, in fact, he has said absolutely nothing that would contribute or communicate anything except some emotional nonsense.

Oh, let us glorify The Lord! sounds very spiritual but what does it mean? Oh, the grace of God! What does that mean? Praise The Lord? Come, let us sit at Jesus' feet; let us feast in His presence! (?) To paraphrase the Apostle Paul: I would rather speak a single word of understanding than ten thousand words of gobbledygook!

And, there are always those that, by simply labeling something, seem to believe they have offered an explanation; that they actually understand when nothing they have said makes any sense whatsoever to the rational listener. Many theologians become practiced in this art.

Sadly, much of what tries to pass for Bible study is no more than a pooling of shared ignorance. The teacher has little or no professional training in the subject and, all too commonly, sincerity is a substitute for knowledge.

Bible study, in common with any other legitimate study, requires discipline, organization and a great deal of that most precious of commodities, time. Unlike the beginning study of a subject like physics, you have to read the entire text, the Bible, before the actual study begins.

Because of this, I recommend a Modern English version or translation like the New International Version. It's not perfect but a good version. The King James is my favorite and I encourage that all memorization be done from it, as a discipline of mind, if nothing else; but the old English is not always conducive to understanding and can even obscure some meanings.

While there is no substitute for knowledge of the original languages, the history and geography of The Bible, neither is there a substitute for its reading. One may well have a satisfactory knowledge of it by reading it whereas another may study theology in all its forms and miss the main point of it all. So, whether you master any of the other things or not, there is no substitute for the complete reading of The Bible from cover-to-cover. And real Bible study begins with that exercise. Only after you have read it, thoroughly, are you ready to begin its study.

At some point in time, a real teacher who knows the Bible academically becomes necessary in order for fuller understanding. The Church was to have appointed qualified men to this task.

Once an overview of all that is in the book is gained, the study of the particular parts can be begun. Along the way, it is most essential that some of the history and geography be learned also.

I use an analogy of the multiplication tables and the necessity of these to make any advances in mathematics. They are the foundation of all mathematics from the simplest to the most esoteric.

I think of the Bible in this regard. It is, I believe, an essential primer of human nature, some important history, and mythology.

But the Bible should never be treated as some kind of rabbit's foot or talisman; it should never be treated superstitiously or ignorantly.

If my point is valid, the Bible being a primer, together with many other even more ancient writings, God expects us to go on with that foundation and continue to learn, to advance in knowledge and wisdom.

There was a good deal of this going on in New Testament times and God's men of the time clearly stated that Christians were expected to go on in wisdom and knowledge. They meant people to go on beyond what was written for instruction, beyond the multiplication tables.

I tell you candidly that once I learned the multiplication tables, if my school had continued to teach only that part of math year-after-year I would have found a different school!

Yet what do we find in the churches? The Same Old Thing repeated endlessly, week-after-week, year-after-year! As a result, I began looking for a different school! I knew there was more to be learned than a constant repetition of the multiplication tables.

It has to be admitted that if a minister were to truly try to teach, he would soon be out of work! We have evolved a system partly due to tax-exempt status in which even the best minister or priest cannot declare the whole council of God, where hirelings preach for a paycheck.

TV evangelists for the most part and charismatics in general, are successful at the church version of Vaudeville. They produce a show and the entire so-called ministry is nothing but a poor, shabby attempt to emulate Broadway and Hollywood.

The progress of doctrine and church growth, I believe, has been stymied by refusing to deal with the hard, but legitimate questions we all have.

I have had to put many of my own prejudices aside in order to even admit of some of these questions. We must face these things much like the Apostle Paul when Jesus made him confront his religious prejudices, those things which he had most surely believed, but had to realize they were only his prejudices, prejudices which he had learned from the venerated scholars of his time.

There has always been a danger in confronting religious prejudices. It is the basis of Voltaire's statement that the greatest crimes ever committed against humanity have been committed in the name of religion!

Would the Apostle Paul have had Michael Servetus burned at the stake as John Calvin did? I doubt it. Did Jesus intend that his followers and disciples should kill or persecute those that disagreed with them? No!

The Gospel is, apart from the mystical nonsense ascribed to Jesus, first and foremost, a message of love and hope. It is to love others and offer them this hope because of the love and hope within us.

The Church is not to invite sacrilege or blasphemy, dissension or chaos. All things within the Church are to be done decently and in order. For this reason, good men of sound mind and exemplary lives are to be the leaders of the Church.

But within the Body of Christ, the Church, there must be room for dialogue, for the progress of doctrine, for the growth of the Church without fear of being burned at the stake.

The views of secular genius must be included in this dialogue. When Thoreau expressed, so well, his criticism of the churches of his time, they didn't listen. They should have. When he said those churchgoers blasphemed God in sermon and song, he was right. And churchgoers today are still doing so!

The fact that Thoreau was only repeating the essence of James in his epistle has gone unnoticed by the churches. It never does any good for the cause of Christ to say: *Be warm and filled* unless you take action to help!

Make no mistake! Christianity is not humanism, but it must always be humane! And, I would add, humanely sensible.

A lack of knowledge of the great philosophers and writers of history has led to a pompous arrogance among many churchmen. There is a very harmful mind-set among conservative Christians that they, alone, are Right! And all others will go to hell!

Yet, to ask the typical Baptist to defend a gospel that would allow Livingston into heaven and consign Schweitzer to hell, to explain how God will cast good men and women into hell who have never heard their version of their gospel, is to watch that Baptist, Lutheran, Episcopalian, Roman Catholic, Nazarene, etc. squirm and wriggle.

As to the Roman doctrines of purgatory and limbo, one can only shake his head at the attempts at answers. But even these makes more sense than many Protestant attempts at answers.

In turning to the hundreds of commentaries on the subject, whether Jewish, Catholic or Protestant is to get an education in obfuscation, of reams of material that attempt, vainly, to address the question legitimately.

Bible study questions of the form with which I began, really belong to those who have already mastered much of systematic theology and have a strong grounding in the various disciplines such as hermeneutics. My point is that while even a child can ask a most profound question, an answer can only be reasonably expected from someone who is qualified in the subject area.

To simply read a commentary on Romans does not qualify

someone to either teach a class on the epistle or pontificate on the various doctrinal issues raised.

Therefore, an understanding of the entire book is based on knowledge of the whole book, not a little here, a little there. The sects and cults are based, primarily, on this approach of taking many things in the book out of context and twisting and distorting them.

Obviously, to undertake the study of The Bible requires a deep motivation. No half-hearted attempt will do as many can testify. The numbers are legion who have started to read, let alone study, the book and given up.

When I first started reloading my own ammunition at the age of fourteen, I read and studied everything I could get my hands on about the subject. I was handling explosives like gunpowder and primers, and I had some idea that these items could do me some hurt if handled incorrectly. I became a real student on this subject and the materials involved.

I approached the matter of using dynamite and blasting caps on our mining claim with the same healthy fearfulness. When I got involved in fast draw shooting, I decided not to follow those that were popularizing the sport by shooting themselves in the foot. And, determined not to become another Toeless Joe Nelson, fastest draw in the West, I got a pro to show me how it was done. I still have all my fingers and toes as a testimony to the fact that I was a good student of these practical arts.

But, amazingly, when you really stop to think about it, everyone is an expert on the subject of religion. The fact that most of such expertise is usually a muddy mix of experience, superstitions, ignorance, bias and prejudice does not prevent such experts from proclaiming their ignorance; sometimes quite loudly.

When I was a young man, I decided to learn to fly airplanes. Like handling guns and explosives, there is something about flying an airplane that brings one into a contemplative state of considering one's mortality. "This thing can kill me!" is one such contemplative state of mind.

Memorization is a marvelous discipline of the mind. But it is now considered as being too time-consuming and too much trouble. The paramount difficulties are a lack of time in a frantic society. Too busy and too tired after fighting the rat race.

Of course, if a man is doing what is right before God, he can expect to find himself in a battle. But, if a good church is there to help and instruct, it makes all the difference in whether he wins or loses blessing for the whole family.

When I get together with others that claim to know The Lord, it quickly becomes apparent where their hearts are. People talk about the things they care about. People who are self-absorbed talk about nothing but themselves.

If they are totally absorbed in their jobs, their troubles, their latest carburetor overhaul or operation, it is apparent also.

God warns about complacency and the things of this world snatching away the things of ultimate value. My soul brother Henry Thoreau has much good advice along this line.

You talk about the things in which you are interested, the ones you love and the work you love. There is nothing revelatory or mysterious about this; it is human nature.

Commitment to the truth, the things of ultimate value, is a natural result of the honest desire for these things on the part of the real philosopher.

The commitment becomes a fact of holy living, so to speak, of daily reading, contemplation, and study, which becomes a witness to others by both your life and your conversation.

If these things are lacking in a person's life, isn't it natural to wonder how much they really care about the truth? Of course it is.

It is an axiom that people might do better if they know better. It requires years to gain any expertise in the subject of philosophy. But there is no short cut to such knowledge that includes systematic theology, hermeneutics, the languages, history, geography, archaeology and cultures of the Bible and other writings of men, including the great literature of nations throughout history.

Chapter fifteen

Our Responsibility as Children of God

It is vital to have all the learning possible as you approach this question of the meaning and purpose of it all. The greatest theologians through the ages have addressed themselves to such study and it would be most unwise to lightly set their efforts aside. But you must also keep in mind the fact that they were acting with limited knowledge compared to the present knowledge available to us.

Were dinosaurs contemporary with Adam? How will the answer to this question effect answers to other questions? Why did God create Satan and what went wrong? Did Satan have creative powers? Why did Satan go to the trouble of subverting Adam and Eve?

It is a common and mistaken notion that people are born with the ability to think critically. Not so. This is a learned discipline with which few are familiar.

So it is that I often find myself threading a very circuitous path, even a seemingly paradoxical or contradictory one, in an attempt to frame questions and seek solutions. But I remind myself that this is the essence of the philosophical methodology.

I often think of Faulkner's comment to the Nobel Committee that the only thing worthy of the agony and sweat of the artist is the human heart in conflict with itself. So I find my ideas, my own heart, often in conflict as I deal with so many unanswered questions.

That this conflict has to have written expression is a matter of the history of philosophy. That such philosophies have excluded women and children, family, throughout history is my own area now of agony and sweat.

No one in the realm of biblical scholarship and the whole of philosophy seems to recognize the detrimental effect of leaving out an entire half of the human race, women, in their attempts to provide answers. This is what I have come to call a six-thousand-year-old problem: The Missing Half of Humanity: Women!

Yet the basis of a civilization is the family. As goes the family, so goes a nation. And that family, its structure, its values, is determined by the relationship between a man and a woman.

When the compatibility of differences is honored, when equal value is recognized, the relationship is a good one. When those differences are used and abused, we have competition and combativeness; this often results in the *Love is Heaven but Marriage is Hell!* Syndrome.

The history of it, the innumerable books on the subject and the history of humankind, evidence that this is a monumentally complex problem and, as a result, being one of constant conflict and warfare.

That the greatest theologians of the churches, the greatest of secular thinkers and philosophers, have failed in an answer, most not even addressing it, should prove something to us. And we would do well to take notice!

The resulting conflict in questioning one's own wisdom and the wisdom of others naturally has a confounding element. Socrates had to die as a result of asking questions that defied simple answers or solutions, questions that hit at the heart of so much prejudice and ignorance, and questions that were determined by those in authority to undermine the Order of the State!

Well, now, if my questions are found to be so threatening to such authority, whether of church or state, questions that trouble minds intent of simple answers to monumentally complex questions and lead men to be troubled with the authority of ignorance and prejudice, my end would seem assured.

This reminds me of the four-page, single spaced, letter I got some time ago from a man I have known for years, Gary North. In fact, I am Gary's spiritual father as he freely admits. He is very church involved and has written many books of a theological nature.

Few people today, outside the area of theology, know that this study was the Queen of the Sciences for centuries. I was immersed in this discipline for years.

But I became what this ex-friend called a Self-excommunicated man some time past by posing some questions to the churches that they have, historically, refused to acknowledge. I did not give up, but

I knew that the development of Church doctrine was stymied by the refusal of religious leaders to be open to new ideas that might lead to a better understanding of nature, of creation, and the relationship between God and people.

For example, the sketchy account of The Creation in the Bible leaves many questions unanswered. So I proposed, as philosophical speculation only, that the creation of the dinosaurs, such monstrous creatures, did not reflect the mind of a God of love and beauty, but rather the malevolent and evil mind of a being like Satan.

The account of Satan, a creature so powerful he thought he could beat God, leaves the possibility that this being has the power of creation. That his creations were ugly and destructive, that God Himself may have intervened by wiping out such ugliness and creating things of beauty out of the resulting void and darkness, is credible and sensible speculation to me.

Satan, in retaliation, came to Adam and Eve, the most beautiful of God's creation reflecting the very image of God, and, I believe, a Mr. and Mrs. God, and succeeded in getting them to rebel against. The result being the blasting of creation and Nature, red in tooth and claw, and Adam and Eve finding themselves in opposition to each other due to God's judgment against them for their disobedience.

Philosophy has been kinder to such questions and investigations than theology. So I had to turn from my theologian friends in the churches and look to philosophy for any encouragement and assistance.

It was asking such questions and suggesting such heterodox possibilities that led to the following.

After reading something I had written, something in which I had posed some of these dangerous questions, my ex-friend wrote that lengthy missive consigning me to the flames of hell unless I publicly recanted.

Like most of you I wonder about that star the Magi followed, I wonder why babies die and what really happens to them afterward, I wonder why good people suffer such injustice and inequity in life, why the wicked seem to prosper and so many murderous animals are never brought to justice, why love isn't the motivating influence in more people's lives?

I even suggested that the Gospel is a great deal more than good

Baptists and Catholics think and preach. I used the example of the inability of such people, by their belief systems, to differentiate between good men like Livingston and Schweitzer. Both lived sacrificially for others. What kind of Gospel would let Livingston into heaven and send Schweitzer to hell?

But the thing that really set him off was my suggesting that God Himself has made mistakes and has admitted doing so. It immediately occurred to him that if God has ever made a mistake it was in creating me! There, I beat you to it.

I suggested it might be that God is learning and in creative activities is trying new things; that as with any artist, errors occur and you learn and go on.

For example, how else explain God's attitude toward his creation of man at the time before he sent the flood? God clearly says he was sorry he had made man! The very words of Scripture declare God was grieved, repentant, of having created humankind and determined to destroy this creation!

But love stood in the way of God's decision. He found a man, Noah, and love took the chance once again. How many of us have been betrayed by love? A very human thing. And, perhaps, a very God-like thing as well, especially when we read that the love of the Son of God was betrayed. The NT writer of this allegory knew somewhat of human nature.

The question immediately presents itself whether an act out of the purest motive of all, love, can be legitimately construed as an error, a mistake?

God is love. And those that love are God's children, so the first Epistle of John declares.

I don't know about you, the reader, but I have made mistakes out of love and I'll bet you have also. And I have had that love betrayed. Several times.

I have beaten my head and breast and called myself stupid for having made these mistakes of misplaced love and trust. But you know something? I haven't let it stop me from loving and trusting again. I pick myself up and do it all over again like the song says. Maybe I'm just kind of terminally stupid that way.

Now no one is sorry for doing something unless they think they have done wrong or made a mistake. This is clearly stated in God's own words according to the Biblical narrative.

God made many choices of men where he was clearly hurt by their failures; men like Abraham, David and some of the prophets come readily to mind. These men failed in God's expectations of them. Did God make mistakes in choosing such men?

If so, he made such mistakes out of a motive and heart of love. The Biblical history of God's dealings with men and women clearly evidences something to me. God made humankind with the ability to choose right and wrong.

God took an obvious risk here. The story of The Fall is a story of choice. Adam made a conscious decision to disobey God. God did not know whether Adam and Eve would be obedient or not! That was the risk.

But it made God the responsible party as Creator for the resulting pain and evil of sin in the world. The Unfolding Drama of Redemption, as Graham Scroggie called it, begins here.

God accepted his responsibility for this by the sacrifice of his Son, Jesus Christ, according to the NT. That is the story behind the Gospel.

A most interesting question arises at this point. Many questions, in fact. But I call your attention to just one.

If it had been in the mind of God to provide Jesus Christ as the sacrifice for sin at the time of The Fall, why would he later determine to destroy humankind from the face of the earth? No commentator to my knowledge has addressed this question.

After The Fall, God says: The man has become like us to know good and evil! Who is the US? Genesis 1:26 reads: Then God said, Let us make man in our image, after our likeness.... Again, who is the US?

Christian commentators would have us believe the Us is God the Father, God the Son and God the Holy Spirit. Thus really straining at a gnat.

And what does that mean, specifically, that Adam and Eve had become god-like in knowing both good and evil?

That tree of the knowledge of good and evil. When the serpent called Eve's attention to it, she saw it as good for food, pleasing to the eye and desirable for gaining wisdom. Look at that last. Just what characteristic of that tree and its fruit made it desirable for gaining wisdom?

Unless you are struggling with an answer that question, you have a long way to go in true, Bible study! Just the fact that Adam was with Eve at this moment, unless you believe he was out mowing the lawn, that Eve was deceived with her husband standing by, deserves study. Was he waiting to see if she would fall down dead before he took a bite? Considering the fact that Adam tried to blame both God and his wife for his own failure as a man, I wouldn't be surprised.

A lot was going on here that neither Jewish nor Christian theologians have never acknowledged or studied. A major problem I have had to confront all my life is the fact that while God may have made us in his image and gave us the capacity to ask the questions, religious scholars seems determined to ignore them or slough them off as though they didn't exist!

Worse; when someone like me raises the questions we are treated as skeptics or infidels! Yet who has more reverence for God, the ones who pretend an understanding they do not possess or those who seek answers to their legitimate questions because they believe God wants us to seek such answers and grow in the faith thereby?

The basis of understanding that has been provided in so much of the writings of the ancients should result in the progress of doctrine, of wisdom and learning. Yet the churches seem to have left off actual study, devoting themselves to repeating the Same Old Thing endlessly; and, as a result, we are left in chaos, unable to come together as that early council in Jerusalem to seek answers that seem good to both the Holy Spirit and to us!

No one can dispute the fact that the churches were to be training institutions, not places where you invited the lost to be saved. But they long ago left off real teaching and turned evangelistic! Wrong! But if you have nothing of substance to teach? Then let's just get together and feel good about each other, stroke each other, and tell the world to go to hell!

You can readily see that giving expression to such ideas would have led to my being burned at the stake in times past.

But, folks, unlike Socrates I'm not going quietly. If they find me guilty and worthy of death, I plan to go kicking and screaming out at the injustice of it all!

How does the account of Satan in the Book of Job and Daniel help us in understanding the enemy? Why does Paul say: We are not ignorant of Satan's devices when such ignorance seems to abound? How did Paul deliver certain ones over to Satan and ask the Corinthians to do so as well? What did they know that we perhaps should know also in this respect?

Great theologians have been drawn to the wonderful names and titles of our wonderful Lord, each with their own significance; but what about the names and titles of Satan? No one would deny that evil has enormous attraction and there is a glory of evil. It is men's inability to compare the glory of good with the glory of evil that leads to such ignorance about the subject.

Adam and Eve became as God, knowing good and evil when they ate the forbidden fruit. What, exactly, did Adam and Eve know in this regard that God had reference to? Certainly Adam and Eve knew the Serpent, who, and whatever she was. And how was it that this creature had such easy access to them in the Garden?

Were there such creatures, able to converse with Adam, among the beasts that Adam named while looking for a suitable helpmeet? That there was thought to be a chance of finding such is certainly implied from the context. Was the Serpent motivated by jealousy that she was not chosen, and, as a consequence, singled out Eve for his deception? Was this an attempt to get Eve and poor, old Adam got caught in the crossfire?

Isn't it possible that God learned from His experience with Satan and made man out of love and loneliness, in His own image, in the hope that Man would fulfill His dreams and plans which angels, including Satan, and, possibly, other creatures like the Serpent, proved incapable of doing?

Now I do not believe in angels. But ancient writings like the Bible give them credence. So, I will postulate the following on that basis.

It is even within the realm of speculation that God limited man in some ways that contrasts with the powers of angels, but gave man far greater capacity in the God-like ability to love, hate, create, choose, build, plan, imagine and dream.

That Satan and the angels have, at least, the capacity to choose; even rebel against God is stated in the Bible. In any event, Satan must have had extraordinary power to even imagine he could beat God, that he could unseat God Himself.

Jude, in his epistle, tells us that Satan's majesty and authority precluded the archangel, Michael, from bringing a slanderous accusation against him but said: The Lord rebuke you! Satan rose up against Israel and incited David to commit an enormous sin in the numbering of the people. (I Chron. 21:1).

He appears with the angels before God in the book of Job. He may be the Prince of the Persian kingdom of Daniel 10:13 who delayed The Angel of The Lord for 21 days from coming to Daniel's aid. We are told that the angel, Michael, had to assist in this case. We see Satan standing with The Angel of The Lord accusing the high priest and being rebuked of The Lord in Zachariah 3:1.

Satan stopped Paul, again and again, from visiting the Thessalonians (I Thess. 2:18). Paul's thorn in the flesh that was to, in Paul's words, keep him from becoming conceited is called a messenger of Satan. (II Cor. 12:7). II Peter 2:4, Jude 6,7 and Revelation 12 give us further insight into Satan's power and work.

Can we at least admit that we are woefully ignorant in this area and should not be? If we are expected to understand anything of the Temptation of Christ isn't it vital to know about the tempter? And I mean REALLY KNOW, not some spiritual mish-mash and mumbo-jumbo that tries to pass itself off as understanding. How is it possible to deal with an enemy when we are so very ignorant of him? The plain answer is that: WE ARE SUPPOSED TO KNOW!!!

So while I do not any longer believe in the Devil or angels, and I most certainly do not subscribe to any words of men like the Bible or Koran being anything more than the words of men, I realize much is to be learned from such writing which has been missed by scholars.

I believe I know what Satan's (by whatever definition) one blind side has to be: Sacrificial love. From the account in Job, it is at least evident that Satan's opinion of men is that they will do anything to save their own skins; that they, like he, are selfish and arrogant liars.

Satan is called of Christ, the Father of liars and murderers, of all that practice evil. An interesting parentage. It is therefore not surprising that the one, single, most distinguishing feature of Christians, children of God, is to be their love for one another. Satan has to be blind to such a thing. He literally cannot understand or conquer those that are truly such people. But he can cause them a world of hurt.

It may be ignorance that causes many to accept the account of Isaiah 14 as an account of Lucifer, literally meaning Son of the dawn. The name, Lucifer, is not in the original manuscripts and the NIV correctly does not include it. This is not to avoid the probable comparison with Satan between the account of Babylon by Isaiah and its obvious connection with the Book of Revelation.

Now there are those that will take vehement exception to some of the possibilities I have raised. But can they disprove them by the Bible alone apart from their preconceived notions and prejudices (blind orthodoxy)? I think not. So, rather than fight against me why not search the Scriptures whether these things be so or not?

Sadly, most will simply be too lazy to even try. But at the very least, if I am attacked for my views I know people are thinking about them. That is worthwhile.

Most of my enemies are those that haven't even taken the trouble to think through their own beliefs. If they did, I believe they would be astounded to discover how much of their own knowledge is based on what they have been told by others rather than what, specifically, God says.

Philosophers from time immemorial have grappled with the paradox of good and evil. But some kind of totally unsatisfactory dualism has always been the result.

For example, some have posited that evil is a necessary corollary to good, that one is essential for the other, Cause and Effect, if you will. But this has never answered well to the basic belief that God is love, that his creation and his acts are motivated by love.

The tension theory, yin and yang, cause and effect, none of these leave us with a satisfactory answer to how a God of love could have been responsible for evil.

I ask in my pet project of a Mathematical Model of Human Behavior whether love divided by hate can possibly equal pure ambivalence? In the infinitesimal calculus, zero represents an infinite point of transition.

But we do not understand that point by labeling it zero. It is a symbol of something we lack the physics and mathematics of understanding.

We use such things as zero because they work, like electricity or magnetism, not because of our understanding them. In fact, we do not need to understand them for workability. But that workability is limited by a lack of understanding.

By delving ever deeper into subatomic particle physics, by our increasing knowledge of astronomy, anthropology and archaeology, answers are coming. In the process we are becoming ever more aware of how enormously complex the beginning of the universe, the beginnings of humankind is.

I do not believe, however, that the paradox of good and evil that has resulted in so much suffering of humanity can be explained in any other way than to accept that God has made errors.

Further, I believe God needs our help if love is ever to overcome evil. If we had such a perfect mathematics that we could say, like dualistic philosophers, that because of cause and effect the evil is an essential corollary to good, that the one results in the other, we are left with no hope of ever overcoming the evil. That is the inescapable and only logical conclusion of dualism.

I cannot accept that. I believe love to be a far more potent force than evil. But it has to be the kind of love that is sensible of the evil; a love that understands that it wields a sword of battle as well as compassion.

The failure of love to overcome is basically the failure to understand love in its divinity. God is not a fool. He, like all who love, takes risks in the hope of having that love returned in kind.

At some point love must understand that a rattlesnake is not going to respond to love and compassion. It is not in the nature of a rattlesnake to be anything other than what it is.

For example, the molesting murderers of children are not going to be rehabilitated by any amount of love and compassion. Love has to take a stand against evil. More, love must, as God has, say: "This far and no further!"

We are in a battle, warfare is waging and the proponents of love and justice are losing because they do not understand that rattlesnakes can only be killed, not reformed or converted!

When the Pharisees attacked Jesus on the grounds that he, a man, made himself equal to God by calling God his father, Jesus replied with Psalm 82 where we read that we are gods. John 10:34,35.

If, as Jesus replied to the Pharisees, the Scripture cannot be broken, if God himself calls us gods, why did they want to stone him? For the same reason that today's Pharisees want to stone those that call attention to their blind orthodoxy by which they continue, as their ancestors did, teachings and dogmas that twist and distort the truth of God.

The Bible says God created us in his image; that man is a distinct creation literally born of God himself! Jesus affirms the family relationship to God, our father. Jesus further affirms that we are his brothers and sisters, family.

Family is not made up of different species. All are of a kind. My children are not the result of my mating outside my species.

Can I perform miracles? No. But I can love, hate, sacrifice for others, imagine, plan, hope, dream, create as an artist and, in short, exercise the god-like faculties that are mine as a child of God, a brother to Jesus.

But I performed miracles for my children! At least that is how children view the acts of their parents. When I am all growed-up as a child of God I anticipate being able to do those miracles he can do. But I further anticipate that state will be reached when I put off this old body with its limitations and have entered into a newness of life, mush as the caterpillar casts its slough.

Now I raised my children in the hope that they would be obedient, that they would learn and grow up to be good men and women, self-reliant, self-disciplined and responsible. I further hoped that everything I could do, they would learn to do better. I hoped they would love me as much as I loved them.

I remain their father no matter how great my children become, no matter how far they surpass me. That is my positional authority and supremacy. In this, the child never becomes greater than the parent.

Just so, I believe God, both father and mother, are family; that we as human beings were created the children of our father and mother God.

I think those that claim such kinship, those that call themselves children of God, better rethink a theology that would make God's children less than gods themselves. And as God's children, I think we better grow up and accept our responsibility as their children, and do the job expected of us in confronting evil.

My eldest son is 41-years-old. Just the other day we were remarking on how wonderful it was that we could talk man-to-man. He knows he has lived long enough to have the wisdom and responsibility that comes with his age.

But will Daniel, or my other son, Michael, or my daughters Diana, Laura or Karen ever tell me they are greater than I am? No. Even if they are, I'm still their father and, in the best of family foundation, the child never is above the parent. There is this thing of honoring the father and mother that must be practiced for the relationship to be a loving and healthy one.

If you want to argue the point from your own religious orthodoxy, you better take a hard look at what Jesus said about our position as gods, born of God himself according to his own words, before castigating me.

Granted we are going to die. And gods don't die.

But what, exactly, is death? According to Scripture we are going to pass on but become immortal in the process. But that immortality is ours now! Eternal life is something we now possess; that which is life, life born of God himself, is deathless!

Some will go on to everlasting punishment. Some will go on to what God has prepared for them. I do wonder if, in our dreams and thoughts, we do not gain some insight into this thing of eternal life? Do the very particles that comprise life and matter determine the final outcome? If my thoughts and actions are evil, do these particles carry the message into eternity for me to live with forever? Now that would be hell!

The point being that only the body subject to death and decay passes away. That which is immortal remains.

As my own, brief span draws to a close, I long for the simplicity of that little church in Little Oklahoma, the security of the love of simple folks who never heard of theology. I long for the heartfelt singing of the Old Hymns of Zion with my grandad's booming voice and grandma's piano accompaniment. How I miss the old, old stories of Moses in the bulrushes, Samson and the Philistines, David and Goliath. Of a truth, as The Preacher so well said: For with much wisdom comes much sorrow; the more knowledge, the more grief.

But the responsibility of knowledge weighs heavily upon me. How to keep from speaking when so many are hurting so in ignorance! God commands us to study to show ourselves approved. The poet may say: When ignorance is bliss, 'tis folly to be wise! But poets are notoriously impractical. The world may bless them in spirit but the world itself is a cruel taskmaster, rewarding results rather than fine words and a sensitive soul.

The Dial could never be a match for The Farmer's Almanac, and, while Longfellow, Lowell and Holmes may have become hobbies for antiquarians while Thoreau still beams brightly, while his Civil Disobedience may have inspired a Gandhi and still speaks to us of much that is common sense, it is well to remember that he finally made pencils.

It is well to know how to make pencils. My soul yearns with longing through Walden, but the world demands that one make pencils. It is, as made in the image of God, that men may possess their souls while making pencils. But it takes good men to distinguish the priority and meet, and beat, the world on those terms.

And well it should be so for: If any not work, neither should he eat! If you wish to starve for the sake of a finer soul than this world seems to appreciate, you should be free to starve. But don't expect me to feed sheer laziness. If you must sweep floors while musing on a higher plane don't complain to those that have given all diligence to the industry of making brooms as though you were made of better stuff.

So it is that one may plant and one may water but God gives the increase. Please note, however, that planting and watering are necessary in God's work. And real work it is unless you are so benighted as to think that memorizing a few Bible verses, letting your hair grow and developing a fanatical gleam in your eyes are all that is required. That may do to fool some, but even this world's wisdom is wiser than that, and you had best heed wisdom on the subject lest you think more highly of yourself than you ought.

As we read through the Bible and other literature, we have to admit that there is much that makes no sense whatsoever according to present orthodoxy. Just the laws of the Old Testament alone, while many attempts are made to spiritualize them, give evidence of God's ways of dealing with people that have changed considerably.

The events of the Exodus alone and the actions of the Israelites are deserving of great attention. There is much in God's dealings with this time in history and the people that bespeaks a situation that is steeped in ignorance and superstitions. The people behave like children and are treated accordingly. Many of God's commands must be understood in this context or they are inexplicable.

By the time of the Church Age, it seems God clearly understood men and expected them to understand Him. But church scholarship, as well as sectarian philosophy, suffered, and still suffers, much from the darkness of prejudices and blind orthodoxies. The so-called Reformation, while doing much good in freeing us from some of these things, failed to address, may, in fact, have been incapable of doing so, much of the results of the Dark Ages. Renaissance art displays a great deal of this ignorance.

The creative process, the gift of imagination, the yearning we have to learn, the ability to love sacrificially, is all a part of our being made in the image of God. As Jesus affirmed, we are gods.

A great scientist and philosopher, John Scott Haldane, made the comment concerning the Universe: The universe may be not only queerer than we suppose, but queerer than we can suppose.

Considering the fact humans have the God-given ability to imagine truly fantastic things, that is quite a statement. Yet I can't help but believe that when Jesus said he was going to prepare a place for us, he meant the creative acts of God are still on going in that vastness beyond our imagination. And I believe we will be involved with that on-going creation.

The Bible declares: Eye has not seen nor ear heard, neither has entered into the heart of man the things that God has prepared for us. It is a part of the creative effort that you should try and fail. We ascribe that to human frailty.

But in this context I believe God is far more human than the churches give him credit. I believe Jesus understood and chose that title, Son of Man, out of pride and hope for all of us as children of God.

There is a work for us in eternity. As we gaze at the stars in wonder and yearning we know, in our souls, that we are going to enter into a work the supposed angels cannot do, a work that requires gods, children of God, born of Him, in His plans for us to help and cooperate in His on-going creative efforts.

A host of godly scholars will have to undertake the New Systematic Theology I have proposed, but nothing short of this will do the job. My question is: Where shall we find such men? And the women who, on the basis of equal value, will be the inspiration and helpers of such men? In the meantime, if we do our part, I believe God will surely do His. If we do all that we are required to do, if we do right no matter what others do, the consequences are entirely in God's hands and we need fear no one or no thing.

As with the problem of the conflict that has always existed between men and women from the allegory of The Fall on, if it were simple we would have solved it long ago. In the speculations of nature and God's plans for humanity, it is not simple. To treat it so is to fly in the face of the facts. God isn't simple and neither are we.

In spite of the enormity of the task of the study required, it pales beside another factor: Our ability to come together and put our differences and prejudices aside in the search for truth.

But I live in hope of this. Why? Because I have changed.

Anyone who knew me fifteen-years ago would have difficulty recognizing me as the man who used to hold some of the views I once held. And to put the best face on it, if a man so obstinate and of such strong opinions (Read: plain bull-headed) as I can change, so can others.

For example, when I was very young in the faith, I became a card-carrying Pharisee of the Pharisees. No exaggeration. The outside of my cup was so squeaky clean that I could quickly judge who was saved and who was not, who was spiritual and who was not.

I ashamedly admit of the time I and a few other young Pharisees of whom I was the leader attended a kind of ecumenical social gathering. At the time I was the president of Christian Endeavor for the Centinella Valley.

There happened to be a young Lutheran pastor in attendance and we struck up a conversation. He seemed enthusiastic and we were getting along nicely until he took out a cigarette and lit it. I rudely and abruptly ended the conversation and turned my back to this young pastor.

If I could speak to him now I would beg him on my knees to forgive me. I was the spiritual giant and how could any so-called minister smoke! God has long since taken me to the woodshed and certainly has not spared the rod on this poor sinner.

The spiritual pride, ego and sheer arrogance of those younger days are long past. But as a result, if any man has more just cause to question his own wisdom than I do, I know of no such man. I am sometimes in amazement and awe of how one man, myself, could, in just one short lifetime make as many mistakes as I have!

And when it comes to raising a family? Name the mistake and I made it. When it comes to selfishness, few could surpass me. If there is one man on the face of the earth more intimately acquainted with the dark side of human nature I don't know of him.

Not one word of this is to be construed as false humility. I have one of the most devious and cunning minds you could possibly imagine. I have lived the life of the most successful con man; that is the one who believes in his own virtue! I know how to manipulate with the best. And I know full well those thoughts that most of us have, those monstrous things that come unbidden to our minds that if any suspected us of such thoughts we would die of mortification!

I was one of God's hard-cases. I could excuse anything on the basis of rationalizing it away. If I was convinced I was right, by the deceitfulness of my own vile heart, I could make it a holy cause with the best of them and bless it with a text!

There is a man I know who has made his family pay a high price for doing what he is convinced is right. He has driven the family into penury for what he believes is a work for the honor of God and the saving of our nation.

He is wrong! I was such a man myself. It took the loss of my family together with some other extraordinary circumstances to bring me to God's view of the matter.

As Christ is the head of the Church, so is a man the head over his family. Well and good. That's Scriptural and men applaud.

However! That man is the head over his family for the good of that family just as Christ is the head over the Church for the good of the Church!

To the religious, as I used to be, I will use the words of Scripture to make a point:

Men, your first responsibility and obligation before God is that family! And in the words of Scripture: If any not provide for his own he is worse than an infidel and has denied the faith! I Timothy 5:8. What, gentlemen, could be plainer?

Looking at this objectively, it makes perfect sense: As goes the family so goes a nation! And so goes the Church!

Because of my own sin and failure, my own mistakes in so many different areas of life, I have become a most unwilling expert on the wrong things to do, of the dark side of our fallen nature, the Old Corrupt Adam!

So when I speak of such things, I know whereof I speak. And the things I have tried to call attention to have been bought with a price. And sometimes the innocent victims of my own self-righteousness paid the price.

With that thought in mind, I close with the admonition that the churches will never be agents of change for morality, for substantive change for the Good, until they examine their wholly untenable dualistic, failed theology. I adamantly oppose the position that evil is essential for good!

No form of Calvinistic lapsarianism, supra, infra, etc. to which all philosophies, non-religious as well as Christian, Jewish, Moslem, Buddhist, etc. subscribe in one way or the other, will do. All dualistic philosophies of men that would try to make God responsible for preordaining evil fail upon honest examination.

If we were on the right track in any of these, war, being the most unreasonable act of man, would cease and peace would reign supreme!

Such an honest examination of the present, orthodox abandonment theology, teaching that God alone will overcome the evil, that we, as gods, are not responsible for subduing evil, would, I believe, be the catalyst for the churches finally finding common ground of agreement.

But I don't minimize the extreme difficulty facing the churches in trying to deal with orthodox prejudices centuries in the making.

Tom Paine, most would agree, was not a nice guy. But without him there would never have been a War for Independence birthing the freest nation in history, a beacon of hope for the rest of the world, legitimate arguments against this notwithstanding.

It was essential that Paine faced the truth and dealt with facts to pull the colonies together in common cause. But it was equally essential that he move the hearts of the people.

Oddly, it was infidels like Paine and Franklin, men who questioned orthodox religion, which gave us a nation conceived in justice, liberty, and concomitant personal responsibility. It was not the churches. But not so odd once you have examined the orthodoxy of the churches.

And in all honesty, we must admit, as Franklin and a few others did, the beginning was flawed on the basis of slavery. Not to mention failing to recognize women as being of equal value to men.

A theology that deals with the facts and moves hearts is essential for these times. The present theology (not to mention the philosophies of men) of the churches has failed to do this, and the price is the potential for our nation to become enslaved to a world dictator, a French Revolution and anarchy. Or, a nuclear Armageddon.

You cannot sugarcoat such possibilities by saying only those things pleasing to the ear and expect action by the people.

By trying to pass off a theology, or any philosophy, that is unable to take decisive action against an evil system, against evil people, you join yourself to accommodating the evil.

I love children. In our present welfare and prisons (our growth industries) society, I confront an ugly fact of present life.

I was a classroom teacher during the change when it became risky to put a friendly hand on your students or give them a hug of encouragement, when the vulgarity and profanity of teachers exceeded that of the students.

A couple of little neighbor girls like to visit me. I'm a grandpa and, at first, I was delighted to see them. There was no father in the home and one could only guess at the circumstances that made them need a loving grandpa.

But I'm unmarried, living alone. I realized that all one of these precious little girls would have to do is make any kind of statement, or be led to make some statement, that could be construed as improper behavior on my part toward them to, at the very least, make me a candidate for prison.

I'm forced under the circumstances to try to make it clear to these little ones that I cannot have them visiting me. That is hard, that is cruel. Especially toward little ones that need all the love they can get.

Now if the molesters of children were killed like the rattlesnakes they are, not many dirty old men would have to be exterminated before they got the message, and little girls and boys would be safe from such predators. But can you imagine the churches of today taking the lead in such action? Not hardly.

There is always a high price to be paid for excellence whether academic, artistic or industrial. Excellence in pursuing the Truth in the cause of freedom and justice requires the very best effort of time and resources.

And allowing the rattlesnakes to have it their way cannot do it by perversions of laws that pervert the cause of justice, and some fuzzy-minded distortion of civilized behavior. Reptiles like rattlesnakes know nothing of civilized behavior, of law, and most certainly have no conception of justice.

By the compulsion generated through long years of experience and study, I am far removed from accepting a status quo that is the enemy of all that is pure and beautiful. Like most of you I want happy endings to love stories, I want Tony and Maria to be the winners in West Side Story. And they could have been if it had not been for the ugliness of orthodox prejudices.

But there are evil, ugly people who, not knowing of the love and poetry of romance and having no chance of such in their own lives, try to profane and destroy all that is beautiful. These children of the devil, as the serpent in the Garden, know how to deceive by bringing God's righteous love into question, by getting others to believe that there is no reward for virtue.

I want to work for a world where the Tonys and Marias have a chance, where my children have a chance for the poetry and music of life. I will never accept that it cannot be done, that good people are going to continue to cave in to the Cainites by default.

But I know this can never happen without just standards of morality, without doing battle against the enemies of righteousness.

And this will never happen as long as the enemy continues to be so successful in subverting the truth by calling people like myself bigoted, homophobic, etc., for standing up for the Truth! These perverted liars have their appointed place set for them in the Lake of Fire (once more, by whatever means or definition). But I will continue my best efforts to make that an expeditious appointment for them.

A race that can produce the music and poetry that we have, that can love as we can, cannot help but have within it the capacity to fight for these things.

I never tire of the great Broadway musicals. I have said that they represent the last time poets worked in America. Why is this? What happened to the inspiration of the genius of romance that produced such masterpieces of the art of love as The Sound of Music? There is a greater and more powerful sermon in this great musical and South Pacific than any I have ever preached or heard!

Why have such beautiful works of art given way to the loss of the hope of such things and fallen into the hopelessness of the ugly, vulgar and profane?

An evil system has been allowed to rob our children of love and romance, of hope of a future. And unless we take a stand, no, more than a stand, unless we decide to do battle, what can we offer our children?

Children have a right to be able to dream. That young girl and boy have a right to hope for love and romance. But only if they are taught to honor virtue.

And where is the reward for virtue to be found if our children are constantly confronted by the successes of evil and the wicked continue to prosper?

Virtually no one would realize or admit that they are blaming God by their prayers. Yet that is exactly what most people do when they ask things of God that are their responsibility!

For example, my children had a right to expect me to act for them in many ways as their father. They had a right to expect me to love, feed and clothe them, to provide for them all the necessities of life.

Of course, in love, I tried to give them all I could, and, most importantly, I tried to prepare them to face an adult world.

But when my children were grown it became their responsibility to provide for themselves, to act and think for themselves.

One thing remained unchanged; my love for them. I continued to work for them as I could, to advise them when possible, but the work of adults was now their responsibility.

If any of my children make a mistake that puts them in a position where, in spite of my love, there is nothing I can do for them, they have to bear the consequences.

For example, a grown son commits a crime and goes to prison. Not all the love of the parent can free the child. If he commits murder, not all the love of the parent can redeem that lost life and make restitution.

The child no longer has a right to ask the parent to undertake for him in such cases. Nor does the child have a right to continue to ask the parent to feed and clothe him, to ask the parent for those things that are adult responsibilities the child should reasonably provide for himself.

As parents, we always want to do all we can for our children. But we realize that once grown, they must bear the consequences of their own decisions.

The one thing that never changes is the love of the parent for the child. It is that constant, never failing love that the grown child should always be able to depend on. And that continuing love is the thing from which the child will always draw strength.

But how much of prayer is actually the adult son or daughter of God blaming him for not providing things that are the responsibility of the adult child? If we are grown adult children of God, why ask him to do things or provide things that are our adult responsibility?

God's love, as with any parent, should be the strength of our actions. We have a right to depend on his never failing love and guidance in making decisions that lead to action. But the actions are now our adult responsibility!

Yet we will come to God asking him to do things that are our responsibility! We ask him to do something about the suffering in the world, about continuing wars and conflict between people!

Are we not, in fact, blaming God for those things that are our responsibility? Of course we are!

We ask God to deliver us, to bring judgment against the wicked when it is our responsibility to take the necessary action to confront evil and overcome it! And then we will blame God for not doing that which is our responsibility!

There are things I cannot do for my grown children. There are things our Heavenly Parents cannot do for their grown children. But unless we stop moaning, bitching and complaining, unless we stop blaming Dad and Mom and do the things that only we can do, not them, nothing will change for the better.

Don't try that "God can do anything!" line on me. It won't wash and it never has. That is a cop-out, pure and simple, that is the party line of man-made religions from time immemorial!

Only when we learn and accept the fact that God is limited in what He/She can do for us will we be able to take our lives in hand as responsible adults and fight to win against the evil! As long as we continue to blame them, making them the scapegoats for our miserable failures, we cannot hope to do battle against the wicked successfully!

While the great majority of people will reject what I have said, I suggest that if they think of this sensibly and objectively apart from their prejudiced, blind orthodoxies, they will see the logic of it.

I have many friends who, out of consideration for my welfare, out of genuine concern for my soul, have tried to dissuade me from some of my heretical views, who have cautioned me not to put such things in print.

My question to you, the reader, and my friends is this: Prove I'm wrong and tell me how your orthodox positions are changing things for the better, how you are fighting the battle against evil to win? Show me how your interpretation of Scripture, how your ideas of the nature of God and humankind are giving you victory against wickedness and wicked people? How are you making a difference in the care, protection and feeding, of the millions of children who are suffering? How does your theology actually work in a practical sense?

Bottom line: My friends have no answers to these questions. They continue to hold on to an abandonment theology, dualistic doctrines that make God responsible for evil, not them. Like the child caught in a lie or petty theft, they will try to deny this. All they know is that I'm wrong and they have the truth. They just aren't able to prove it.

And, after all, since God is in control of everything, since Jesus is bound to show up eventually, it isn't even our responsibility to fight!

But to continue to hold the view that God can do it on his/their own, that they do not need our help and cooperation, that we are not, in fact, gods ourselves with that family responsibility, is to face the continued successes of the wicked.

Now you know the title of this book is not intended to convey the idea it is all up to God to fix that which is our responsibility. But to sincerely ask, "Hey, God! What went wrong and when are you going to fix it?" is a perfectly legitimate question.

Yes, I believe God, our Heavenly Parents possibly, made errors out of love just as we do. But we learn through the errors of love, we learn to discriminate as we grow up. Yet the ideals of love never change. Love cannot live in suspicion and distrust; it never becomes cynical. It never fails in hoping that this time, it will work; that the one loved and trusted will never betray.

I will probably die a poet. Why? Because in spite of the many errors and failures of love, in spite of the continual betrayal of love and trust, I cannot let go of the dream and I cannot stop loving. It's a gift. And perhaps I have just described the heart of God.

It takes two artists working together to make the dream come true as God intended between a man and a woman. But when the dream comes true, you have the foundation for virtue and goodness in a family. And from the family comes the virtue and goodness of a nation. When those things are being done that make children and the family the most important priority in our nation then we will be able to have hope. And only then can we offer such hope to our children!

Chapter sixteen

Some Closing Thoughts

Being a simple country boy, modest, unassuming and self-effacing (to a fault some have said), and of no particular ambition but going fishing and making love to every beautiful woman I meet, it seems patently ridiculous for me to be writing books. But I have written a book. Actually, I've written several and they are good books; however, with "HEY, GOD! What went wrong and when are you going to fix it?" I have written a book.

During the research and writing I had to put off many tasks that had a cumulative detrimental effect. For example, I had to forego the semi-annual (more or less) washing of my windows and chores such as dusting and removing cobwebs from implements of infrequent use like the TV, stove and vacuum cleaner.

Some correspondence suffered as well. I lost $10,000,000 by failing to mail my guaranteed winning number to Publisher's Clearing House and a free Caribbean cruise, a free trip to Vegas and my free gift of Ex-in-laws, Episcopalians and gopher repellent, satisfaction guaranteed.

But there was one benefit from the total absorption of the book, I forgot to shave. As a result, my beard, requiring little effort on my part to grow, will be suitable for playing Santa Claus for the grandchildren this Christmas.

Of course Walt Kelly and Tom Lehrer made their contributions and deserve honorable mention. Tom's Vatican Rag, The Old Dope Peddler, I Wanna Go Back to Dixie, Smut and National Brotherhood Week has always provided me inspiration and hope for the human race.

With HEY, GOD! I know I have written a book; a book some have told me would change the world if enough people read it. That's nice. The world needs changing. Of course if that should happen, reserving the caveat that the book results in changes for the better, I deserve the Nobel and Pulitzer.

Because I'm a poet, musician and romantic, I lose myself in the great Broadway and film musicals. I have sung to women and had some sing to me. It hasn't been a fantasy, it has actually happened. I've loved several women and they have said they loved me. But the music ended quickly in most cases. Maybe because I needed Audrey or Maria but never found her. The idealization of the poet's love is holding that woman, looking into her eyes, singing to her and having that look and that song returned in kind. Failing this, the best I could do was to offer my faithful love, the kind of love that keeps its nose to the grindstone, caring for wife and family and, in short, working out your love in the traditional ways.

Tragically, the poet may slumber, but he never dies. He lies there, growing restless and, at last aroused, becomes something the great majority of women do not know how to accept. But the majority of women don't know how to have a man look into their eyes while he sings to them.

The majority of men and women know nothing of writing love letters. The poet is compelled to write them. The majority of men and women know nothing of opening their very heart and soul. Again, this is a compulsion of the poet. A poet knows little of secret compartments of the heart and mind, he tells all, even when that all is hard and ugly. He does not know how to practice the hypocrisy of presenting a carefully barbered and perfumed, well-tailored facade in the place of the truth.

But it doesn't take a poet to dream or want those dreams to come true. All those possessed of a conscience, a soul want to love and be loved. We want an ending where the lovers live happily ever after. And we want that happy ending for ourselves.

What does it take to play a part convincingly? How did Shirley Jones and Julie Andrews learn to sing to a man and look so convincingly in love with Gordon MacRea and Christopher Plummer? Shirley and Julie knew how to love. They were in love as they played their parts. For the men and women who give us our enduring fantasies of such love and romance, the best know how to love and, while the play goes on they live that love.

But you must be practical! Yes, there is no getting around that one.

Love and romance don't go well with an empty stomach and no roof over your head. However, even provided the necessities, few women ever find their Knight and few men their Audrey Hepburn, Shirley Jones or Julie Andrews.

Now, in the September of my life, I have come to some conclusions as to why this seldom is the case, why the right man and woman have such difficulty meeting each other; if I have to settle for Audrey in my reverie if we are only able to have each other in our dreams that will have to do; at that, it is more than most ever have.

Why? Because I know my Audrey, wherever she is, is faithful to our love in spite of the fact that we never found each other in this life. Granted that sounds a poor substitute for the reality. But I maintain it is more than most ever have. Why? Because Audrey and I know real love and romance; we know there is no substitute for this regardless the realities. Somewhere out there is Audrey; a woman who knows the love I have just as I know the love she has, a love that regardless of never finding its fulfillment in each other keeps the dream alive, keeps us alive.

It is the kind of love that inspires to the best art, music, literature of humanity, the kind of love that moves hearts and minds in these things, that has true immortality, deathless because it is the very heart of God himself!

There is a faith in love to be considered. Those who have such a faith are saved by it. They are the true believers that know, in their hearts, that no matter what, love conquers all! I live, and move and have my being in love. I live in the music, the poetry, literature and art of love. I always have, though the poet gave place at times in order to meet the necessities of practicalities and the too oft times ugly realities of life.

I nourished the poet at times with a wilderness trout stream where the joyous, chuckling, sparkling water cascading over rocks, spraying and flashing into countless diamonds shooting off refracted, iridescent rays of dappled sunshine, plunging through short rapids became gleaming waterfalls descending into crystal clear pools. I would take him to the oceans where the scent and sound of the sea and the crashing of the waves against gleaming sands or rocky shore left marvels in their retreat. And watch a bloodburst sunset in wonder at that magnificent vista of water across which lay the islands of imagination, of the Bali Hai's of the mind and soul. Then we would go to the desert, so clean without the corruption of fences, asphalt, concrete and man-made structures and marvel at the sere vastness with nights so clear we could count every grain of sand in the moonlight.

When I made music with clarinet, saxophone, guitar or my voice, the inspiration in the music was Audrey. Her name at the time might have been Susan or Ann, but it was Audrey that remained; Susan and Ann never did.

In the yard of my little house in the country, I sit outside of a summer evening and watch the sunset gradually give place to a platinum-colored twilight. The trees and the hills in the distance become dark silhouettes and stars begin to appear in the canopy of heaven and I listen to my private, heavenly choir of the rustling of the leaves and branches by a warm, scented breeze and the last music of the birds now beginning to be replaced by the peeping of tiny frogs and the chirrup of crickets.

Evening deepens into the quiet, smooth velvet of darkness and I gaze at the stars, Ursa Major and the immense Milky Way and Audrey is with me though I sit alone. And at that, I'm not nearly as alone as countless who don't even see the stars or even consider sharing them with another.

I don't blame Susan or Ann for not being able to abide the poet; they felt ignored by him. His thoughts were on Audrey and they simply couldn't be her; it wasn't their nature. At first, they thought they were Audrey. There were the times when they thought they shared the enchantment of God's marvelous creation, that they even thanked the poet for pointing such things out to them.

The poet would place a rose on their nightstand. He would try to tell them the thoughts of his heart. He believed the closeness of their warmth and softness as women a sacred thing. But invariably, Susan and Ann would prove they didn't really value the things of the poet. They couldn't be Audrey. The poet, because he couldn't betray, would simply retreat and go to sleep. Eventually, Susan and Ann would find someone else, someone more practical with common sense and not given to dreams.

I don't know that Audrey would have agreed with some of the things I wrote in my book, HEY, GOD! but I know she would have agreed on one of the direct results of the book for the protection of children. Looking at my criticism in the book of the churches failing to take the leadership in being agents for positive change, it occurred to me that I should put my money where my mouth is.

As a result, I have proposed a Constitutional Amendment for the protection of children. I wish Audrey were here to help me with it. I know she would.

The proposed amendment reads as follows:

AMERICANS FOR CONSTITUTIONAL PROTECTION OF CHILDREN

Proposed amendment to the U.S. Constitution

An adult convicted of the molestation of a child will be sentenced to prison for a term of not less than ten years.

If the child dies as a result of the molestation, the person(s) convicted of the crime will be sentenced to life in prison without the possibility of parole.

A child, as defined by this amendment, shall be a boy or girl who has not attained his or her sixteenth birthday.

This amendment clearly defines the felony and punishment, but the powers of enforcement, prosecution and penalty are reserved to the states respectively or to the people.

There is not a single Constitutional Amendment that specifically addresses children. Yet we pay lip service to the dictum that: No nation that fails to cherish its young has a future as a nation. I always add: Nor does it deserve one!

With the help of California State Senator, Don Rogers, I initiated a proposal for an amendment to the U.S. Constitution that would protect children at the most fundamental level, protection from molestation.

It is essential that such protection be universal. An amendment would serve this purpose. If child molesters knew they faced federal prosecution and life in prison without parole, it would be the strongest kind of deterrent and save many of the Polly Klaas's.

People have lost faith in our system of government. And how

can the people have faith in a system that cannot even protect their children?

An amendment would empower the people by giving them a chance to stand up and take action in a cause that declares our love for our children. It simply cannot be left to the several states to do this on an individual basis. The laws protecting children from molesters are too ambiguous, voluminous and far from being in accord from state-to-state.

For the first time parents, family, a nation can directly address a specific, positive step by which We the People can show we care about children and family values. It is my earnest conviction that this would be a mechanism that could draw our nation together in common cause.

When you consider the fact that fully one-third of little girls suffers some form of molestation, this goes a long way in explaining some of the major problems in America. This amendment would serve notice that the people of America intend to protect the rights of children to be children in all innocence, that Americans cherish their young, our posterity, that we are, in fact, a moral nation.

Just the fight for such an amendment will pay vast dividends in making the enemies and predators of children, of family, the enemies of our posterity, declare themselves. I can think of no better way of bringing good people together in common cause. Our children have no voice or choice. It is our duty to speak and act for them.

Such an amendment will reduce prison and welfare populations. In the shorter term, it is well-substantiated fact that babies having babies are to blame for an enormous burden on taxpayers. These babies of girls as young as eleven-years-old are invariably doomed to substandard care which increases medical costs. As such children grow, they are far more likely to be anti-social, illiterate and begin early, criminal activities loading our juvenile justice systems, and, eventually, our courts, jails and prisons.

If adult molesters of such girls faced life in prison, I guarantee there would be an immediate impact on this problem that is contributing to so much heartache and fiscal difficulty in our nation. In the longer term, there will be fewer such children growing up to a life of crime, thereby reducing prison populations. Fewer such children being born will have a dramatic effect on our economy by reducing the problems they create for the schools, medical care and other financial burdens to the taxpayer.

A somewhat more subjective, but to me, major factor is what this amendment will do for a lower divorce rate and the strengthening of family in this nation. Women will be forced to a much more careful consideration of choices of stepfathers or live-ins if divorced, particularly the mothers of young girls. Better to make the marriage work.

Unquestionably, when we are dealing with the fact that over one-third of our little girls are molested in one way or another; the trauma carries into their adult relationships, especially marriage. By radically reducing such molestations, we have taken a huge step toward establishing healthy marriages, and, by extension, a healthier society.

Consider the boys that are molested and the enormous cost, mentally, socially and fiscally to America. Such boys are far more likely than others to be involved in crime and sociopathic, anti-social behavior are. This amendment will virtually eliminate the inhumanity and national disgrace of child prostitution. By force of law, it will encourage sexual restraint, self-discipline and responsibility and greatly reduce the number of abortions.

It will also dramatically impact Child Protective Services, forcing that agency to act in a far more humane, responsible and professional manner. There is no doubt in my mind, having worked in this agency myself, that with the power of such law as this amendment, CPS will have to do a better job of identifying, establishing factual case evidence and removing the predators of children.

Even if this were not a question of morality, the fiscal impact alone makes it deserving of our best efforts.

My hope for passage of such an amendment is based on several facts. One being that it hits at the heart of all Americans regardless of race, creed or political views. Also, if the fiscal impact can be made clear to Americans, this alone would insure passage.

For my part, I will try to make the message one of empowering the people to take action against an evil on which we all agree, action that We the People can take in spite of Caesar! If we can succeed in just this one thing, you know the hope it will give Americans that we really can do something positive for the future of our children, for the future of America!

With success in just this one thing to start, imagine where Americans, inspired with such hope that they can take control and make positive changes for the better, might be able to go from here in correcting some of the other evils that are destroying America!

Few people know the actual laws concerning molestation. Having worked in the schools and CPS, I had to know them.

In dealing with the arguments against this amendment, I have to confront much ignorance on the part of those who do not know such laws but have much assumed knowledge about the subject.

One example of such ignorance is the person who said to me: "You can be arrested if a child accuses you of molesting him!" Incredible as it seems, this man actually believed this. Why? Because he had heard something somewhere! You would think such ignorance impossible. But it's out there and has to be confronted.

No one can be arrested on the basis of a child's accusation. Yes, the police and/or CPS might take a report. But an arrest is predicated on evidence and investigation, not simply an accusation whether by child or adult. In this respect, the laws concerning suspected or alleged molestation are no different than the multitude of other laws governing the actions of police leading to arrest and prosecution for a crime.

Yes, the reputation of a person can suffer simply on the basis of such an accusation. But that is true of any number of other things that can destroy a person's reputation regardless of guilt or innocence. As with any crime of which a person is accused, guilt must be established beyond doubt. The amendment must automatically follow due process, a right already established and guaranteed by the Constitution.

What the amendment will accomplish by federal guarantee is prosecution of those who have enough evidence against them to be arrested and charged for the crime, not suspicion of the crime.

The most pervasive argument against the amendment comes from those who believe the amendment is too draconian, from those that believe that the child molester is sick, not a criminal. The crux of this argument is the perception that child molestation is not the result of criminal intent, that it is not serious enough to incarcerate a person for life. I will answer this by saying that first and foremost, a child has a right to be a child, to be raised in a loving environment in all the innocence of childhood. No one would disagree that molestation emotionally scars a child for the rest of his or her life. Try living with that! The molester has done something to the child that literally imposes a life sentence on the child!

The molested child is likely to engage in aberrant, sexual behavior. This perpetuates a vicious chain of victims. I know personally of one case where there were 32 counts of molestation involving eighteen children molested by one person! Out of those eighteen children, some will go on to molest others. Only keeping the molester in prison will break this chain.

As to being sick, this is a sickness that admits of no cure in spite of claims to the contrary. You're a psychologist or psychiatrist who subscribes to the sick theory. Very well, treat the molester in prison where he belongs! I suggest, however, that the molester be kept apart from the general, prison population or that separate facilities be provided.

The molester is a predator. If a mountain lion leaves its natural habitat and starts preying on pets, even children in another environment, we don't say: The poor lion must be understood and treated for its aberrant behavior. No, we hunt down and shoot the lion if it has attacked a person. Why? Because we know an animal like a lion that behaves in such a manner is not susceptible to treatment to correct such behavior. It will never learn not to attack people.

Few of us would have any compunction about shooting a lion or mad dog that threatened a child. "That thing is trying to kill the child!" you say. Since the molester, in most cases, is not trying to kill the child we don't consider him a mad dog. But he is.

In the instance of a molester who makes a child of thirteen pregnant, what happens; Abortion. But if not abortion and she has the baby, what happens? Typically she goes on welfare. And, as happens many times, the baby is born with defects and the hospital and medical costs ($5,000 a week to keep a crack baby breathing!) to the taxpayers are enormous!

If the molester is arrested and imprisoned he gets out and continues his depredations. Will the molester be responsible for the babies he has fathered? You know the answer to that one. The baby and typically the child-mother become a lifetime cost to the taxpayers. The victims of molester's go far beyond the child molested.

Because the victim of molest is not murdered the death penalty is not appropriate for the child molester. There is a victim but the victim's life has not been taken. As to the murder of the innocence of the one raped or molested? They will have to cope as best they can.

But it will help immeasurably for the victim to know that the mad dog, the predator will never have opportunity to do such a thing to someone else! And it will help immeasurably for the victim and witnesses to know they need never fear this animal coming for them when released from prison, that there will never be another victim of his depredation! And I maintain the victim has this right to that much peace of mind!

Ask yourself why molestation is not taken as such a serious matter in society? You may surprise yourself at some of your answers. The bottom line to this is that we, as a society, have been trained not to think about it so seriously.

Since girls, far more than boys, are the victims of molest, this points out a problem of tremendous magnitude concerning a society's attitude toward molestation.

Girls and women are there to be used by men! Girls and women do not have the value of men!

My books: Hey, God! Birds With Broken Wings, and The Missing Half of Humankind: Women! address the truth, the facts of this problem. But you would have to read these books to gain an appreciation of the monstrous magnitude of the problem, its history and dimensions, its impact on the whole history of the human race and how it affects virtually everyone today!

Suffice it here to say that the problem of the relationship between men and women is the most difficult, intractable problem with which the human race has to deal, a problem of such complexity and intractability that it has never admitted of a solution!

Yet look at its importance. As goes the relationship between the sexes, so goes a nation. But, I ask in the book: "Why are women totally excluded from philosophy and theology?" I answer: "Because they have no value beyond sex!" The natural, historical resentment of women is thus easily understood. Molesters act on this premise. They know girls and women have no value apart from sex and as a result society, led typically of men, will not act against the molester effectively.

We keep boys and girls in school until they are 17 or 18 years old. But do we consider such teenagers children? No. That is the reason for the amendment dealing with children under the age of 16. It isn't because 17 and 18 year olds are adults. But our society treats them as such sexually. These children are marrying in our society. Our entertainment media encourages, extols their sexuality. We have taught such children that they should be sexually active or there is something wrong with them!

It would be naive indeed to think that children as young as six and seven aren't getting this message as well and responding to it. And just as children are now raping and killing children thanks to the messages received primarily through the sex and violence of TV, videos and movies, the so-called music they are exposed to, the pornographers, pedophiles and molesters have taken advantage of an amoral climate to increase their activities to the most dreadful detriment of our future as a nation!

I can think of nothing as effective to changing our direction as a nation, to tell our children that we do love them and care about their future as this amendment. Draconian? Only in respect to what we, as a society, have been taught to accept and live with.

But who have been our teachers? The psychologists and university professors that have multitudes of theories but do not contribute anything in the way of substantive solutions aided by the entertainment media that is selling the sex and violence as normal.

Or are they those homosexuals and molesters in the Congress and judiciary who like little boys and teenage girls? Nothing you can name will so expose and call down the wrath of the enemies and predators of children, and our nation, as this amendment! But parents, people who love children and America, who know the future of our nation rests on our children will be in favor of the amendment.

This is not to say that some honest people won't have difficulty with it. And that is their right as Americans. I ask these, however, to examine the amendment and its ramifications as objectively as possible. This, I fully realize, is asking a lot, especially in view of how we, as a society, have been so successfully propagandized and brain washed in viewing molesters as poor people who need treatment for their sickness.

But unless the chain is broken, it will continue to grow worse and worse with no end in sight. I have a perfect example of how difficult it is to face our prejudices.

A friend of some years recently dissociated himself from me for a short time because of a letter to the editor I wrote. This friend was ordained as an Episcopal Priest but went into selling real estate. I quoted Sam Clemens' remarks concerning an Episcopal minister, one reverend Sabine, which were not complementary of this man of the cloth. I certainly did not, nor did Clemens, denounce all Episcopalians. And in Sam's defense, he had the highest regard for the Gospel and Jesus Christ and had some close friends who were ministers though he loved poking fun at the hypocrisy of religiosity.

To make matters worse, I mentioned something in the letter about the distrust people have of used car and real estate salesmen. This friend, this outstanding example of Christian living, a man with a good heart astounded me by calling and abusing me terribly for the letter.

I was dumbfounded by his hypocrisy! I never thought him capable of such a thing. I pointed out to him, when I could get a word in, that if Clemens had made his remarks about a Baptist minister, my friend would have laughed. I pointed out that next to congressmen and lawyers (samo samo) used car and real estate salesmen come next in public distrust.

Now I have a good friend, a state senator, who never takes exception to my generic remarks concerning politicians. I know this man, an honorable man, is the exception to the rule and he never takes my remarks personally knowing full well that politicians, by and large, are scoundrels.

But my friend, a good Episcopalian and real estate salesman, could not see the hypocrisy of his stand. He could not accept that while he might be the exception to the rule, the public opinion of used car and real estate salesmen is one of proverbial distrust. Worse, he took my letter as a denunciation of him personally. He had no basis whatsoever for doing so.

The point being that when blind orthodoxy and prejudice hold sway, it is extremely difficult for the person to recognize it in their own life. Like the religious person who reads the Scriptures and never sees the obvious contradictions and corruptions in the texts, who knows nothing of good textual criticism and scholarship and worships a book rather than the truth of God, there are those like those Pharisees of old who are willingly blind!

Go ahead and knock the Baptists and Catholics, lawyers and used car salesmen but Episcopalians and real estate salesmen are sacrosanct and above reproach! Right. But my friend needs to take a look at the vast number of complaints to the state real estate board and lawsuits against realtors. They run a close second to auto mechanics that still hold the top spot.

Does it occur to people like this good Episcopalian, since he is so righteous, to fight for cleaning up the mess in his own backyard so he has an organization that is, in fact, above such reproach as that of Sam Clemens? Not likely.

Whose ox is gored? In the case of people who are merely religious, people who have no interest in the real truth, I expect no help with this amendment. While there are good people in the churches who will help in its passage, it is not a church issue; it is a We the People issue.

Further, I think it reasonable to accept as a fact that a Hindu, Buddhist, Moslem, Jew, Republican or Democrat loves their child as much as any calling themselves Christian.

But there is a most disturbing factor that has to be considered in this. I deal with it in my book. The fact is that we may be talking about a genetic factor, at least in part. There is such a thing as learned behavior. In other words, there are behaviors that can be learned or changed and have nothing to do with genetics.

I suggest in my book that in some cases we are dealing with people that have no conscience, people like the serial killer that may, in fact, be of another species. Before you write this off, let me offer one point for your consideration. Recent studies with mice have located a mother gene. Mice without this gene do not nurture their young and let them starve to death.

In my book I write of studies in subatomic particle physics and how such things may impact on behavior, especially in the paranormal having to do with things like precognition, prescience and telepathy. No one questions that such things are factual; we just don't understand the mechanism at work in such cases. And, to date, they are not understood well enough to submit to strict, scientific examination in a controlled environment making replication nearly impossible.

I also suggest in the book that when the Bible refers to the seed of the woman and the seed of the serpent, we are talking about two, different species of creation. The cold-blooded murderer and sadist may be a child of the devil quite literally. The compassionate children of God may be another species quite apart. Now if studies in genetics, together with studies of subatomic particle physics and PSI (paranormal research) should determine that there is, in fact, two species of creatures called Man?

Ion therapy works. Anions, negatively charged atoms, are beneficial in cases of depression. We don't know why. The discovery of the antiproton in 1955 and the antineutron in 1956 proved the existence of antimatter. A mirror, opposite image or doppelganger, of the proton, neutron and electron means, theoretically, that there may be planets and stars out there somewhere made of antimatter. But such material could not exist with what we call normal matter. The two different charges, brought together, would result in their mutual destruction with the resulting release of tremendous amounts of radiant energy.

I mention these things only to point out the fact that with the existence of things beyond our imagination, beyond our field of reality, there exist realities we know little or nothing about. As with my story of Karrie and the bear, in the HEY, GOD! book I warn there is a bear coming that, like the Scopes trial, the churches and religion in general are not prepared to deal with.

The recent announcement of a computer to be completed in 1999 that will have such huge capacity as to be able to emulate an atomic explosion may be the leading edge to astounding discoveries in particle research. What we have been lacking in studies of PSI is the ability to discover patterns of brain function and how atomic and subatomic particles impact on our emotions, even physical health and how gene patterns predict certain behaviors.

A computer that can emulate a pattern in an exploding star could conceivably discern patterns in brain function, those fractal/symphonic billions of firings of neurons, and account for anomalies of behavior, even PSI abilities.

We have a long way to go but I maintain hope. Perhaps, as with Napoleon's dream of wars fought and won without cannon and bayonet, we can let go our prejudices, the solution of the paradox of good and evil may yet be understood. But it will take Renaissance Men, men and women, studied in a multitude of different disciplines rather than specialists, to discern the patterns in so much seeming chaos enabling us to make sense of it all and suggest courses of action.

Some of these people will have to be expert in the philosophy of physics as well as human behavior. They will have to have the genius to be able to bridge the gap between the hard and the social/behavioral sciences. To bring the arts and the sciences together on a common ground of understanding has been the Holy Grail of the true poet, his personal Grand Unification Theory. While people tremble in fear of a bloody French Revolution in the near future, if enough of us help God as is our responsibility as gods ourselves according to Jesus Christ, as adult children of God we can resist the Devil and prevent his having it all his way.

When I was a very young man, I had the privilege of the intimate friendship of one of the greatest scholars of the Bible of modern times, Charles Lee Feinberg, Ph.D., Th.D. Dr. Feinberg, a converted Jew, was the Dean of Talbot Theological Seminary at the time we met. For whatever reason, he took me under his wing and one of my most prized possessions is an autographed, Pilot Edition of the New American Standard Bible which he helped to translate.

A master of Semitic languages, his major area of study at Johns Hopkins University, Uncle Charlie, as he asked me to refer to him, gave me much needed and expert guidance in my own scholarly study of the Bible for which I will always be grateful. In regard to the Bible, I have always maintained that no one has any right to consider themselves truly educated who has not read the one book that has had a greater impact on civilization than that of any ever written, the Bible.

In the course of my own study, I amassed a personal library of some 5,000 volumes of the finest, most scholarly works about the Bible, its history, the geography, languages, and mores of the peoples of Bible times. From earliest childhood I was raised in a church environment and taught the lessons of Scripture. The study of this book has been, virtually, a life-time habit.

Because of our extraordinary relationship, Uncle Charlie advised me to get a university education from non-religious schools; which I did. As a result, I was thrust into an academic environment that saved me from many of the myths and superstitions that hold sway in religious institutions, something that Uncle Charles recognized would eventually be my undoing as a scholar in my own right.

Early on, I realized there was something fundamentally wrong with a gospel that could not discriminate between an Albert Schweitzer and a David Livingston. What kind of a gospel would allow Livingston into heaven and consign Schweitzer to hell? Both men lived sacrificially for others.

Yet to watch the average minister struggle with such a question is a study in human behavior as they attempt to contrive an answer that is inevitably a conflict with the very doctrine of Soteriology they espouse. No one has a higher regard for the Scriptures than I. But my regard for the book does not blind me to scholarly, textual criticism. And this is the reason for my letter.

One of the marvels of the Bible is that it is so free of the myths and superstitions that held sway during the historical period covered. One could say it is a virtual miracle that stories such as that of the fabulous Phoenix are not contained in Scripture.

There is no more credible history of the times covered by the Bible. Yet, to say that it is without error flies in the face of irrefutable, scholarly evidence to the contrary. While the Bible might, as claimed, be without error in the original autographs, none such exists to our knowledge.

The best manuscript evidence at our disposal shows corruptions of the texts in several places, even some, what I call, holy tampering of the texts by both Jewish and Christian copyists and translators.

People make the ignorant statement that the Bible is without contradictions. I will cite only two of many examples I could give:

In the 27th chapter of Matthew, Judas goes to the chief priests, throws the betrayal money into the temple and goes out and hangs himself. They pick up the money and buy the potter's field to bury strangers. But the story as given in the first chapter of the Acts of the Apostles is that Judas, personally, used the money for a real estate investment! In the 2nd chapter of Exodus, Moses flees Egypt in fear of his life. But in the 11th chapter of Hebrews, Moses is portrayed as not fearing the wrath of Pharaoh!

In both of these examples, the contradictions are evident. Yet the twisted and distorted attempts by otherwise honest commentators and preachers have been a history of obfuscatory language and reasoning that flies in the face of honest scholarship. Such attempts to reconcile the irreconcilable have brought rightful suspicion of ministers and Bible commentators. If they cannot be honest in regards to textual criticism, where else might they be practicing such intellectual dishonesty?

My years dedicated to work in the churches, among the books of the great Bible scholastics led eventually to an honest appraisal of much dishonesty and, even, the hypocrisy of much so-called orthodoxy.

The greatest of the heresies of which I am accused of the brethren, the thing that brought a breach between me and those orthodox brethren with whom I used to have sweet fellowship, was my finally accepting the fact that God has admitted to making errors.

Granted these errors were made in love, they remain. The most obvious was God admitting he was sorry he made man and determined to destroy him from the face of the earth. But God risked it all again, in love, on Noah. The Bible is filled with such errors of love as God sought for men to do his will, men like David and Solomon who failed of his expectations for them.

I have made many errors of love. They are those of loving and trusting only to have that love and trust betrayed. Yet neither God nor I have given up loving and trusting again and again.

If God is love, and I believe he is, love always takes such a risk. An error? If so, it is a risk all those that follow the teaching of Jesus Christ take in practicing the real Gospel, that of loving others. The kind of blind orthodoxy of religious men led to the Dark Ages and some of the cruelest treatment of human beings imaginable, all in the name of God and Jesus Christ.

Christianity was to be distinguished by love as opposed to the false religions of the world. Tragically, the churches took a wrong turn and are noted for the confusion and chaos of today. In the words of an old friend, J. Vernon McGee: "These Christians may love God but they sure seem to hate each other!" However, the real love of God and others inspires hope; hope of salvation and a hereafter where we will once more be with our departed loved ones and friends.

At a time when the charismatic antics of pulpit, TV and radio so-called evangelists are making every attempt to make God look foolish, when men seem to think God places a premium on ignorance, the world has a right to look askance at the churches.

Tragically, this condition will persist until Christians are willing to question their own blind orthodoxies and honestly answer to the legitimate questions we all have a right to ask of God. Anyone who has read the Psalms knows those men were not afraid to confront God on the issues of the pain, suffering and injustices of the world.

Where did the church take a wrong turn in attempting to make God something he is not? God is not perfect by the definition of men; he is perfect by his own. And he is a lot more human, for lack of a better word, according to the Bible, than the churches give him credit.

Omniscience, Omnipotence and Omnipresence are religious inventions of men, they are not characteristics God claims for himself. Until those who profess to speak in the name of God begin to be honest, I have small hope things will change for the better in the churches.

About the author

Samuel D. G. Heath, Ph. D.

Books in print:

BIRDS WITH BROKEN WINGS
DONNIE AND JEAN, an angel's story
TO KILL A MOCKINGBIRD, a critique on behalf of children
THE AMERICAN POET WEEDPATCH GAZETTE for 2008
THE AMERICAN POET WEEDPATCH GAZETTE for 2007
THE AMERICAN POET WEEDPATCH GAZETTE for 2006
THE AMERICAN POET WEEDPATCH GAZETTE for 2005
THE AMERICAN POET WEEDPATCH GAZETTE for 2004
THE AMERICAN POET WEEDPATCH GAZETTE for 2003
THE AMERICAN POET WEEDPATCH GAZETTE for 2002
THE AMERICAN POET WEEDPATCH GAZETTE for 2001

Dr. Heath was born in Weedpatch, California. He has worked as a manual laborer, mechanic, machinist, peace officer, engineer, pastor, builder and developer, educator, social services practitioner (CPS), professional musician and singer. He is also a private pilot and a columnist.
Awarded American Legion Scholarship and is an award winning author.
He has two surviving children, his sons Daniel and Michael. His two daughters Diana and Karen have passed away.

Academic Degrees:
Ph. D. – U.S.I.U., San Diego, CA.
M. A. – Chapman University, Orange, CA.
M. S. (Eqv.) — U.C. Extension at UCLA. Los Angeles, CA.
B. V. E. – C.S. University. Long Beach, CA.
A. A. – Cerritos College. Cerritos, CA.

Other Colleges and Universities attended:
Santa Monica Technical College, Biola University, and C.S. University, Northridge.

Dr. Heath holds life credentials in the following areas:
Psychology, Professional Education, Library Science, English, German, History, Administration (K-12), Administration and Supervision of Vocational Education and Vocational Education-Trade and Industry.

In addition to his work in public education, Dr. Heath started three private schools, K-12, two in California and one in Colorado. His teaching and administrative experience covers every grade level and graduate school.

Comments by some who have read the authors writings

After reading your book I will only say this...you are so far into flagrant heresy that it is highly unlikely that you are saved...you are in the position of a self-excommunicated man...that you are on the road to hell.

I would not waste even this much time on you except for my personal debt to you for having presented the gospel to me. That would be the great irony: the man who led me to Christ roasts in the lake of fire forever...you are a perpetually lawless man whose wives treated you just as you have treated the Church... be not surprised at your present lonely condition. It will get worse. Much, much worse. In hell, it will be forever... here is my counsel...recant publicly and send out a newsletter telling your readers that you have done so.

(Comment by Gary North, friend of the author since high school, son-in-law of Rousas J. Rushdoony and founder of INSTITUTE FOR CHRISTIAN ECONOMICS and leader and publisher for CHRISTIAN RECONSTRUCTION).

I am truly moved by your art! While reading your writing I found a true treasure: Clarity! I felt as if I was truly on fire with the inspiration you invoked! L.B.

I started reading your book, The Lord and the Weedpatcher, and found I couldn't put it down. Uproariously funny, I laughed the whole way through. Thank you so much for lighting up my life! M.G.

You really love women! Thank you for the most precious gift of all, the gift of love. Keep on being you! D.B.

Your writing complements coffee-cup-and-music. I've gotten a sense of your values, as well as a provocativeness that suggests a man both distinguished and truly sensual. Do keep up such vibrant work! E.R.

Some men are merely handsome. You are a beautiful man! One of these days some wise, discerning, smart woman is going to snag you. Make sure she is truly worthy of you. Desirable men like you (very rare indeed) who write so sensitively, compellingly and beautifully are sitting ducks for every designing woman! M.G.

Now, poet, musician, teacher, philosopher, friend, counselor and whatever else you have done in your life, I am finally realizing all the things you say people don't understand about a poet. They see, feel, write and talk differently than the rest of the world. Their glasses seem to be rose colored at times and other times they are blue. There seems to be no black or white in the things they see only soft pastel hues. Others see things as darker colors, but these are not the romantic poets you speak of. C.M.

Before reading your wonderful writings, I had given up hope. Now I believe and anticipate that just maybe things can change for the better. J.D.

You are the only man I have ever met who truly understands women! B.J.

Doctor Heath, every man with daughters owes you a debt of gratitude! I have had all three of my daughters read your books. D.W.

Your writing is very important. You are having an impact on lives! Never lose your precious gift of humor. V.T

Dr. Heath;
You are one of the best writers I've had the privilege to run across. You have been specially gifted for putting your thoughts, ideas, and inspirations to paper (or keyboard), no matter the topic.
Even when in dire straits, your words are strong and true. I look forward to reading many more of your unique writings. T. S.